# KEY
# ACCOUNT
# MANAGEMENT
# in FINANCIAL
# SERVICES

*To Caroline* – Peter Cheverton

*To Jean, Laura and Alec* – Tim Hughes

*To my wife and children, Carol, Simon and Helen and to our extended family* – Bryan Foss

*To my wife and daughters, Ofra, Maya and Talya* – Merlin Stone

# KEY
# ACCOUNT
# MANAGEMENT
# in FINANCIAL
# SERVICES

## *tools and techniques*
### for building strong relationships with major clients

## peter cheverton, tim hughes, bryan foss & merlin stone

IBM®

**KOGAN PAGE**

London and Sterling, VA

**Publisher's note**

Every possible effort has been made to ensure that the information contained in this book is accurate at the time of going to press, and the publishers and authors cannot accept responsibility for any errors or omissions, however caused. No responsibility for loss or damage occasioned to any person acting, or refraining from action, as a result of the material in this publication can be accepted by the editor, the publisher or any of the authors.

First published in Great Britain and the United States in 2004 by Kogan Page Limited

120 Pentonville Road
London N1 9JN
United Kingdom
www.kogan-page.co.uk

22883 Quicksilver Drive
Sterling VA 20166–2012
USA

ISBN 0 7494 4187 9

---

**British Library Cataloguing-in-Publication Data**

A CIP record for this book is available from the British Library.

---

**Library of Congress Cataloging-in-Publication Data**

Key account management in financial services / Peter Cheverton ... [et al].
    p. cm.
  Includes bibliographical references and index.
  ISBN 0-7494-4187-9
  1. Financial services industry—Management. 2. Selling—Key accounts. 3. Marketing—Key accounts. 4. Customer services. I. Cheverton, Peter.
HG173.K49 2004
332.1'068'8—dc22

                                            2004019046

---

Typeset by Saxon Graphics Ltd, Derby
Printed and bound in Great Britain by Scotprint

# Contents

# Foreword

The world of business-to-business financial services is intriguing for the marketing expert. At the high end, the risks associated with individual products or customers are high. Failures in governance can bring whole companies down, and have done. Many contracts for particular deals involve legal advice and legal fees can be hundreds of thousands or even millions of dollars. While the prospective gains and losses may be much smaller for bank or insurance branches managing their local key accounts, the need for professionalism for a balance between marketing, sales and service on the one hand and risk management and prudence on the other, is just as great.

This book is about professionalism in selling to large financial services customers. The principles are the same as in all business-to-business markets, though the way they are applied may look different. Perhaps the most important step that banks and insurers must take is to recognize that they are in the same sales boat as industries ranging from logistics and engineering to defence, where customers have much greater expectation of professionalism in sales than they used to have.

This book is designed to help financial services companies meet the expectations of their larger customers, and to do so profitably. The authors have an unrivalled pedigree in business-to-business theory and practice and all are experienced and widely-read authors. They have drawn on their enormous expertise in marketing, selling and financial services to produce a straightforward, readable, reliable guide. Good luck in using it.

*Professor Malcolm McDonald*
*August 2004*

# Foreword

In marketing and selling, so much of what is written in professional and consumer press is about retail customers or consumers. But many, possibly even most, financial services companies make their money from their business customers. These range from the very largest corporate customers, through large intermediaries (eg bancassurers as customers for insurance companies), to medium sized businesses which are the key accounts of regional or local banks or insurers, or of the local branches of national or international banks or insurers. Managing these business customers often involves a complex relationship, with the customer being both an intermediary and a final customer. Many customers are global, and they expect the best standards of global account management. All customers expect their suppliers to use the best information technology that money can buy to support relationship management. They expect best practice in every area, and they expect their suppliers to recognize what best practice is – anywhere in the world – and to know how to use it.

Managing these larger or key accounts requires top standards of professionalism, because the on-demand nature of business and tougher competition has given them a much wider range of choice than they once had. These accounts expect their suppliers to be the best – in terms of the speed, quality and relevance of their proposition – and best in terms of how suppliers manage that proposition to their benefit. As customers, they have mostly looked hard at their core skills and activities, focused on what they should do and what they should outsource, and they expect their suppliers to do the same. If a financial services supplier claims to manage its key accounts properly, then customers expect them to do so.

This book is about the professional management of the sales force that deals with these key accounts. It explains the fundamental principles of key account management in financial services. It provides lots of ideas and models to help you understand how well you are doing in managing your key accounts, and to improve how you manage them.

This book encourages you to join the journey IBM is on, in managing its key accounts and helping these companies to manage their customers too. We understand that it is a journey and not just a question of reading a book. It takes years of steady improvement to people, skills, processes, systems and strategies. But we know it is worth it, and also that it should be worth it for you. We also know that this book will help you make the journey.

*Mark N Greene PhD*
*General Manager*
*IBM Global Banking Industry*

*Thomas (Tom) K Swett*
*General Manager*
*IBM Global Financial Markets*

# Acknowledgements

We would like to thank everybody who helped us with our research for this book. Their input has been crucial in clarifying issues and in providing case studies and examples.

As always, the very best people to ask, and the most important people to listen to are our customers: thanks to them all.

*Peter Cheverton*

Thanks to Bristol Business School for supporting my research efforts and to my colleagues for their encouragement. A particular thanks to all those involved in the financial services industry who allowed me to interview them for this book.

*Tim Hughes*

Thanks to all those that continually encourage me, including my worldwide network of IBM colleagues, client contacts, IBM alliance partners, academics, professional body members, and not least my mentors and mentees (you know who you are).

*Bryan Foss*

The list of those I have to thank grows every year and is finally too long to include particular names. It includes anyone who has ever contributed to my thinking or publications (this book being a good example); the many financial services companies who have allowed me to dig into them, and even paid me to do so; the senior professionals who have mentored me; my fellow directors of the various companies I am involved in for their desire to work with me; the academics who have encouraged me over the years and tolerated my intolerance of some academic ways; the professional institutes who have listened to me – and even those who haven't; the many publications, publishers and conference organisers who have disseminated my work; and, most importantly of all, my close colleagues at IBM who have ensured that I can continue to irritate people productively.

*Merlin Stone*

# Part I

# Defining Key Account Management in Financial Services

# 1

# Why financial services are special

*(with Gary Wright)*

Why have a book dedicated to key account management (KAM) in financial services (FS)? Are not the principles the same in all sectors? What makes FS so special? In this chapter we address some of these questions before considering the principles of KAM and how they apply in FS markets. This book is a response to the demand from managers in the FS industry for more information and training on KAM. As the FS market has become more competitive, customer relationship management (CRM) in its widest sense has become a big issue for FS providers. In the business-to-business context, understanding the KAM approach is an essential part of effective CRM.

## DEFINITIONS AND SCOPE

The FS market includes many types of institutions, as follows:

- retail, corporate, investment and private banks;
- mutual funds, investment trusts;
- personal and group pensions;
- life and general insurance and reinsurance companies;
- credit card issuers;

- specialist lending companies;
- stock exchanges;
- leasing companies;
- government savings institutions;
- brokers and agents;

and many others. Other companies, such as motor manufacturers, retailers and telecommunications companies have also entered the market.

## Consolidation and convergence

Traditionally the consumer side of the market is separated into the two main market sectors of banking and insurance. However, this distinction has become less meaningful recently, as many companies in each sector now sell both product ranges. This 'bancassurance' model exists in many countries. Mergers and takeovers between banks and insurance companies have accelerated the process. Deregulation has allowed organizations formerly restricted to a limited product range to sell a wide range of FS. This has removed traditional barriers. Thus, in the UK, building societies were restricted to providing home loans, savings accounts and closely related products. The Building Societies Act of 1986 and other legislation allowed these mutual organizations to offer a fuller range of banking, insurance and investment services. Many building societies demutualized, converting into banks. In the US, the same has occurred.

Meanwhile, in business-to-business FS, there have also been changes. Whether through deregulation of retail and investment markets or the emergence of new markets, corporate customers can buy services ranging from traditional banking and insurance to issue of new financial instruments and derivatives from a much wider range of providers across the globe.

Consolidation and convergence of FS have happened globally. In the US, many bank mergers have taken place, resulting in a major transfer of assets from small US banks to very large institutions. In the European Union the level playing field concept, under the Single Market Programme, is predicted to increase banking concentration as European Monetary Union creates incentives for cross-border and in-country mergers. The worldwide growth of financial transactions has presented unprecedented opportunities, but the risks to FS firms have also increased. World economic trends have created volatility and risk. Stakes are higher. These trends create pressures for globalization in FS, where an international presence is now needed to underwrite and distribute corporate debt and enterprise risks.

## New competition

While traditional FS suppliers consolidate, many new operators have entered the market. These tend to be companies with an existing customer base to whom FS can be sold. Many organizations now have some kind of involvement in marketing FS. Supermarkets sell both insurance and banking. In the corporate world, leasing is frequently packaged with commercial equipment. This trend has been accelerated by the availability of new technology, enabling FS to be sold, transacted and serviced remotely and yet in a more packaged and integrated manner.

# MARKET SIZE AND SECTORS

The FS industry is big! The three largest banking centres in the world (US, Japan and UK) hold 10.5 trillion dollars in deposits (IFSL, 2003). The three largest insurance markets (again consisting of the US, Japan and UK) attract over 1.5 trillion dollars in gross premiums (IFSL, 2003). In the UK, FS accounts for over 5 per cent of GDP and employs over a million people. The FS industry affects virtually all adults. Consumer FS covers products ranging across current accounts, savings accounts, home loans, personal loans, credit and debit cards, life assurance, pensions, general insurance, endowments, mutual funds, unit trusts, stocks and shares, warrants, options, spread-bets and many more. In the UK, 43 million adults, representing 94 per cent of the population over 16, hold one or more financial products (Mintel, 1999). Expenditure on FS has tripled, from £3.35 billion in 1988 to around £10 billion at the turn of the century (Mintel, 1999).

The corporate and intermediary sector is no less impressive. Life insurance is still predominantly sold through independent financial advisers and tied agencies in the US, UK and elsewhere. Much general or property and casualty insurance is also sold through brokers, whether face to face or using call centre or web technologies. In banking, the commercial sector is larger by value than the retail sector in most major markets. US commercial banking reached $6,300 billion asset value in 2002, accounting for 79 per cent of the US banking market (Datamonitor, 2003b, 2003f). US banks are very important to the long-term financing of state and local government projects and are often the most important source of financial advice and other FS to state and local jurisdictions (ABA, 2003). The biggest commercial banking market is Europe with an asset value of $16,500 billion in 2002 taking 61 per cent of the total European banking market (Datamonitor, 2003a, 2003d). Elsewhere commercial banking was worth $8,100 billion in the Asia Pacific region (Datamonitor, 2003c) and $6,300 billion in Japan in 2002 (Datamonitor, 2003e).

# WHY ARE FS MARKETS SPECIAL?

FS affects all our lives and makes up a significant part of the world economy, but which of its features demands special treatment in a book on KAM?

The FS industry is undergoing the greatest period of change since modern international markets began. Changes vary by sector and affect product suppliers, wholesale and retail intermediaries and the end-client. The changes include regulation, clearing, settlement, technology and client service. Coping with these changes while meeting client needs is vital for customer retention, and this means having key account managers (KAMs) whose knowledge is constantly updated by education.

The balance sheet power of global banks has supported the world's FS industry in the last 15 years and has created an elite group that now struggle to maintain growth. Their main growth in recent years has been through acquisition and merger. Organic growth has not been strong enough, despite the globalization of markets and the growth of population and – in the case of the richest economies – growth of personal wealth.

## The internet

The internet has had a dynamic and dramatic effect on the industry. It has changed the relationship with the end-customer and the investing public by enabling investor access to wholesale markets. Disintermediation of inter- mediaries has generated a return to old client service values and a move towards outsourcing of non-profit-making business. The industry's supply is built on historical foundations rather than from a logical or cost-effective service standpoint. Business relationships with a historical foundation and built on strong trust and loyalty can be very strong, assuming a reasonable level of service at a reasonable price. However, suppliers must not rest on their laurels and expect that times will not change and the clients will not alter the benchmark standards they use to judge suppliers. The industry- wide take up of the internet, from wholesale to retail intermediaries to client connectivity, has threatened firms relying on traditional relationships. New entrants have emerged and offered cost-effective access to markets that enables clients to cut out the middleman. However, the fact that clients can buy direct from wholesalers has created an opportunity for supplying advice and information.

The dot com boom and bust can now be seen as a blip rather than the terminal decline of the web. In the next few years it is likely the many good ideas from that period will re-emerge, this time with better financial business planning. There is no doubt that the internet has brought account management and client relationships back into prominence for suppliers and clients.

## Outsourcing

Outsourcing on a global scale is in vogue for many different types of firm, as the costs of non-core business continue to rise and sometimes threaten the profitable part of the business. This applies particularly to IT costs. With the growing threat of regulatory enforcement, many firms see outsourcing as an escape route. However, the outsourcing of non-core activities can have hidden costs and business risks. Today, there is strong reliance on people and on enterprise-wide communication, especially for client relationships. Outsourcing the customer support desk seems curious! The internet has made outsourcing more attractive, but it remains to be seen whether outsourcing in general results in better client service. Outsourcing has created problems where the supplier–buyer service relationship is broken and the third party manages the client. This weakens the pressure the client can exert on the supplier. Low client satisfaction may result.

## Government and the investors

Government policy in most countries is to encourage individuals to take more control over personal finances, especially pensions. The coming investing generation is comfortable with new technology and aware of performance and will be the most demanding customers ever seen. Brokers will be challenged to provide a greater array of services and at a lower cost and increasingly an international investment strategy. It will not be acceptable to investors in the future just to invest in a narrow range of funds and products. Retail investors will insist on better financial performance, to sustain their lifestyle and debt position. Suppliers must meet industry challenges, but still produce better services and build client relationships.

## Industry challenges

Market structure changes, increased regulation, increased reliance on technology, and the need to keep staff and maintain margins can be barriers to firms maintaining a high level of service for buyers. Individually, each barrier can be dealt with. In combination, they have created a problem that most firms have found hard to manage.

Market structure challenges include:

- implementation of the euro;
- consolidation of exchanges;
- consolidation of clearing and settlement;
- introduction of central matching;

- escalation of SWIFT;
- introduction of new technical message standards.

Regulatory challenges include:

- harmonization of international rules;
- implementation of domestic rule changes;
- legal requirements;
- government policy;
- governance, eg Barings, Enron and so on;
- operational risk management.

Technology challenges include:

- internet;
- new developments;
- legacy replacement;
- shortening the settlement cycle;
- real-time management;
- straight-through processing;
- database management;
- mergers/integration;
- staff turnover.

## The regulatory environment

Firstly, regulation plays an important role in the selling of any FS product. This varies between countries. Until now, differences between national regulatory regimes have been a major factor in limiting the competitive development of global FS operations. However, increasingly we see similarities in regulatory trends in different countries and pressures towards global harmonization as cross-border transactions increase with the globalization of other industries that use FS.

The UK banking market provides an example of the effect of deregulation. In 1980, relaxation of restrictions on domestic lending allowed banks to compete in the home loans market. Further legislation relaxed the Bank of England's control of interest rates and opened access to wholesale funds to building societies. Under the FS and Building Societies Acts of 1986 and the Banking Act of 1987, clearing banks, building societies and insurance companies were allowed to compete directly. New controls, checks and balances accompanied this opening up of the banking industry. In the UK the FS and Markets Act (FSMA) provided for a statutory regulator of the banking industry. In Europe the FS Action Plan (FSAP) is intended to remove remaining barriers to a single market in FS across the EU. At the same time the Bank of International Settlement's Basel 2 Accord is an example of a move to impose internationally consistent compliance and reporting processes for dealing with risk.

Opening up the FS industry through deregulation has made it far more competitive and led to widespread consolidation of what was a very fragmented and localized industry in many countries. The pressure to compete more effectively has led the larger organizations to buy smaller or complementary operators. At the same time, there remain, at the bottom end of the market, thousands of small independent financial advisers and insurance brokers. The industry has become more polarized with the large operators having grown at the expense of those in the middle.

Meanwhile, the likely cost of providing pensions for an ageing population is causing governments and employers everywhere to shift emphasis from state and company pensions to private provision. The move to private provision has been accompanied by pressures to provide customer value and has led to the requirement for products with a 1 per cent cap on charges in the US, the UK and elsewhere. This means a limited (perhaps even insufficient) margin for the manufacturer and for any intermediary selling the product.

Changes such as these demonstrate the impact of the regulatory environment on the shape and development of the FS industry in any given market. While deregulation opens up opportunities for FS providers, it often goes hand in hand with checks and balances that limit profitability. In less regulated markets, increasing pressure for a low-cost operating environment together with intense competition is affecting the shape and efficiency of the FS industry.

## Product complexity

FS products are complex. At one end of the scale are no-risk savings products, at the other sophisticated instruments for managing unique types of risk. Retail and corporate customers have a wide range of needs and frequently require professional advice. Customer contact personnel are not only part of the product, but may also determine what the product will be. In the corporate market, tailor-making of individual solutions is commonplace and expected by buyers. Here, the provision of FS often requires close collaboration between supplier and buyer. Customers must not only specify their needs but also, because the service is ongoing, provide feedback as it is delivered. In doing this customers must collaborate with suppliers. They also need a high level of support and interaction to get the product's full benefits.

In complex and evolving businesses, customer needs are often also highly complex and individual. Sellers need to consider how the buyer is going to use and benefit from the product and (where relevant) how this will benefit the end-consumer. Suppliers of FS, whether in corporate markets or supplying intermediaries, must understand their customers' businesses intimately if they are to deliver valued services and gain competitive advantage.

## Uncertainty of performance

The level of risk involved in some FS products makes KAM in FS special. The institutional investor in an organization often acts in a custodial or fiduciary role and must be very sensitive to risk management. However, uncertainty of outcome means it may be hard for the buyer and seller to judge realistically the likely return on the product. The return on risk products may have a complex relationship with the overall performance of domestic economies and the world economy. In this situation a high level of trust and commitment may be needed between service provider and client if the relationship is to survive difficult times.

## The problem of measuring profitability of products, operations and relationships

This stems from the last two points. Where products are complex and returns depend on risks taken it may be hard to measure returns from a customer relationship in the shorter term. On the other side the cost of servicing the relationship may involve a high level of investment in the short term with commercial benefits arising only in the longer term. While measurement of key customer profitability is difficult for many industries there are some special challenges in this area for FS.

## Role of technology in planning and delivery

Information technology (IT) is a strategic resource in FS organizations. In the past, technology was seen mainly as a way to cut process cost. Recently, the internet and call centres have developed as added-value delivery channels, bringing with them the need for effective data integration for organization-wide initiatives such as CRM and knowledge management. The FS industry has been quick to adopt these new technologies, recognizing them as fundamental to organizational development and growth. However, the deployment of the technology has sometimes had mixed results, with the differences in the requirements for successful deployment often not fully recognized. Competitive advantage arises from the effective deployment of new technology rather than from the technology per se.

The pressure to compete cost-effectively has stimulated the application of technology to provide new sales and service routes. Traditional face-to-face contact is an expensive way of dealing with customer transactions. It costs at least twice as much as dealing with the customer through a central call centre, which in turn is at least twice as costly as dealing with the customer through the internet. Good data management is fundamental to managing customers, from understanding different customer segments to providing the information needed at point of sale or service. Technology is at the centre of the competitive battle of FS. It is predicted to open the industry up to even more intense competition, domestically and globally. So its deployment is very relevant in managing customer relationships cost-effectively.

The 20th century closed with most of the FS market investing heavily in technology as a solution to one or more of the major challenges listed and it is here that the 21st century has to find the answers to the mistakes made by the selection of the wrong technology. PCs began to explode across the FS business in the 1990s and companies shifted away from mainframes. This allowed FS suppliers to meet an immediate business demand and maintain a healthy profit margin and keep the employers and shareholders happy. However, the very flexibility of the PC created massive challenges. Networking of PCs and integration with legacy mainframe demanded middleware solutions to connect systems by transforming or translating electronic data and transporting it to the destination, which was inevitably a mainframe system. The effect was to paper over the cracks of the systems' architecture. It enabled a relatively cheap method of maintaining legacy systems and providing some flexibility to meet immediate business require-ments. The result has been that the systems inventory of most firms is now quite complex and expensive to maintain. The knowledge of what is under-pinning the front layer disappears as staff leave. In many cases this has already happened, with many suppliers building their new technology on sand as the foundations have long been lost. This has created a technology time bomb for all but a few suppliers.

The role of technology in FS client services is vital for the development of bespoke services, particularly if manual non-client service processes can be eliminated. Staff time saved should be taken up with direct client services responsibilities. This will demand retraining of existing staff and occa-sionally redundancy if retraining proves beyond them. However, the industry has never selected or implemented the right technology for their business. In fact, many investments are driven by fear or greed, eg a major regulatory breach or a large commercial opportunity of new market or client. The internet has had the most dramatic impact of all technologies. Firms slow to take up the technology have suffered lost opportunities at best or at worst suffered terminal decline and merger. The internet enables the retail customer to go direct to the wholesaler and select a best-value product.

This applies particularly to a new rich generation, who have the technology capability and are not scared of the internet. The growth of internet sales demonstrates the increasing comfort level of the buyer.

## Channel complexity

One impact of the application of new technology has been proliferation of distribution channels. The mix of distribution channels has become a major issue for banks and other FS providers, with new channels increasing coverage and allowing cost reduction. FS is well placed to adopt new channels because there is usually no physical product to deliver. Traditional distribution channels have not delivered the results needed to meet growth and profitability targets. This has forced banks in particular to focus on re-engineering distribution. Call centres and e-commerce are now rapidly augmenting the traditional channels of branch offices, sales forces and account managers, intermediaries and direct marketing.

Most banks follow a multi-channel strategy. A multi-channel offering gives customers different access options in buying and using FS. Customers use channels in different ways. They may use the web for getting the basic research information, use a call centre to get further details and buy the product face to face. A multi-channel strategy opens up many different ways for a supplier to service corporate customers more cost-effectively, perhaps to align the level of servicing resource with the value of the customer, or to manage cost-effectively the complex pattern of transactions and contacts with very large customers. The appropriate channel mix depends on the needs and maturity of particular markets. Thus, telephone distribution is important in wholesale money markets, foreign exchange and securities markets.

## High degree of intermediation

Intermediaries are an important channel for many financial services. Companies often market through a number of partner channels and routes to market. A large proportion of life insurance and investment products are sold through financial advisers. Various kinds of brokers are involved in the home loans market and sometimes a number of intermediaries are involved in the supply chain. For example, a broker may be involved dealing directly with the borrower, a packager may deal with the loan administration set-up, a bank may provide the loan and an insurance company may provide the home insurance. Although the agreement is packaged, each supplier may be directly involved at any stage of the relationship, for example in administration, customer servicing or product maturity processes.

This has several implications. Product providers may be distanced from end-customers for much of the relationship, yet must act with consistency when delivering some services direct. Their primary focus is on the needs of the intermediary. Their ability to run relationship programmes with end-customers is likely to be limited by a lack of end-customer information and contact opportunities. In this case the intermediary could be a key account for the supplier, because of the amount of business the intermediary is generating through the end-customers. However, the intermediary might also be a corporate customer of the service provider. For instance, a large mortgage broker could be a corporate customer for a bank for which it sells mortgages.

# WHY KAM MATTERS IN FS MARKETS

There are then several aspects of FS with a particular impact on KAM in FS:

- The regulatory environment requires a high degree of expertise in providing compliant advice and legal products, particularly across geographical and political boundaries.
- Product complexity and the risk dimension imply the need for a very close and trusting working relationship with corporate customers.
- Technology is playing a strategic role in FS, in particular in transforming the pattern of distribution and delivery.
- The management of multiple distribution channels has major implications for management of the overall relationship between the supplier and its key accounts.
- The business customer may be an intermediary or the end-customer or both. This provides extra complexity for the KAM approach.

At the same time, several pressures can be identified that are increasing the need for KAM in FS. These broadly relate to:

- market maturity;
- consolidation in supplier and intermediary markets;
- consolidation amongst corporate clients;
- increased competition;
- pressures for better cost control;
- trends towards globalization.

KAM is vitally important in any service supply business. In FS it is no less important. One can liken the FS KAM to that of any profession where markets are in constant change and buyer risk is involved. KAM is making a strong comeback as FS undergoes rapid and uncoordinated change. One example is the effect of e-business. It threatens intermediaries who base their business on execution and settlement values. Relationship and value-added services become enterprise differentiators. Intermediaries must protect their value to the client and improve the quality of their supply chain by improving their relationships and their ability to offer important clients bespoke services.

The pace of change in FS has increased greatly. Many changes are associated with technology, but there have also been changes in market structures and in legal and regulatory areas. All affect supplier costs and, when passed on, client costs. Despite the worthy objectives of risk reduction and client protection, much of the development budget of FS suppliers has not been spent on improved client services. It will be some time before we see the client receive better service at a lower cost.

As competition increases and clients are more valued by suppliers, the best firms will ensure that their KAMs are experts in their products and their clients' industries – indeed, they should know more about the client's industry than the client. They also need the personal skills of client management. Knowledge is power. The service supplier must not be in a position of relative weakness, putting clients in a more powerful position. Sadly, there is no global certification for the knowledge and capability needed to service clients.

Wealth management firms tend to have good account management, due to historical, long-term relationships based on service and trust, complete understanding of client needs, knowledge of their market and products, access to superior delivery channels and good personal skills. Retail banks have been weakest, owing to their historical position as relatively reactive suppliers of a very broad range of services, ranging from being first resort for clients with urgent financial needs to longer-term business and personal provision. Service was seen as less important as a way to making profits out of retail assets than just being there. Today, all large suppliers realize the need for good account management, but they should learn from the mistakes in this case study.

## How not to do it

A particularly difficult client was very upset with the service it was receiving from the supplier. The service involved a newly developed and implemented technology to achieve a business benefit for the client, which in turn was offering its new service capabilities to its clients. Over several months, technical people, normally followed by business people, spent much time at the client site, but problems continued, to the increasing frustration of the client. As more people got involved to solve the problem and more solutions were tried, more time, money and effort were lost on both sides. Inevitably the client lost patience and threatened to withdraw and look elsewhere as the problem was no nearer to a final resolution and confidence was being lost. Near the point of no return, as a last resort, a senior manager from the supplier was called in. The immediate problem of regaining the client's confidence was sorted out in a single sentence! 'Don't worry about this problem: it's ours and we will resolve this for you.' The eventual solution included:

- clear and accurate diagnoses of the problem;
- understanding the client's industry and business;
- clear understanding of what resolution the client expected;
- an agreed timescale for implementation;
- no charge to the client!

With mergers of FS companies, particular customers may become more significant and need more effective KAM. Consolidation among clients means that many FS companies are now selling a wide range of products and services to larger customers. There may be different decision makers, with the situation complicated by the existence of networks and alliances, necessitating a more effective KAM approach. At the same time competitive pressures put existing relationships under the spotlight. Pressures on margins mean that controlling expenses is a major issue. Nowadays many companies review their relationships on an annual basis. Clients are better informed than ever and more discriminating. In particular, major clients are often concentrating their business with fewer stronger suppliers so as to maximize their competitive advantage. Clients themselves are focusing on how to manage their suppliers to their own advantage. The principal reason for corporations changing their supplier of FS is the quality of the relationship team. As never before, suppliers need to understand their client's business environment, markets, corporate policy, and organizational and decision-making structures. In an increasingly global market place this may entail developing capabilities and alliances across the world.

Better client management is no longer optional. To keep their corporate clients and manage their business through intermediaries, FS suppliers need to manage relationships with them better, for mutual advantage. That's what this book is all about: providing tools and techniques for profitably achieving key supplier status through KAM.

# 2

# What is a key account in financial services?

In the last chapter we discussed the reasons why FS is different enough from other sectors to merit a separate book on KAM. The complex industry structure, with a high proportion of corporate sales and complex intermediation, means that KAM takes place on several levels and in varying circumstances. In this chapter we examine this complexity in managing business customers and intermediaries.

## GENERAL DEFINITIONS AND THEIR LIMITATIONS

'Key account' is a relative term. For a multinational organization, it usually refers to the largest national and global customers. For others, a key account may be a large regional business. For a bank, a key account of a local branch might be quite a small business. So we prefer a soft definition. 'Key' means an account that needs to be managed closely so that its needs are fully met and so that it yields its full value to the supplier. It is one that if lost, would significantly affect the current or future income to the business or business unit. Key account strategy is perhaps best seen as an investment in the future. KAM is about managing that investment effectively. Various terms are used in different organizations as alternatives to the term Key Account Management. These include Partner Relationship Management (PRM); Strategic Account Management (SAM) and National Account Management (NAM). The first of these is sometimes used where the customer is an intermediary. We have used the term Key Account Management (KAM) in this book as the generic terminology that best covers the field.

# CATEGORIES OF KAM IN FS

Business-to-business markets in FS can be split broadly into corporate and intermediary sectors. In the corporate sector, suppliers provide directly for the needs of business customers. This is distinct from the intermediary sector where suppliers provide products for selling on to end-customers. We also separate investment banking as a category. Investment banking is a sub-sector of the corporate category, but has its own character and merits coverage in its own right. Table 2.1 summarizes our classification.

## Corporate KAM

Companies and organizations at all levels, from self-employed individuals to global corporations, from private to public, need FS. Their needs vary widely, according to factors such as size, industry sector and style of management. Generally, the larger the organization, the more complex its needs. However, this does not mean that the principles of KAM apply only in dealing with very large organizations. It really depends on the current or potential significance of the customer to your business. A company that is very small for a global bank may be very large for an insurance broker! So, we start discussion of corporate KAM at a regional level.

### Small to medium sector KAM

In every country, millions of small businesses have banking needs, but most are mini-businesses, mainly the self-employed. This is a very important sector but one best dealt with mainly by mass-market methods, which use and personalize aspects of KAM at low cost, rather than the more expensive and traditional forms of customized KAM. It may be useful to distinguish between those that are more like personal customers and those that have the potential to grow into tomorrow's large accounts.

At the level of mid-size businesses, KAM starts to become relevant. For example, medium-size professional customers or group practices (such as solicitors, accountants, doctors, dentists) may be important for banks on a

**Table 2.1** *Categories of KAM*

| Category | Market | Scope of KAM | Examples of Product Needs |
|---|---|---|---|
| Corporate sector: general | Very wide: all types of corporate companies and public sector organizations. | Enormous range of levels of KAM, from regional through to national and global accounts. | Banking, insurance (property, people, vehicles), reinsurance, pension schemes, investment. |
| Corporate sector: investment banking | Corporate clients and other FS companies. | Narrower – mainly at international and national levels. | Specialist investment services, capital raising, mergers and acquisitions, risk management. |
| Intermediary sector | Historically, mainly FS companies to other FS companies, though now other players have entered (eg supermarkets, car dealers, telcos). | A wide range of levels including joint ventures (such as HBOS and Sainsbury's), partnerships (such as Bristol & West Bank providing savings products through Saga), tied agents (an insurance company selling through a third party as sole supplier), multi-ties, and sales through networks of independent financial advisers (IFAs), agents and brokers. | Insurance (life and general), pensions, investment products, mortgages, banking, savings. |

regional basis. Here, a local supplier of FS may have the advantage of local business awareness and intimacy of contact. The supplier will need to demonstrate this with an understanding and empathetic approach and high responsiveness. However, the size of the business generated may limit the amount of tailoring of the service to the client's needs. It may also be very demanding on the skills of the account manager, who may need to provide a range of services across different industries and professions and so will need broad knowledge. Smaller companies often need higher levels of servicing from their FS suppliers than the latter are prepared to give. This mainly relates to the relative size and profitability of the business generated by the company compared with the cost to the supplier of servicing it.

## Large corporate sector KAM

Here, there is generally a different balance of power between client and supplier from that in the relationship with small to medium organizations. Large corporations typically have complex needs, and suppliers compete aggressively for their business. For instance, corporate customers may have multiple banking relationships, traditionally using (in the UK) between 11 and 32 banks to service their business (Tyler and Stanley, 1999). Generally the larger the corporate customer the more banks it uses, though many companies are now reassessing this approach as they consider that fewer suppliers are easier to manage while retaining competition and choice. Usually suppliers are ranked in importance and it is important to win lead bank status in the ranking process, as this ensures the largest slice of the business (Holland, 1992).

The immense bargaining power of large organizations makes them very demanding customers, requiring tailored products at low prices and an in-depth understanding of their business. In addition they often have their own expert knowledge through their specialist financial functions. Hence they have a high degree of knowledge of the services offered by different banks and of their method of delivery. They expect excellent operational service quality and this perhaps explains their preference for managing multiple banking relationships (Tyler and Stanley, 1999). This puts great pressure on their suppliers to perform effectively, in providing routine services and also strategic support. The supplier must have in-depth knowledge of the client's market, a wide range of product capabilities and good knowledge of regulations and laws. For clients dealing in imports and exports, the financial service supplier must offer additional services like export factoring, guarantees, indemnities, currency exchange, rate protection, knowledge of regulations and even local support in other countries. In this sector, effective KAM is needed to manage the many operational relationships between corporate client and supplier and to maximize the business development opportunities that arise from the relationship.

## Investment banking sector KAM

In the large corporate sector, with trends towards internationalization and globalization, there has been a steady growth in the demand for investment banking services. The main activities of investment banks relate to advice on mergers and acquisitions, raising capital for corporations and providing sophisticated products for managing risk. The market has developed greatly in the last 25 years, stimulated by a general increase in the volume of trade across national borders. Global investment banking has also benefited from a climate of deregulation and the relaxation of exchange controls, weakening divisions between national markets. At the same time, technological developments have enhanced investment banking by supporting sophisticated hedging strategies requiring global data processing.

Investment banking is characterized by two types of relationships with clients (Foss and Stone, 2002). The first type is share of mind relationships, where the bank focuses on a few large high-impact transactions for the client. They require intense investment of time by key people in the bank, to build access and influence with the right decision makers within the client organization before doing the deal. The second type is share of wallet relationships, involving large-scale coordination of many people. With consolidation and mergers between clients, the scope and complexity of these relationships have increased. The challenge for KAM in this situation is to transform individual relationships into a broader institutional relationship.

Several factors in the investment banking market increase the importance of effective KAM:

- With the growing trend towards serving large global clients, a few large clients tend to have a big impact on business performance.
- Developing a global account management strategy requires a bank-wide understanding of the overall profitability of each client and its worldwide situation and needs.
- Banks are facing increased competition and there is overcapacity in the sector.
- Investment banking has become very competitive, with performance under scrutiny from customers, shareholders and regulators.

## Intermediary KAM

A significant feature of the FS market is that much business is done via third parties acting between suppliers and customers. The supplier's focus tends to be on managing the relationship with the third party, while the third party often has the primary relationship with the end-customer. This creates a new sphere of business-to-business activities where KAM principles can be applied. Intermediary relationships are complex and take many forms. The main types are discussed below under the following headings:

- traditional brokers (including financial advisers, tied agencies, mortgage brokers);
- non-traditional partnerships;
- other intermediary arrangements;
- hybrid situations.

## Traditional brokers

Brokers perform an important role at the interface with the customer. They develop a trusting relationship with clients, advising on products to meet complex needs. Typically they sell one or more of life, general insurance, investments and home loans products. The FS business may be a by-product of their main area of operation, as is the case with accountants providing investment advice or estate agents selling home loans. Depending on their business, intermediaries may focus only on customer acquisition, passing customer support and long-term relationship opportunity to the provider (for example, an estate agent would pass management of the relationship to the mortgage or life assurance provider). Here, the provider is free to cross-sell other offerings as it builds a relationship with the end-consumer. In other situations, the intermediary retains the customer relationship (as is usual in general insurance or long-term financial advice). Any attempt to step into this primary relationship by the provider would be fatal.

In the UK life insurance market an important distinction is made between independent financial advisers (IFAs) providing advice across a full range of suppliers and tied arrangements. In cases of single ties and multi-tie arrangements a close working relationship is probably required, in particular because the supplier has additional accountabilities for ensuring that the agent complies with legislation in providing advice on products. Regulation also allows the supplier to give more assistance to the intermediary than to an independent adviser. In these more closely tied cases a KAM approach may be applicable. In the IFA market KAM may have been less developed in the past because of the diversity of the sector. While it is large, employing around 50,000 people in the UK, this is made up of around 9,000 organizations (Foss and Stone, 2002). However, there are pressures towards consolidation and rationalization through both mergers and acquisitions and common interest networks, as follows:

- The application of technology for providing quotes and for transacting business is leading to the development of larger networks of IFAs, benefiting from common systems support.

- Requirements to comply with legislation and to ensure that staff who provide advice are fully trained favour the development of larger networks.
- The pressure on margins for investment products may favour larger intermediaries with increased bargaining power, which can do deals to the benefit of their customers.

So even in the diverse IFA sector it is increasingly important for suppliers of products to deal effectively and efficiently with networks that deliver volume business. A KAM approach is increasingly relevant. Another example of the increasing relevance of KAM can be seen in the broker sector of the home loans market. While lenders used to deal with small mortgage brokers through their branch networks, now these arrangements are becoming more centralized. A new sector has grown up – the packagers. These further intermediate this market, by providing an interface between small brokers and the lenders. The packager deals directly with the smaller broker and undertakes the set-up administration on behalf of the lender. The increasingly centralized lenders now often deal with a small number of packagers and directly with large brokers, rather than with a myriad of small brokers through local branches.

## Non-traditional partnerships

A significant trend in recent years has been the entry of new players into the FS market. These include retailers, such as Wal-Mart, with a strong brand and access to a large customer base. The new entrant acts as an intermediary, with a traditional financial supplier providing the actual product. This model is also being adopted by other non-traditional providers attracted into the FS market by higher growth opportunities than those available in their own industries. Utilities, telecommunications companies, car manufacturers and other retailers use their product as a gateway to sell FS to their large customer bases, often using a banking partner for the licence and product capability. Some, such as Sony, IBM and Ford, have gained sufficient licences to provide these financial services directly, without the need for a partner. They may affect the traditional balance of the industry. Thus, Wal-Mart has used its strength to challenge the traditional card charges and payments systems. Developments in technology have enabled the provision of FS through these non-traditional suppliers, who often use call centres or the internet as primary interfaces with their customers, to support their low-cost retail operations. In banking, ownership of an expensive network of branches and ATMs is no longer a precondition of market entry.

So, the FS market is becoming more competitive, with the entrance of these new players with their powerful brands and large customer bases. But many new players do not have either the expertise or infrastructure to create and manage the financial products themselves. Invariably many deals require working with an FS partner. This means the two organizations working in a relationship that may range from a one-off promotional agreement through to a full-scale joint venture.

For traditional FS companies faced with this new competition, the choice is between competing head-on with new players or working with these new players, or both.

## Other intermediary arrangements

Many other intermediary arrangements exist in the FS industry. One is the selling of financial products through the workplace. In this case the workplace company can be seen to be an intermediary channel, offering access to its employees for pension schemes, health and other such products. Worksite marketing has grown rapidly in the US in the last decade and is probably set for a similar growth in the UK market (Foss and Stone, 2002). Where the workplace organization is large, this could extend to the development of tailored and own-branded products. These workplace services can be made available via corporate intranets, relieving the buying company of much of the administrative cost and effort of providing differentiated employee services.

Another arrangement is agreement between separate FS organizations to provide tailored products to the customer base of other financial organizations to broaden their product offering. For example, an insurance company might sell an own-branded credit card to its customers, sourced from a banking partner, or consumer goods may be ordered online with associated loan and insurance products.

## Hybrid KAM

The previous sections demonstrate that much FS business is done through organizations acting both as corporate customers and as intermediaries. So, a complex web of relationships often exists between organizations and there may be a mixing or blurring of KAM categories. A client company or individual decision maker may be a final customer and at the same time also an intermediary (a general insurer may insure a bank's physical property and also sell insurance through the bank). A client may be a key account for one division of a company and not for another division of that same company. Reinsurers sell to insurers, who take on some of the small risks and reinsure large ones, so the customer may also turn out to be a competitor. All this highlights the complexity of relationships between the organizations involved. It also affects how organizations deal with regulations with regard to the separation of roles and the creation of 'Chinese walls' within FS suppliers. For instance, in the US, rules that apply to the independence of analysts in investment banks may limit the access to research that a reinsurance arm of that bank may wish to provide as an added-value service to its clients.

# MANAGING THE COMPLEXITY

In this chapter we considered the scope of KAM in FS and discussed the context in which FS suppliers are faced with the task of managing a web of relationships. This task is becoming more crucial and complex as consolidation occurs amongst customers and in the FS industry itself. Many banks have moved away from local relationship management, reorganizing into centralized units and using technology to support service delivery. Many insurance companies have moved away from large sales forces to remote servicing through call centres and the internet. However, in their search for service efficiency, FS companies should not lose sight of relationship quality. A selective and appropriate approach to KAM is needed to manage interfaces with corporate customers. Let us now consider some basic ideas of KAM and how they can be applied in FS.

# 3

# Competitive advantage through managing the future

## MANAGING THE FUTURE

The increasing emphasis on managing corporate and intermediary relationships has long-term implications for FS suppliers. As we outlined in the previous chapter a key account is an investment in the future. Key accounts are customers that promise to take you where you wish your business to be. In view of this, identifying them is as important as choosing a portfolio of investments – some must give a quick return, some are longer-term, while others are speculative, balanced by those that offer more certainty. KAM is about managing that investment. It is about managing a very different kind of relationship with the customer. It is about managing the implications of that relationship for the supplier's own business. In other words, KAM is about managing the future.

## YOUR BUSINESS STRATEGY

If KAM is about managing the future, then we must understand how that can be done in the highly complex and ever-changing market environment for FS. Business strategies are instruments for managing the future, and they seek to balance three important elements (as shown in Figure 3.1):

**Figure 3.1** *Managing the future*

- The *business objectives* are concerned with where you are trying to get to – what sort of business you want to have in the future.
- The *market opportunity* is a consideration of the forces that help and hinder. Among the latter are your competitors. Among the former are those customers that will best help you get to where you want to be.
- The *business resources* are those things that support, or constrain, your progress – your capabilities, range of products, ability to tailor-make solutions, systems, capital and, not least, your people.

This is not a static model. As the future gets closer, so it changes and, as opportunities alter, so you must modify your objectives to match any new resource requirements. The all-important 'balance' will shift almost continually as the market changes, which, as we know, is now almost a permanent experience. Managing the future is a continual process of analysis, reassessment and change.

# WHERE TO START?

## Objectives?

Starting with objectives is the easiest, which is why most start there, but the perils are clear. Too many hockey-stick graphs in business plans project splendid growth after a period of no growth or even decline. When you see such graphs, ask two questions: what has been proven to have changed with the market opportunity, and how are you using your resources differently to take advantage of this? If the answers are 'nothing' and 'we're not', then ignore growth projections – why should they happen just because someone writes it down?

*Resources?*

Sounds sensible, but here's a thought for you. Your current resources are probably ideal for the opportunity of about two years ago. So why start with what you've got today? This can only restrict your view even before you start your journey.

*The market opportunity?*

But it's not so easy. You are already plunged into the market, already responding to today's demands. Stepping back and viewing the future is not easy, but it is vital. More than that, it is one of the purposes and one of the benefits of the KAM approach.

# THE IMPORTANCE OF BALANCE

The balance between these three elements is critical. Objectives must be balanced by the realism of the opportunity and the resources available. All too often, in the real world, we see how resources lag behind the opportunity, while the objectives surge ahead of it.

Such an imbalance can be damaging in any business circumstance, but particularly in KAM. We are dealing here with customers and how they see us as a supplier. It is easy to profess objectives that, unmatched by adequate resources, are not met. Where this results in customer discontent or disillusion, the penalties can be severe indeed. Realism is vital in the management of expectations, in enhancing your customers' perceptions and in winning the support of your own colleagues – something, as we shall see, that is fundamental to successful KAM.

Realism is not to be feared as suggesting any lack of vigour or ambition. Wild hopes may seem brave, but they can be the source of stress that pulls you and your business apart at the seams. George Soros, the international financier, said that when he was hopeful he didn't sleep at nights – it was worrying that made him feel secure! It is only through balancing these three elements that you can properly define your key accounts. Objectives and resources rarely lie entirely in your control. Shareholders demand returns, and constrain your ability to invest; but of the three elements it is market opportunity that is most fickle, and so needs most study.

## When things become unbalanced…

The most common example is where a supplier is not sufficiently aware of changes in a customer's needs, for example when the end-consumer's needs have changed, it is struggling with value creation and differentiation, and is more likely to search out or respond to a more innovative offer from another supplier. For example a few years ago, Royal and Sun Alliance (RSA) were suddenly surprised to hear that the Halifax might be looking for new insurance suppliers, despite their relationship going back as far as anyone could recall. RSA identified that their 'key account team' was just an administration team with little understanding of the client's needs, especially the deteriorating competitiveness of block policies – ones where the insurer sold to the bank coverage for a certain number of customers, irrespective of their risk – in a market where the new direct insurers could 'cherry-pick' the best risks at the most attractive premiums. So RSA appointed and trained key account managers using IBM Account Management courses, ensuring that they had a competent executive sales team who were in touch with market and client demands, and able to coordinate a combined response. This initiative enabled RSA to retain their position with the Halifax at the time.

# ASSESSING THE OPPORTUNITY

Can we predict the future shape of FS markets? Trying to read the future is tough, but we must try. The good news is that there are a number of tools and techniques that can help us:

- PESTLE analysis;
- Porter's analysis;
- the 'opportunity snail'.

Each of these tools has one thing in common – the pursuit of long-term competitive advantage.

# PESTLE ANALYSIS

In considering 'Why financial services are special' in Chapter 1, we emphasized the importance of the regulatory and political environment in the way that FS markets have developed in many countries across the world. We also demonstrated the impact of technological developments in providing new distribution channels and opening up opportunities for new market entrants. In the light of this the market opportunity in FS can be seen to be subject to many forces and the acronym 'PESTLE' is particularly relevant in reminding us to consider some of the larger-scale factors:

**P** – Political changes.
**E** – Economic changes.
**S** – Social changes.
**T** – Technological changes.
**L** – Legal changes.
**E** – Environmental changes.

Change throws up new challenges, but also new opportunities. Considering these larger-scale factors and identifying where your organization can gain an advantage in dealing with its key customers are what start to differentiate the key account manager from the traditional salesperson. This is a longer-term strategic approach rather than a short-term sales drive.

# PORTER'S ANALYSIS

In developing a strategic approach, Michael E Porter (1980) provided a model much used to assess the different competitive forces that bear in upon a business and so formulate strategies that aim to raise barriers to those forces, or take advantage of them (Figure 3.2).

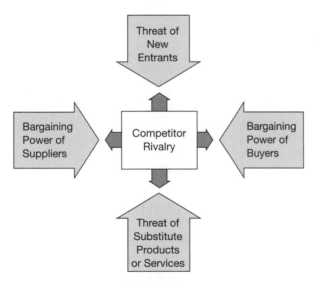

*Figure 3.2*  *Porter's model*

Porter shows how any business operates within the ferment and flux of five different competitive forces, putting aside regulatory and other forces for simplicity. As well as some general comments on each, we might look at UK and other FS markets to illustrate the different forces at work:

- *The current competitors – each 'jockeying' for position through price, quality, or service.* Financial markets have generally become more competitive in recent years, putting pressure on margins. In corporate and investment banking, large organizations prefer to have a range of suppliers to choose from so as to negotiate the best overall package of product terms and service levels. However, some have cut the costs and complexity of supplier management through reducing this approved list, while maintaining multi-sourcing and price negotiation capabilities. Largely as a result of the highly competitive market situation the actual number of traditional competitors in UK banking and insurance markets has fallen.

- *The threat of new entrants – replacing the traditional competitors.* These have often come from the opening up of domestic markets and also from aggressive global FS providers. For example in the UK market Alliance and Leicester Bank, formerly a building society (ie mainly consumer savings and home loans), is now competing aggressively in providing commercial banking services. Global players such as MBNA and American Express have for many years been establishing their presence in the UK market. Investment banks with global reach are gaining the business of the largest corporate clients. The presence of new entrants on many fronts is reshaping the dynamics of the market.

- *The threat of substitute products or services – replacing your offer, perhaps through the use of new technology to provide a lower-cost alternative.* New delivery channels such as the internet (allowing self-designed products and packaging, or self-managed accounts and services) and call centres have not only helped new competitors enter the market, but have also changed the costs of providing many FS products. While technology has its limitations in relation to expectations of personal service, there is no doubt that developments in its capabilities and in its use and acceptance by customers will continue to have a major impact.

- *The bargaining power of customers – amalgamation in many industries is increasing the buying power of corporate customers.* Larger customers have bigger budgets and may need proportionally less account management, but tend to drive a harder bargain. They have access to specialist expertise. As their business becomes more important to the supplier (as a proportion of total income), they are often in a stronger negotiation position. New entrants to FS with large end-customer bases, such as telcos, retailers and car retailers may be in a powerful negotiating position in relation to the FS company ultimately providing the service. They control access to the customer, own the brand that the customer deals with and can deliver a high volume of business.

- *The bargaining power of suppliers – often through the provision of increasingly specialist, high-value or unique services.* Major suppliers can wield their own power where they offer something that their competitors can't. In the IFA market, advisers must have certain strong product provider brands available for customers. In investment banking, global reach or particular specialist expertise may give the supplier power. Provided that retailers and others don't wish to or are unable to move too far back up the FS supply chain there will still be many situations where the product supplier can wield some power!

How these forces appear to you will depend on your starting point. An organization with a well-established position in the market is at the centre of the model and will tend to see these forces as threats to its position. Its strategy might be to raise barriers to each one of them. A company seeking to enter a market will be on the outside of the model – a new entrant – and will tend to see the various forces as either obstacles or opportunities. Its strategy will be to find means to overcome them, or take advantage of them.

**Retention or growth? KAM can be designed to pursue either**

We have just summarized two broad, almost generic, sales strategies, each stemming from a relative position in the market. These are further illustrated in Table 3.1.

**Table 3.1**   *Sales strategies based on market position*

| Market Position | Sales Strategy |
| --- | --- |
| Established position | Retention through raising barriers |
| Potential entrant into a growth market | Growth through finding ways to overcome barriers to entry |

In both cases, the nub of the matter is the same: one thing is required, either to defend or to assault a market position – *competitive advantage*. And here we come to a central plank of most KAM strategies, indeed a key purpose for KAM: KAM is a means to gaining competitive advantage.

We will talk about competitive advantage on many occasions, principally in Part IV, but for the moment let's just consider the problem of competitive advantage as a route to a secure future.

## A SECURE FUTURE THROUGH COMPETITIVE ADVANTAGE?

Competitive advantage and customer loyalty result from many things: products, services, people, declining competitors, changing circumstances or just good fortune. All, including 'earned luck' (which you make for yourself through analysis and planning), are of interest to the key account manager, but as sources of competitive advantage they may be fragile. Competitive advantage, like loyalty, unless continually earned, is easily lost.

## Times change

What are your sources of competitive advantage in relation to your key customers? Are they the same as five years ago? How do you see them changing over the next five years? You may well have seen major changes over the last few years. Laws that once favoured you turn against you; competitors in decline find new leases of life; superior products become ordinary; the buyer who loved you leaves you; temporary cartels break up. This is particularly so where a supplier becomes 'lazy', perhaps having enjoyed for too long a position of power and security. Pent-up customer dissatisfaction can suddenly blow up, producing a big change in a short time.

### Size alone does not bring security

Large companies are most exposed in periods of rapid change – they either respond or lose ground. In the 1980s the UK pension market transformed due to government regulation changes in both corporate and consumer pension markets. While Prudential Corporation and Legal and General (amongst others) recognized this opportunity and took brave growth decisions, others such as Royal and Sun Alliance Life failed to keep pace. Over a few years RSA Life dropped rapidly through the list of largest life companies, losing ground particularly in corporate pensions and eventually becoming insignificant compared to its non-life insurance operations.

## When customers 'snap'

When there is little competition and customers have few options for changing suppliers, customers must be very dissatisfied before they put in the effort of finding an alternative. There is inertia in the market (Figure 3.3).

Add competition – new suppliers eager to win new customers – and the picture changes. Now, small lapses in a supplier's performance result in lost business. Small increases in customers' dissatisfaction cause them to 'snap'. The market becomes fluid.

In assessing the future opportunity, an FS supplier seeking to retain its position must heed these lessons. This means not only understanding the competitive and environmental forces that affect its customers, but also having an intimate knowledge of what is happening within the customer.

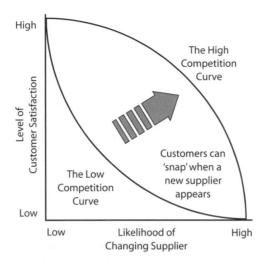

**Figure 3.3**   *When customers 'snap'*

## Proactive customer support in the insurance market

Allstate Insurance (US) is a major provider of life insurance and investment products via independent financial advisers and intermediary groups. In the 1990s competitive pressures led insurance carriers to higher marketing costs and lower sales conversion rates, while intermediaries struggled to compete with each other and to cut marketing and administration costs. Regulation limited the cooperation and support provided by the insurer, to ensure independence of the intermediary's advice to the consumer. Allstate combined and cleaned many external data sources to create a prospect database. After de-duplicating its own customers against it, it analysed the database (using best-practice data-mining techniques) to identify prospects most likely to buy. Through simple and generic browser-based technology, intermediaries could access details of the top prospects in their geographic area. In return the intermediary was encouraged (through assured access to the next 20 prospects) to respond with limited data that confirmed follow-up actions and whether the customer had eventually made a purchase. Because of the intermediaries' independence they were not confined to selling Allstate products to these prospects, but the combination of timely prospect data, supported by relevant product information, often ensured that Allstate products were an obvious best fit. While this pilot project was constrained to a limited period, it was the basis for trialling new techniques of intermediary cooperation and joint value management that continue today.

# THE 'OPPORTUNITY SNAIL'

Finding opportunities from within the customer often demands going beyond the people you might usually deal with. It is no great surprise that, without an active plan to do otherwise, customer contacts tend to settle down to a few regular meetings with the same faces. In FS these are often faces within the finance department. The feeling of comfort and stability that this can bring is dangerously illusory. When the face changes so can your fortune. Genuine security is usually the result of deep relationships with as broad a range of contacts as possible. Even while the face remains the same, the supplier is in danger of missing out on the real opportunities. Working in the realm of the gatekeeper can be a very limiting experience.

In the best KAM examples the supplier has contacts across the buyer's organization, to link into business strategy and new growth initiatives, generate demand for the supplier's products and prove value for services provided, and ensure that products and services are exploited by the buyer for business benefit and that the overall relationship is well administrated with rapid problem resolution where required.

If we consider how ideas and decisions are generated in the customer's organization, we might begin to see the way to uncovering real opportunities, whether for new business or to add value to existing arrangements. Many decisions involving buying FS involve the chief executive and executives on the board. Understanding the motivations and plans of each director involved could be invaluable to you as a supplier in coming up with new ideas and in persuading the board to take them on.

One example concerns intermediary markets where your company is supplying a product that is actually sold further down the value chain. Your primary contact may not be in the department where the real opportunities lie.

Figure 3.4 shows an example of what we will call the 'opportunity snail', as it exists in your immediate customer. The snail represents the typical route a new idea takes as it develops from 'wouldn't it be great?' through to a product launch. In this company, the initiator is the marketing department with a hundred bright ideas a year.

*Figure 3.4*   *The 'opportunity snail'*

Each of these ideas proceeds through checks and developments, often called 'stage gates'. These include: Market Research, to gain ideas and to see if the market is interested in specific new products; Systems and Administration, to see if it can be administered; Legal and Compliance, to make sure that it is within the law; Sales and Training, to find out what needs to be done to ensure that the staff are capable of effectively selling or administering the product. This snail is a simplification, as in reality there would be a complex series of loops, and loops within loops, but it illustrates the problem of making contact with the customer only at the outer edge.

## Penetrating the snail – in search of the real opportunity and the real value

In many cases contact with these internal departments may be a necessary part of the process of supporting your customer. Often systems links are needed between your respective organizations as part of processing of the product. In many cases your organization may have obligations in terms of legal, compliance and training issues. But in addition establishing these links could also bring you a significant advantage. You are now involved with potential products where decisions are not yet made and there is much to influence in the decision. Possibly the 'idea' might not see the light of day but this simply highlights the skill required in managing a key account – where to invest your time and energy.

Should we penetrate further into the snail, right back to the marketing department? There are pros and cons to doing this. Reasons in favour of penetrating to the centre:

- You can discover the real hopes and ambitions of the customer.
- Your expertise and skill in your particular product area can help the customer improve its success rate – surely the route to being considered a key supplier?
- Early contact allows you to set the criteria so that you are the only viable choice, and price is a very minor issue when it comes to the final negotiations.

Reasons against penetrating to the centre:

- What do your primary contacts make of you talking to Marketing? For some this would be tantamount to dealing with the enemy!
- If only a small percentage of new ideas see the light of day, couldn't this close involvement lead you horribly astray, sucking in far more resources than the potential business merits?

## The need for a key account team

Could you do this all alone? Should you do this alone?

The example above relates to product development, but there are many other situations where it is necessary and beneficial to penetrate the key account snail. The more complex the snail, the more it involves people in specialist functions and the less likely it is that sales professionals can do this alone. Even if they can, perhaps it is still best that they don't try to go it alone:

- Penetrating beyond the buyer is never easy, but if it is someone other than the salesperson doing the penetrating that can sometimes ease the way.
- Can the sales professional really be credible in so many different guises and areas of expertise?
- Why should these specialists see a salesperson in any case – wouldn't they prefer to speak with someone who speaks their professional language?
- You'll be amazed at what real experts can uncover when speaking with their opposite number.
- Where is the KAM going to get time to do all this penetrating and follow-through work?

## Putting chains and snails together

What do we conclude from these thoughts? To succeed at the centre of the snail, we must understand the customer's business as well as the customer does. One very successful KAM summed it up succinctly as 'the need for a degree in horse racing – you had to know which opportunities to back'. We would add that you probably need to know which executives in the buying organization to back as well! Each snail is unique, with its own challenges, its own driving force at the centre – sometimes Marketing, sometimes Finance, sometimes Sales, often 'the boss'. Time taken to understand your customer's snail will be time well spent.

The advantages of penetration are substantial but the potential pitfalls are serious. The answer is to manage the penetration so as to avoid the pitfalls, and here we come to the heart of what KAM calls for. Relationships must be managed so that they develop to your advantage and not to your detriment. As they develop, so must your understanding of the customer's business and market, ensuring that you can take advantage of the information the relationship brings without suffering the pains of an 'anything the customer says is right' approach. One way to avoid such pains is to remember the reason for wishing to penetrate the customer's opportunity snail – the pursuit of a long-term competitive advantage.

# LONG-TERM COMPETITIVE ADVANTAGE?

Competitive advantage brings key supplier status, which brings competitive advantage. Is this the Holy Grail of KAM? Undoubtedly, one focus of KAM must be on securing something sustainable, something that will last (if looked after) through all the vicissitudes of the market. And here we come to another central plank of many KAM strategies, indeed another potential key purpose: KAM is a means to key supplier status.

What does this mean? What is a key supplier? How can you achieve key supplier status? We answer these questions, from the customer's perspective, in Part II. For the moment, note that key supplier status is rarely the result of products, technologies or service alone – however superior they might be. It involves developing relationships, building trust, building customer knowledge, using that knowledge to deliver value and, very importantly, jointly managing the future to avoid surprises.

First, we should continue where we have just started, by looking at the future – identifying the purpose of KAM, the objectives part of managing the future.

# 4

# Key account management – its purpose

## WHY KAM?

Chapter 4 may seem rather late to be asking such a fundamental question, but it is hard to show what it will do for you before you understand what KAM is and what it might involve. Choosing an objective before considering the opportunities is an all-too-common mistake that we should avoid.

**Do you need 'good' reasons, or will 'bad' reasons work just as well?**

There are many good reasons to practise KAM. Then there are the reasons that have driven most businesses in this direction. What do we mean by this? The truth of the matter is that many businesses across many sectors have developed KAM strategies because they had little choice, and that's rather sad. Here are some reasons behind the development of the KAM approach in FS:

- customer consolidation;
- global customers demanding a uniform approach and service;
- the supplier's own complexity, often as a result of mergers– many business units selling to the same customers;
- the growth opportunity requires the prioritization of resources;
- the requirement to sell solutions rather than just products or services.

Consolidation is a feature of companies in many industries competing in mature markets. Larger companies offer higher potential sales, but are often more demanding on their suppliers. Concentrating more resources on to those growing fastest is a good idea – and so KAM is born. Global customers may demand a consistent approach across the world and a sharing of information and expertise across markets – and so KAM is born. It is not just about consolidation amongst your customers – many FS organizations have grown through mergers and acquisitions. This creates stronger entities, but also creates complexity with more representatives calling on client companies – and so KAM is born. Customers often demand a more strategic approach to addressing their business challenges – and so KAM is born.

And often, that's it – KAM is the result of outside pressures. The supplier is made to do it. There is good and bad news in this. The good news is that pressure makes things happen. The bad news is that nobody wants to do it! **Defensive...?**

The final two motivations listed above are of a different nature – KAM because it will do something for us, gives us an edge, gives us competitive advantage. Surely these sound better reasons, but sadly they are often not sufficient to make the supplier take on the challenge of the changes required. This is one of the ironies of the story – KAM is often implemented the fastest for the least good reasons, and sometimes not at all, even though the best of reasons are there to be seen. **... or offensive?**

Before you proceed any great distance with your own KAM journey, be sure you know what you want it to do for you. If your reasons are defensive, then you will have a lot of pressure from outside to make things happen, but there will be plenty of resistance from those who don't understand the need. If your reasons are offensive, don't expect your organization to change overnight just because you think it's a great opportunity. **Be very clear what you want from all this effort**

## THREE SIMPLE PURPOSES

The previous chapters have raised three very clear purposes:

- KAM is a process for attempting to manage the future.
- KAM is a means to competitive advantage.
- KAM is a means, if possible, to lead or key supplier status.

And we now add an extra requirement: that it should do all this profitably. Perhaps this was already clear to you? It certainly isn't to all. A client interested in KAM training for its team once told us, with some pride, that it had 72 key accounts. Our interest was suddenly raised – 72 key accounts; it must have an enormous number of KAMs – and we saw the number of events running into the distant future. It turned out that there were four KAMs, so that was 18 key accounts each.

We asked a few questions:

- How does the label 'key account' help in allocating resource, time and money?
- How do you behave differently with those 72 customers compared to all the others?
- How do those 72 customers see their own business enhanced as a result of this label?

The answers, after some pressing, were: 'It doesn't, we don't and they probably don't.' In addition to the reasons cited above, the purpose of KAM is to ensure that you have positive answers to these sorts of questions. We might have asked further:

- Does it mean anything?
- How does the label 'key account' help to manage the investment in your customers?
- How does it help you to manage the relationship between the two businesses – supplier and customer?
- How does it help you to manage the future?
- How does it help you to balance sales objectives with resources and with the opportunity?
- How does it help you to identify activities that would give competitive advantage?
- How does it help you to secure lead or key supplier status?

The purpose of KAM is to have positive answers to all of these questions. KAM is, in short, a *means* to achieving your objectives – not an objective or an end in itself. There is too much effort involved in establishing and maintaining a KAM strategy for there to be no better purpose than being able to say that you did it.

## SALES AND BUSINESS OBJECTIVES

In the previous chapter we discussed broad sales objectives. We have seen already that there is plenty that KAM might do for your business. Let's consider just six possible objectives:

- retention of customers in a competitive environment – *building barriers to entry*;
- growth through entry into new customers – *overcoming barriers to entry*;
- growth with existing customers – *finding new opportunities*;

- managing customers with a cross-territory perspective – _global account management_;
- managing customers serviced by several different business units from within the supplier – _uniform service_;
- going beyond product and benefit selling – _selling solutions_.

Remember, from Chapter 3, that KAM is a means of managing the future, and that requires a balance of _objectives_, _resources_ and _opportunity_. We should consider these objectives then in the light of those other two elements. We like to think of this as a series of 'sanity checks'.

# SANITY CHECKS

Does the _market opportunity_ exist to achieve these objectives?

- _Building barriers to entry._ Do you have a sustainable competitive advantage? Can you secure lead or key supplier status? With which customers?
- _Overcoming barriers to entry._ Do you have a unique value proposition? Which customers would consider it? Are your competitors failing anywhere?
- _Finding new opportunities._ Have you identified and fully exploited the range of opportunities with this customer? Is the customer generating new needs?
- _Global account management._ Do such customers exist? Are they organized to operate 'globally' (as opposed to just being in lots of places)? Do they want a global service?
- _Uniform service._ Are there benefits from the customer's point of view of providing homogeneity in the services you provide across business units? Which customers would benefit?
- _Selling solutions._ Do you understand their challenges? Can you help them, and in turn make profit out this?

(This last question is a big one, and we will return to the notion of the needs of key accounts driving and directing a supplier's wider business activity in Chapters 19 and 20.)

Do you have the right _resources_, and deployed in the right way, to achieve these objectives?

- _Building barriers to entry._ Do you have the right team? Is it deployed correctly?

- *Overcoming barriers to entry.* Is the team sufficient to seize the opportunity, and is it deployed correctly? This is not just a matter of size of the team. The approach is of far greater importance.
- *Finding new opportunities.* Is your team still looking, or have you grown complacent? Do you penetrate your customers' snails?
- *Global account management.* Is your business globally orientated – physically, or psychologically? Will teams work to such objectives?
- *Uniform service.* Will different units collaborate?
- *Selling solutions.* Can the business cope with the diversity of solutions? Are all functions organized to be responsive?

Table 4.1 provides a summary of these thoughts, against these six objectives. A similar table should be completed for your own circumstances.

# IMPLICATIONS OF KAM

Some issues will doubtless be starting to arise by this point in our assessment of KAM. However far you intend to take KAM in your business, the following implications may have occurred to you:

1. *How many key accounts can you have?*

   **Most businesses have too many key accounts...**

   Everything we have said so far suggests that it is relatively few – if you are to prioritize your resource on these customers, if you are to behave differently, if you are to allow their needs to drive your business processes, etc. Part IV looks at the question of identifying your key accounts, looking at the link between market segmentation and KAM and providing a process for making your selections. Leaving it till Part IV may appear rather late in the day, but it is important to understand what KAM actually involves before making these decisions.

2. *How should you use your team?*

   **KAM is not for loners...**

   This is really the heart of KAM in practice, and Parts III and V look at this in detail – asking who is in your team, how should they contribute, and what skills and support (including systems) will they require?

3. *How will KAM affect the running of the business?*

   **KAM is not just a sales initiative...**

   Depending on how far you wish to take it, KAM might be anything from a sales initiative (rarely successful!) through to a revolution in how you run your business. Chapter 14 looks at some of the obstacles that obstruct implementing KAM in a FS business and helps you answer a key question: just how far do you wish KAM to change the way you operate?

**Table 4.1**  *Sanity check summary*

| Objectives | Market Opportunity | Resources |
|---|---|---|
| Building barriers to entry | Do you have a sustainable competitive advantage? Can you secure lead or key supplier status? With which customers? | Do you have the right team? Is it deployed correctly? |
| Overcoming barriers to entry | Do you have a unique value proposition? Which customers would consider it? Are your competitors failing anywhere? | Is the team sufficient? Is it deployed correctly? |
| Finding new opportunities | Are you at full capacity with your customers? Do you penetrate their 'snails'? Are they creating new needs? | Is the team still looking? |
| Global account management | Do such customers exist? Are they organized to operate 'globally'? Do they want global service? | Is your business globally orientated – physically, or psychologically? Will teams work to global objectives? |
| Uniform service | Do customers really want it? Which ones? | Will different units collaborate? |
| Selling solutions | Do you understand their challenges? Can you help them, and make a return on your investment of time and resources? | Can the business cope with the diversity of solutions? Are all functions organized to be responsive? |

## SO, WHAT WILL KAM 'FEEL' LIKE?

How will you know that you are doing anything different from before? If we summarize some of the varied purposes of KAM, we might be able to draw some simple conclusions.

First, we hope we have demonstrated that the title 'KAM' is not a badge of status, like the key to the executive washroom. Nor is it a response to the too-simplistic notion that the biggest customers must have our 'best' salespeople – whatever that means. Nor is it an internal process about selecting, labelling and pigeonholing customers. So what is it? There are several possible purposes and objectives of KAM, which are to:

- manage the future;
- identify customers that will help us achieve our objectives;
- retain and grow customers against competitive forces;
- gain entry to new customers;
- develop intimacy with customers' needs and values;
- gain competitive advantage;
- increase long-term customer loyalty;
- secure lead or key supplier status;
- balance business objectives, market opportunity and business resources;
- allocate and deploy resources, particularly people;
- identify customer-focused activities, and commit to them;
- direct and drive the business, particularly support functions;
- secure a profitable future.

### Being single minded is OK too!

We have one client that uses KAM for a very special purpose. Its business relies on continuous innovation, which is expensive. Often the benefits are short lived. If it is not careful, the choice to do nothing can be strangely tempting, with disastrous results in the longer term. It chose to identify key accounts as customers that will not only force it to innovate, but will support it in its efforts. In practice this usually means customers who will promise to take its innovations on board, before they are actually begun! It is a good idea to innovate alongside customers, but this approach has an added benefit. The customer can be used as a kind of battering ram to break down internal inertia and complacency.

## GOOD PRACTICE?

The following elements of KAM practice always appear in the most successful applications, those in which the supplier achieved its aims, and on those grounds we feel justified in calling them elements of good practice:

- Relationships with the customer go further than the first layer of contact.
- A key account team composed of commercially aware functional experts maintains multiple contacts.
- The KAM is of sufficient stature (and perhaps seniority) to win credibility with the team and with the customer.

- The supplier understands the customer's business and market as well as, perhaps better than, the customer.
- The supplier sees KAM as a cross-business process, not just a sales initiative. This is supported from the top.
- The supplier is prepared to invest in KAM and measures performance over the long term.
- Key accounts are identified on a rational basis that takes into account both your customer's view of your capabilities and your view of the customer's attractiveness.
- Only as many key accounts are selected as the business can manage. There must be a balance between objectives, opportunities and resources (see Chapter 3).

And the conclusions? In all likelihood there will be two features of KAM that stand out above all others – we might even call these the defining features of KAM:

- **developing the nature of the customer relationship in order to enhance understanding;**
- **aligning the business to act on that knowledge in order to secure competitive advantage.**

The first of these two features is the subject of the next chapter. We will return to the second in Part IV. This will be quite a journey. This is something beyond 'selling' in the traditional sense. Some say that KAM isn't about selling at all; rather it is about relationship marketing, ie forging partnerships with customers that are designed for mutual benefit. Perhaps you define 'selling' like this already? If so, you have less of a journey to make.

## IS THERE A KAM PROCESS?

In the next chapter we identify five stages through which a customer relationship develops as a result of KAM. We describe the kind of activities that might apply at each stage, although this is not a prescriptive process. The activities described are in response to the nature of the relationship and in turn help to define its nature – a virtuous circle when it goes well. One thing is clear: by the time the relationship reaches what we call the 'partnership stage', you leave behind any simple linear process of 'do this, then that and then, bingo, the sale'.

If there was any such linear process at the outset of the relationship, then it soon becomes a question of everything happening at once. Not only that but, as the relationship develops, so the intensity of the activities in this process increases. To bring some order and structure to what could soon become an overwhelming situation, we might try to identify a process or series of activities, even if this does not represent a purely chronological sequence. This process is shown in Figure 4.1, but care should be taken not to oversimplify this into a series of separate steps; rather it is a collection of activities that proceed sometimes in sequence and sometimes in parallel.

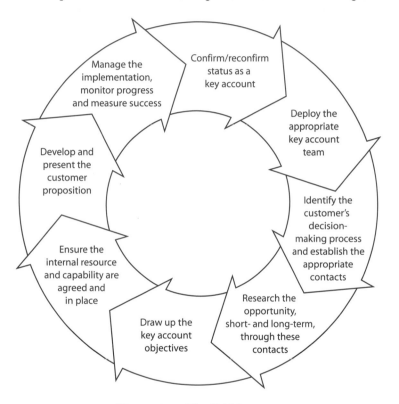

*Figure 4.1*   *The KAM process*

# 5

# Developing the relationship

What constitutes the best relationship depends on the circumstances. If your ambitions are high with a particular customer, and the customer in turn thinks well of you, then perhaps anything short of a deep relationship might be a missed opportunity. However, if the customer does not deserve much attention and asks only for the briefest of contacts with you, then the deep relationship you have envisaged could be inappropriate. Before turning to a model that helps us understand the different kinds of relationship (for example, what is a deep relationship and how does it differ from a shallow one?), let us consider three different sales approaches and the kinds of relationship they engender. We will call these sales approaches the *milk round*, the *hunter* and the *farmer*.

## THE MILK ROUND

This is (or rather was) the classic sales scenario in an established market: a team of managers or sales representatives trying to service a large group of business customers. Examples of this in FS are bank branch managers maintaining a wide range of relationships with many customers at a local level, or insurance salespeople armed with weekly journey plans covering hundreds of contacts.

### When your bank manager was just round the corner

Back in the 1960s and 1970s in the UK there was a rapid expansion of bank and building society branches in every city, town and village. The local manager was a pillar of the community and took personal responsibility for developing his or her business contacts. Often the manager was a generalist and was equally responsible for developing business and retail customers. However, throughout the 1980s and 1990s the number of branches declined. Many banks recognized that a regional or centralized approach was more cost-effective. For example, in mortgage lending, local mortgage introducers (such as accountants, solicitors and estate agents) who formally put business through a local building society branch are increasingly routeing them through centralized operations. Technology has also hastened the reduction in local contact, with staff and branches being replaced or supplemented by the more 'efficient' methods of telesales and e-commerce.

The milk round approach (so named after the milk delivery person who knows the same customers in the same streets over a long period of time) still exists in FS. No one can deny the benefit of local knowledge and person-to-person relationships. However, narrow margins and cost-reduction pressures will maintain the trend towards smaller sales forces and closing local branches.

# THE HUNTER

The hunter approach to selling is most common in fast-growing or acquisition-driven markets. It is all about taking an aggressive approach with an emphasis on gaining new business. It is therefore applicable to particular FS markets at particular stages in their development.

### Chasing the sale in a growth market

During the 1990s, investment banks operated in an especially beneficial environment as a result of developments in securitization and corporate bonds. At the same time the globalization of corporations stimulated the investment and restructuring side. As a result, it could be argued that many investment banks developed their business in hunter mode and became rather transaction- and product-oriented so as to generate new fee income. However, the hunter mode doesn't encourage customer retention and development. This is not so serious while business is booming and relatively cheap to acquire. However, it is of grave concern when the market matures, where acquisition costs are high and poor retention levels add to the required acquisition targets. In a more mature market, clients begin to evaluate supplier banks more critically in relation to long-term commitment. So, if an investment bank is too much of a hunter and not organized to serve the client in an integrated way, it stands to lose the client. Of course, the cost of replacing this relationship with a newly acquired customer is great.

There are many problems with the hunting mode, especially if you are seeking to develop a key account strategy:

- It lives for the moment. Investment is of little consequence to a sales-person focused on this month's commission and who may not plan to be on the team next year.
- It does not discriminate – a kill is a kill. Think of a real hunter, a lioness surveying the ever-moving herd of wildebeest. Does this lioness pick out the healthiest-looking specimen, the one with the most meat and the longest eating potential, or does it prey on the sick and the weak?
- It is fun – at least the successful hunter will regard it as so and, when compared to the plod and the slog of the farmer, who would want to change?

Of course some KAMs are natural hunters. They are well suited to identification, targeting and rapid development of new key accounts. However, it is best to ensure that they are motivated to continue this acquisition approach and not expected to farm the key accounts they have found and developed. Move them on to develop new markets and clients!

# THE FARMER

This approach seeks to develop the customer's potential over time. Investment is the name of the game – investing time and effort for a pay-off next year or beyond. Customer retention is paramount. This long-term view encourages, indeed necessitates, broad and deep contacts with the customer, nurtured in anticipation of a future beyond today's sale. We are describing KAM, of course, but it is not as easy to operate as it might first appear. A number of things can work against the farmer's approach:

- short-term targets imposed from above;
- inappropriate commission or reward packages based on volume today;
- sales management that favours efficiency over effectiveness;
- the insistence that all customers are equal – you can't farm them all.

The farmer is well suited to developing existing key accounts, but perhaps not to identifying or the initial contacting of others. A balanced business depends on identifying new accounts to be farmed, allocating your best farming staff to the best opportunities (while maintaining relationships through limiting changes of account managers) and reducing the focus and resources applied to accounts that are no longer as key.

# FROM HUNTER TO FARMER

The very nature of a sales force makes change difficult. It is made up of people who have emotions and are unpredictable. A big issue is the time taken to bring about change, whether through training, new processes or replacing those people. Replacement is often required. Perhaps only one-third of people can make such substantial transitions, even when well supported. By the time the shift is completed, the circumstances that gave rise to the change may be quite different. If the farmer mode is the essence of KAM and this is what you seek, but your current sales effort is mainly milk round or hunter, then you have a challenging journey ahead of you. The relationship model described in this chapter will serve as your route map.

**The new journey plan**

Most salespeople, at some stage in their career, have had to draw up journey or calling plans – where will you be on Thursday at 10 am? Have you got your regulation six calls in the day? Did you drive the most efficient route? Did you schedule your time and the customer calls effectively? KAM is about managing a journey, but a very different kind of journey plan is required. This is a longer-term journey that proceeds from the first one-to-one contact through to a complex and profitable relationship based on trust and mutual interest. Perhaps the main tasks of the KAM are to plan this journey and to manage the developing relationship.

As with any journey, knowing where you start from is always a good idea. Where you are going comes next. Add to this some good landmarks and milestones along the way and you have the basis for a successful trip. This is the aim of the KAM model – a means of charting your course, as illustrated in Figure 5.1.

***Figure 5.1*** *The key account relationship development model*
Adapted from a model developed by Millman and Wilson (1994)

# THE KEY ACCOUNT RELATIONSHIP DEVELOPMENT MODEL

This model, first developed by Professor Tony Millman and Dr Kevin Wilson in 1994, was further researched and developed at Cranfield University School of Management by Professor Malcolm McDonald, Tony Millman and Beth Rogers. Their findings were published in a research report, *KAM: Learning from supplier and customer perspectives* (1996). The model describes the developing relationship between supplier and customer, from pre-KAM, through early and mid-KAM, on to partnership KAM and then synergistic KAM.

The following pages trace this development as both seller and buyer **Contact and** increase their 'strategic intent' for the relationship, that is to say as each side **collaboration** sees more value gained from putting greater effort into the relationship. As it develops, that 'effort' can be detailed by two main factors. First, there are increasing points of contact between supplier and customer, from simple one-to-one through to more complex matrix or team contacts. Second, the nature of the relationship builds from one based on short-term 'transactions' – doing deals – to one of genuine 'collaboration' – working together towards joint objectives and aspirations. Several points should be noted about this model:

- Progress doesn't happen of its own accord – it needs proactive management.
- Progress takes time – more likely years rather than months (at least to achieve major developments).
- Progress requires mutual intent from supplier and customer – not forcing it on customers.
- You don't have to proceed beyond the point that satisfies your, and the customer's, intentions – partnership KAM is only *better* than early KAM if the circumstances demand it and there is mutual gain.

# CHARTING THE COURSE

At each stage, the relationship has particular characteristics. Begin by defining the nature of your current relationship, by identifying its characteristics, and then target how you want it to develop, noting the characteristics that need to change. Each stage has strengths and weaknesses, for both parties, with attendant opportunities and warnings. Progress from stage to stage may require changing skills and capabilities. KAMs must develop their own skills and those of their team as the relationship develops. It may not be possible to proceed all the way along the line – the customer may call a halt at any point. Setting realistic targets saves you frustration and helps you form more appropriate, and so stronger, links with your customer, at whatever level.

The KAM charts a course. Navigation rules are clear: have goals, look out for helpful signposts, take comfort in milestones passed and keep good track of your progress. This way, not only do you know where you are headed, but you will also recognize the scenery when you get there. The following pages describe some of those signposts and milestones (Figures 5.2–5.6). At each stage, the characteristics described are likely, but by no means universal. They are described to help you establish the status of your current relationship.

### A note on the diagrams

The labels used to denote functions and departments are of course just examples. There is no rule that says these are the people who should be involved. Nor is there any rule that says how many people should be involved. Diamond teams (see Figure 5.5) can have anywhere between 3 and 30 members, perhaps more.

## Possible characteristics of the pre-KAM stage

**Keeping your eyes and ears open...**

- Simple, one-to-one contact.
- Supplier presentations focus on their own issues and concerns.
- Response to customer enquiries is yes or no, based on assumed customer needs and supplier's current capabilities.
- The seller will be assessing volume potential.
- The customer will be seeking evidence of competence and competitiveness.
- The customer will judge competitiveness on price.
- The customer may require trials, perhaps at the supplier's cost.
- The initial contact may act as 'gatekeeper', denying access to other contacts.

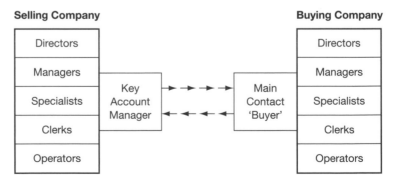

***Figure 5.2*** *Pre-KAM stage*
Adapted from McDonald, Millman and Rogers (1996)

## Possible characteristics of the early KAM stage

- Principal contact between two people.
- The relationship may be competitive, each seeking to gain advantage.
- At worst, the relationship may be confrontational.
- The client contact may see attempts to access other contacts as a threat to his or her position and power.
- Price discussions dominant – focus on cost.
- The supplier focuses on increased volume.
- Suppliers are judged on unspecified performance criteria.
- The customer is still assessing alternative suppliers.

**Control, but learn to let go...**

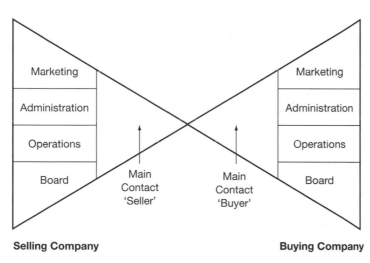

**Figure 5.3** *Early KAM stage*
Adapted from McDonald, Millman and Rogers (1996)

## Possible characteristics of the mid-KAM stage

- Principal contacts start to facilitate other contacts through mutual desire to increase understanding of customer's processes and markets.
- Increase in time spent in meetings and/or working together.
- Focus on reporting those meetings, action minutes, achievements, etc.
- Increased trust and openness developing.
- Links are informal, still facilitated by the salesperson and the principal contact within the client company.
- It is perhaps at this stage that the greatest chance for 'mishaps' occurs – expect setbacks.
- This is a lot of work for both seller and buyer!

**Hard work... but worth the effort in the long run**

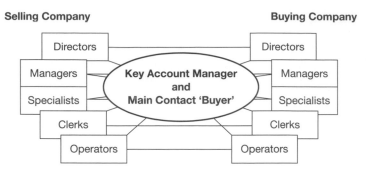

**Figure 5.4** *Mid-KAM stage*
Adapted from McDonald, Millman and Rogers (1996)

# Possible characteristics of the partnership KAM stage

**Enjoying the**
**benefits of KAM**

- Key supplier status is awarded.
- Relationships are based on trust.
- Information is shared.
- Access to people is facilitated.
- Pricing is stable.
- Customer gets access to new ideas first.
- Continuous improvement is expected.
- Clear 'vendor ratings' and 'performance measures'.
- Possible customized contractual arrangements.
- Value is sought through integrated business processes (see Part VI).
- Value is sought through focus on the customer's markets (see Part VI).

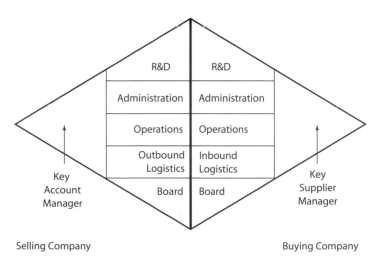

**Figure 5.5** *Partnership KAM stage*
Adapted from McDonald, Millman and Rogers (1996)

- Differences of opinion are allowed.
- The KAM's role is one of coordination, orchestration and responsibility.
- The supplier's main contact now focuses on developing rather than challenging the supplier's capabilities.
- The supplier's total organization is focused on customer satisfaction through 'supply chain management'.

## Possible characteristics of the synergistic KAM stage

- Joint R&D.
- Transparent costings and margins.
- Focus on innovation.
- Collaborative approach to customer's markets and end-users – actively working to develop those markets. Shared market and customer data (where appropriate and allowed by regulation).
- Joint business plans.
- Joint marketing plans.
- Shared communications network.
- Shared training.
- Shared resources – including people.
- Exit barriers in place.
- Focus teams involve members of both companies, led by either supplier or customer.

**Working as one… rare but not impossible**

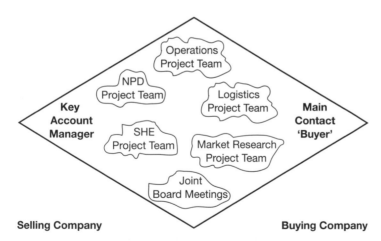

***Figure 5.6*** *Synergistic KAM stage*
Adapted from McDonald, Millman and Rogers (1996)

# SOME PROS AND CONS OF EACH STAGE

Each stage has its own attractions and attendant challenges for both supplier and customer. You must understand these pros and cons if you are to progress from one stage to the next. Each stage brings greater effort, greater commitment and increasing potential for mishap. To take your whole organization with you on this journey (and it is no use getting there on your own if the rest of your team is still standing at the station), you must be able to sell the benefits of moving forward, while assessing the obstacles and making plans to overcome them.

## Pre-KAM

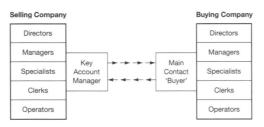

*Figure 5.7    Pre-KAM*

Not many positives for this stage, but a good supplier will be on a voyage of exploration and discovery, asking questions and uncovering customer needs. Done well, with the focus on customer needs and not on satisfying its own requirements, this exploration can show the supplier in a very good light.

**Reconnaissance is about listening – not telling**

The downsides of exploration are only too obvious – the great unknown: sudden barriers to entry, surprising competitor strengths, obscure customer requirements and, hardest of all at first, unclear customer style and culture. Making the 'big presentation' too early, if it hits the wrong nerves, can spell the end before you really get started. Descending on the customer with a busload of senior managers, brochures and a 'flash' presentation can be the very last thing to do at this stage. Many businesses feel it necessary to do this at the early stages of their life – to get out there and spread the word about themselves. Resist the temptation; it rarely works.

For most FS sellers, effort is better spent in researching the customer – seeking for clues as to what makes it tick, what it might need and what it might value. Of course, we are in classic 'chicken and egg' territory here. Without knowledge of the customer, how is it possible to assess its potential as a key account? If you cannot define it as a potential key account, then how do you justify the time and effort for research? To escape from this vicious circle you must recognize that, as well as research, you need persistence, gut feel and faith – not a bad definition of the start of many success stories, but be prepared for the ones that don't come off. Be prepared for one more problem – the customer may regard the salesperson as only a messenger, and the salesperson's own colleagues may regard him or her as an irresponsible 'champion' (often of the customer)! Nobody in their right mind will want to hang around at this stage too long!

## Early KAM

This is probably the most typical sales relationship in many markets, the classic 'bow-tie', and it is a dangerous stage. It is all too easy, and apparently attractive, just to stay here. The salesperson is in full control, with no distractions from badly informed colleagues – and gets all the praise for success! This is the stage that promises 'a place in the limelight' at the next sales conference. The client may also

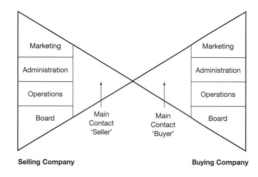

**Figure 5.8**   *Early KAM*

be happy with this state of affairs – it is secure, knows all that goes on with the supplier and can keep its carefully guarded secrets. However, unlike in other industries, this situation may be difficult to sustain in supplying FS. This is because in many situations you need to set up integrated processes and support for the client organization. Most business-to-business FS involves more than a simple product sale! Multiple contact points between selling and buying organizations tend to build up rapidly and from an early stage. As well as the inevitability of the range of relationships developing, there are a number of other general reasons for moving on from this stage:

- Expertise on both sides is seriously underutilized.
- Seller and buyer are expected to be all-round experts – an unlikely scenario.
- Information flow is restricted as buyer and seller jockey for negotiating position.
- When information does flow, it is littered with 'Chinese whispers' as it is translated along the chain – expert to non-expert, to non-expert, to expert... and back.
- Projects and activities are held up by the sales/purchasing bottleneck.
- There is over-reliance on one relationship, and if it breaks, the whole thing must start again – the future of the company-to-company relationship is permanently at risk.
- Salespeople become 'kingpins' who cannot be moved on, or requested to accept major operational change, for fear of losing the business.

A limitation of this kind of relationship in intermediary markets is where the supplier is denied full access to customers' internal processes and also to their markets. A salesperson might know very little about how his or her immediate customers operate in their own markets and still less about the needs of the end-customer. Sometimes denial of access will be deliberate. It is a matter of power and ownership of the customer. An intermediary may have spent many years building up a customer base and an understanding of its particular customers' needs. This knowledge is central to its business success and why should it be shared?

There are advantages to this kind of relationship – it is simple, relatively low-cost and controllable – and if it gets what you want, there may be no need to go beyond it. However, as discussed above, it is often unrealistic to maintain this one-dimensional approach, and it may not allow full development of business potential.

## Mid-KAM

*Figure 5.9    Mid-KAM*

This is the transition stage between the classic 'bow-tie' and the 'diamond' of the partnership KAM stage. It is a stage full of sensitivity and, if the supplier is wise, slow, measured steps forward. As noted above, in FS, in managing the relationship, many contacts need to be developed. The principal contact may feel threatened by any increase in contacts 'beyond his or her own control'; the KAM must ensure that new contacts are cleared with him or her and will almost certainly have to be involved in putting the contacts together, attending the first meetings and perhaps further. Ideally, the primary contact will also be involved in these meetings, but if not, their outcome must be reported to the primary contact in full.

**Hard work – but well worth the effort**

Add to this a briefing-and-coaching role and we can see a potential overload of activities for the KAM. Realizing the work involved, we should look again at the model of managing the future, introduced in Chapter 3, and consider the resources required. How many key accounts can an individual manager have responsibility for at this stage? Add to this the fact that the mid-KAM stage can go on for many months, perhaps even years, and we must think seriously about how many customers can be classified as key accounts. As the benefits of moving towards partnership KAM are unlikely to flow immediately, this mid-KAM stage could be seen by some as not worth the effort. The temptation to go back to the relative comforts of the 'bow-tie' is strong. Resist!

### But we might meet someone important...'

One company was struggling to get past this stage. It had plenty of its people working alongside the customer, but not in any coordinated way. The biggest frustration was that people with contacts were reluctant to go any further than achieving their own narrow objectives – they were not part of a team with bigger ambitions. The KAM told us that most of these people were scared to go further. One of them said, 'When I visit the customer I get in and out as quickly as possible. What if I was to meet someone important and they asked me something really difficult?' Easy to laugh, or to be cynical about the capabilities of non-sales professionals, but if you are to get to true diamond teams such fears must be thoroughly overcome.

## Partnership KAM

This is where the benefits should start to flow. With the proper deployment of expertise on both sides, with the more open and honest transfer of information and with the resultant improvement in customer understanding, the supplier has the potential to move towards significant competitive advantage. Where both sides have made an

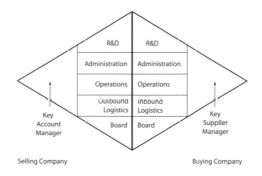

**Figure 5.10**  *Partnership KAM*

investment in time and resources it may be problematic for the buyer to move to another supplier. As a supplier you often have access to privileged information in relation to your client. If a major downside to the 'bow-tie' of early KAM was the denial of access to customers' internal processes and to their market, the main advantage of the 'diamond' relationship is in seeing those conduits of understanding opening up.

Be careful. As contacts proliferate, so does speed of activity – and the risk of saying and doing the wrong things. People without experience of 'sales' will be put in front of customers, and might panic at the prospect. The KAM's role changed through the mid-KAM stage from 'super-salesperson' to 'super-coach'. It now moves on to 'super-coordinator'. If it doesn't, then the potential for losing control is great, resulting in well-meaning, but misdirected, individuals charting their own quite separate courses. Without clarity of objectives and shared understanding of what the customer values, you could just be about to race down some blind alleys. Your enthusiastic IT expert, working with an equally keen counterpart, might see this new road as an opportunity to try some unaccustomed speed. Accidents can happen if they don't stick to the rules of good driving.

**For many, this stage will be the ultimate goal, but arriving here is no cause for complacency...**

---

## The tale of the CEO

The CEO of a regional bank was visiting one of the bank's home loans distributors – a major mortgage broker. The broker requested a self-certification mortgage product that was already available to its major competitors (self-certification mortgages are primarily designed for self-employed people who have difficulty in proving their income). The CEO readily agreed but unfortunately the CEO had not been aware of the essential facts. He didn't know that the distributor had a variable track record in the quality of its mortgage advisers and his own underwriters had resisted using this distributor for this type of product. The distributor had been hassling the KAM for many months and consistently been given the answer: 'not until we can be sure that sufficient quality controls are in place'. Both the CEO and the KAM were put in a very difficult position. So, whose fault was this? Of course the CEO should have known better, but the KAM is equally, if not more, responsible. The KAM should have briefed the CEO. KAMs are responsible for all communications, transactions and activities between supplier and customer. Sure, it's not easy briefing the boss, but nobody said KAM was easy!

---

## The three golden rules of partnering

Achieving this partnership stage may be the hardest bit of the journey. Much stands in your way, but the benefits are so great that it deserves all the effort. Three golden rules will speed you towards genuine partnership:

- Work with a long-term perspective.
- Seek out the 'win-win' solutions.
- Recognize that trust is more important than money.

None of these rules is easy to stick to if short-term gains tempt you. Only you can take the decision as to which is more important: short-term gain or long-term security and prosperity; or perhaps it is the realistic achievement versus the jam-tomorrow dream?

## The importance of the partnership model in FS

FS often requires integration of processes and systems between supplier and buyer. This means that operational, administrative and systems staff from the supplier may need to work closely with their counterparts in the buying organization from an early stage. A high level of trust and understanding needs to be established across a number of levels and functions of both businesses. In this situation it is essential to transform the role of the initial sales contact from that of lone hunter to that of business manager and team leader. There are of course degrees of application between these two positions, and Figure 5.11 illustrates a typical mid-point where KAMs continue fully with their previous role as prime sales contact, but in a very different environment.

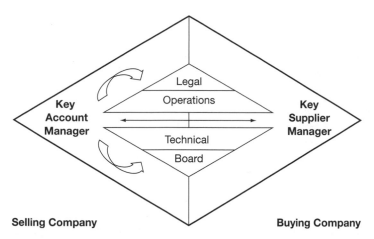

**Figure 5.11** *Partnership KAM – a variation on a theme*
Adapted by Peter Chiu of Huntsman Taiwan, from McDonald, Millman and Rogers (1996)

Of course, the diamond model doesn't propose that salespeople no longer have significant customer contact – or 'touch time' as many like to call it – and neither do they stop selling. What changes is the fact that they play their selling role in new circumstances, as a part of a team sell backed by delivery of promises. There are many demands on them. They must promote their colleagues' roles, and avoid stealing the limelight, but their own personal selling skills must be raised to new heights – they must now become examples of sales excellence and customer management for the rest. As ever, these tools and models are used to stimulate thought, not to impose a strait-jacket. Remember rule number one: you make the rules.

## Synergistic KAM

The experience gained at the partnership stage – coordinating the team sell, coaching the team on their customer interface roles and learning to work within the customer's values and culture – stands you in good stead for moving to synergistic KAM. But do not try to get there too quickly. It is tempting to force the pace, before either side is

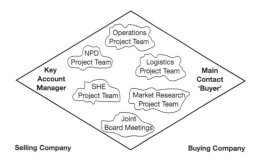

**Figure 5.12** *Synergistic KAM*

ready for the requirements of working in this way. The result could be the breakdown of a relationship, through confusion, and, after all the effort and good work of the partnership KAM stage, that would be a tragedy.

There is another problem: if managed well, the partnership stage will be seen as successful for both supplier and customer. It will have been a novel experience for most, and the idea of changing to something even *more* unusual will raise many barriers. 'If it ain't broke, don't fix it.' You will hear this many times as you try to move both sides of the relationship on, but it will be worth the perseverance. The benefits are enormous – a truly symbiotic relationship where values are shared and so needs are more easily identified and met. The security of this relationship is enormous; a competitor will find it very difficult to break into this account.

On the other side, the supplier's commitment will be almost total by this stage, so be certain that this really is an account worth the effort – withdrawal will be difficult, embarrassing and, perhaps, terminal. One possible characteristic of this stage is collaborative focus on developing the customer's markets. The supplier must ensure that it has the expertise needed to play its part in this activity, or it will soon be seen to be a hollow offer.

This stage requires strong but subtle management, particularly in setting up the teams. These self-managing focus teams must not be allowed to develop into island activities, divorced from each other and heading in ever-divergent directions. But the solution is not heavy-handed supervision, which would defeat the whole purpose of devolving control and empowering the team. The way forward must be through a commitment by all members, supplier and customer, to the joint goals, roles, objectives and expectations of the relationship.

The focus teams should not be functionally based. This would encourage the island or 'silo' mentality that you have taken so long to escape from on this journey. They should be based on projects or programmes, each with clear customer value goals and performance measures. They must exist for their goals, not for themselves. The measure of success for many will be disbanding the team on completion of their task – harder than it sounds. Resist the temptation to keep a good thing going beyond its useful life. There is space for at least one team not based on a finite project: a 'long-term vision' team, a strategy team, focused on managing the future.

One feature of a synergistic relationship is openness of both organizations to each other. This may involve allowing customer access to your own operational processes (setting up products on your systems) and access to privileged commercial information. If this frightens you, then you are probably not ready for this stage.

# SOME THINGS TO WATCH OUT FOR

This is a journey and, with the right customer for your companion, it is one worth making. But remember, it is a journey of exploration and discovery; expect the unexpected. All worthwhile activities bring problems, which must be overcome with patience and resolve. The risks may be high, but not desperate, the obstacles large, but not insurmountable. The possible disasters seen at the outset seem many, but they are not certain and, by thoughtful planning, most can be prevented. And if the journey is made for good reason, you can expect the support of your team, your management *and* your customer. The hardest part of the journey will almost certainly be the transition from 'bow-tie' to 'diamond'. Working through the transitional mid-KAM stage can be very hard work. At times, it will seem more effort than it is worth, to both sides. This calls for all your patience, resolve and understanding. It will call on every skill and tool you have, and some you don't. At this point, you will need friends and allies. This is not a task for loners, so:

- Don't expect your journey to be one way; there will be U-turns and side alleys.
- Remember that the strategic intent must be mutual and, even then, don't expect the customer to make it easy for you. You must lead a lot of the way, and while stamina and persistence will be two valuable assets, so will subtlety and finesse. You will know when you are getting there, when the customer starts to pull.
- Remember, principal contacts have a lot of power when they are the only point of contact. Your efforts to develop broader contacts might be for the good of their company, but they might not see it as good for them! You are about to threaten their control.
- To sell or not to sell? If the customer sees your 'selling' activity as a pushy concern for satisfying your own needs, don't be surprised if you come up against obstacles. If the customer sees it as seeking solutions to its problems, the doors will start to open.
- Some customers will demand that the KAM should not be a 'salesperson' at all, but a business manager and a relationship manager.
- Some customers might not like being called 'accounts' – so this is a word for internal use, not your business card (in the end, you can call them whatever makes everyone feel good!).
- Don't let your organization loose on theirs with no direction and no control – chaos can be the only outcome, quickly followed by a rapid raising of the customer's drawbridge.
- Don't allow commercially 'innocent' members of your team to be taken for a ride by the customer – brief them first and, above all, train them. This includes the boss (actually, especially the boss).

- Don't describe this journey, internally, as an 'initiative' – many companies have had 'initiative' overload and your own team will steer clear of this latest 'seven-day wonder'.
- One sure killer of progress, from early to mid- to partnership KAM, is the unrealistic tightening of travel budgets – strong relationships require personal contact.
- Be careful how you present your intentions to the customer: being told that you wish to be more 'intimate' may concern or confuse the customer, or worse!
- Take care if you are the first to use the word 'partnership'. Try to hear it on the customer's lips first.
- Perhaps your customer will use 'partnership' as a trap. 'Let's work in partnership', the customer says, meaning, 'You tell us your cost breakdowns, and then we'll take you to the cleaners.'

### The tale of the pig and the chicken

Is this last point unduly cynical? Perhaps you should be a little wary until you are sure?

Remember the pig and the chicken that decide to go into partnership together. It was the chicken's idea. They go into the catering business, specializing in traditional breakfasts. At their first business meeting, the chicken explains its ideas.

'Tell you what,' it clucks, 'why don't I supply the eggs and you supply the bacon…'

The moral of the tale? If you don't mean it, and they don't mean it, stick to old-fashioned selling – the early KAM model is fine for relationships that don't aim to progress beyond the transactional.

# MAKING DIAMOND TEAMS WORK

This challenge will be discussed throughout the rest of this book – it is after all perhaps the biggest of them all. For now, there are two almost mandatory actions to ensure that diamond teams work well and avoid the pitfalls that are just waiting out there for the unwary – a contact matrix and clear GROWs. The contact matrix is discussed fully in Chapter 24. It is not a complicated tool, simply a chart that lays out all the points of contact between supplier and customer – who is responsible for seeing who. GROWs, also described in Chapter 24, are a little more involved. GROW is an acronym:

**G** – Goal.
**R** – Role.
**O** – Obligation.
**W** – Work plan.

Each point of contact in the matrix should have a set of GROWs to express its purpose.

These two simple tools (and keep them simple, please!) help you to direct and monitor and control the activities of the key account team.

## The diamond team – core and full

How big should a diamond team be? This depends on your circumstances, but there is a more general answer. A team of anything more than six people is going to start hitting problems of getting together, communication and all the rest. Yet there may be more than six people involved with the customer – so what to do? A good solution is to identify what we might call the *core team*, the few people, probably three or four, who meet and discuss the customer very frequently and are responsible for the key interactions. They are rather like a steering team. Around them is the full team, as many as required, and a changing group as projects come and go. The core team should meet regularly, and be copied on all significant developments. The full team might meet only once or twice a year, and be copied on developments on a 'need-to-know' basis.

# AVOIDING FRUSTRATION

Developing a relationship requires mutual intent. The result of any imbalance in that intent will be frustration, sometimes minor but sometimes resulting in the termination of the relationship. The relationship zones are depicted in Figure 5.13.

## Seller's frustration zone

If the supplier's intent outpaces the buyer's, then the attempt to involve the key account (KA) team in front of the customer may not result in any change in the nature of the relationship – it does not progress from transactional to collaborative and the contacts are rejected. At best, the supplier is frustrated. Worse, the supplier wastes the customer's time. Worse still, the KAM wastes his or her own company's resources, and this is hugely damaging to the profitability of that customer. Worst of all, the supplier's frustration may lead to undue pressure on the customer, with serious, potentially terminal, consequences. If the supplier *is* ahead of the customer in strategic intent (and this will often be so), then develop a KA team by all means, but don't foist it on the customer – prepare the ground so that, when strategic intents *do* match, the team is ready.

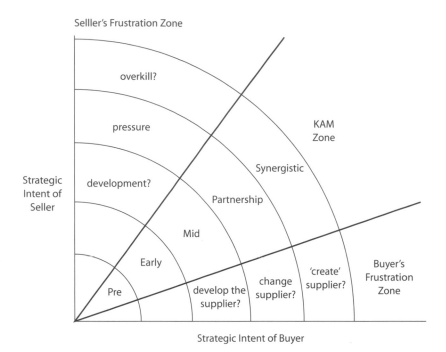

**Figure 5.13**   *Buyer–seller relationship zones*
Adapted from McDonald, Millman and Rogers (1996)

## Buyer's frustration zone

If the supplier's intent lags behind the buyer's, then the customer may have to take steps to develop the supplier. If the supplier still lags behind, the customer will soon be seeking a new supplier.

## Getting the right match

Are customers at their most demanding at the early stages of the relationship, the 'show us what you're made of' phase? No! While the deeper relationship found in the partnership or synergistic stage is more stable, it is also more demanding. The expectations placed on a supplier increase with each stage of the relationship:

- At the *early* KAM stage, the main expectation is that the supplier should be proficient.
- Entry into the *mid*-KAM stage suggests that the customer is looking for more; it now expects the supplier to be a problem solver.
- By the time the *partnership* KAM stage has emerged, the customer's expectations of the supplier will have risen to just that – a genuine business partner.

So, a supplier should understand where the customer sees the relationship. Misunderstandings can lead to more than just frustrations; they can be terminal. A customer once stated that a supplier was fired because the supplier thought that being proficient was enough. The customer was looking for something beyond the _early_ KAM stage and the supplier didn't read the signs or recognize the frustrations. We have also heard a customer say that a supplier was fired because it had ideas beyond its station. A mismatch of perceptions about where the relationship lies is more damaging when the relationship is quite advanced than in a basic relationship in which both sides can see it for what it is. It is worth monitoring the joint perception of the relationship to ensure that these damaging mismatches don't occur.

## AN UPDATE TO THE KAM PROCESS

Chapter 4 suggested a KAM process: a series of activities, not necessarily linear, shown in Figure 4.1. At each stage of the relationship described in this chapter, these activities will be pursued, each in more depth and with greater accuracy, efficiency and success as the relationship develops. The process builds on itself and thus the relationship advances. Rather than being a flat circular process, it can now be seen as a spiral working upwards, with the activities being carried out on ever-higher planes. Of course, sometimes the spiral will work downwards and steps previously covered, which might appear rather mundane from your until-recently high vantage point, will have to be repeated. There is little place for false pride in KAM.

# 6

# The good, the bad and the sad

This chapter gives several examples of experience from FS markets. They are all real cases, based on our own experiences and on the research we conducted in preparing this book. To preserve the anonymity of our sources, some details have been changed and the names of some of the companies involved withheld. Of course, it is usually easier to come up with bad or sad stories than good stories about KAM practice. This is not because there are more failures than successes, but because we usually learn more from failures. Good stories sometimes suffer the problem of context – it worked, but only in those circumstances, people will say. In this chapter we present a mixture of positive and negative examples. While it is useful to show failures, as a warning of what to avoid, it is more valuable to show how critical turning points have been addressed. So, in providing these examples, we include the bad and the sad, where neglect and lack of fore-thought are often the issue, but also some good stories, to show how KAM methods have been successfully applied.

The bad stories show two examples of ineptitude in KAM. The first is by taking things for granted at the client end, the second by being proactive, but making a mess by not understanding the customer's needs. The sad stories include one where a proactive approach to the intermediary's end-customers is let down by the quality of customer data. The other sad stories relate to communication and how appropriate communication at the right time can make all the difference in key account relationships. To finish on a more positive note, we include a couple of examples of good practice. The first shows how a relatively small provider of banking services gained a competitive edge through after-sales service, the second a turnaround situation where a niche supplier partnered with a larger supplier to retain an account that would otherwise have been lost.

# SOME BAD STORIES

This one comes from an international reinsurer. It concerns a typical contract initially introduced through a broker. It involved reinsuring an insurance company in the US in respect of its medical expenses book. On the face of it, the rate applied looked set to make a healthy profit for the reinsurer. However, about three months into the contract, claims data from the insurance company (normally sent every month) stopped coming through. The reinsurer's medical underwriter made repeated requests to the initial point of contact, the broker, to get updated claims information, and the broker in turn passed this on to the insurer. This went on for months. Meanwhile, the insurer continued to pay its premiums regularly. This situation continued until annual renewal of the contract. Then the reinsurer indicated that it would not renew without full claims data. Finally, the requested data were received and the reinsurer hit with a large claim. The lesson relates to the need to penetrate down the supply chain into the client's organization. Here, the nature of the financial risk being taken required much closer monitoring than was possible at arm's length. Rather than complaining to the broker that he wasn't doing his job, the reinsurer should have taken direct and speedy action. As an employee of the reinsurer concluded, 'one of us should have got on a plane and visited the ultimate client with a view to immediate cancellation if figures were not produced'.

**What happens when you ignore 'snails' and 'chains'…**

This example comes from insurance. It is common practice for insurers to support large brokers by setting up events for the broker's members. In this case a target-hungry account manager, desperate to make a relationship with a major broker work more effectively, agreed to sponsor a national conference. It is common to invest a lot of money, literature, promotional merchandise and other resources into national conferences, given who will be there. Therefore one might expect the account manager to think through the benefits to be obtained and at least make an attempt to quantify these. But here, little research had been done to see whether the broker would merit priority treatment. Worse, the account manager betrayed lack of understanding of the account, by bringing totally unsuitable presentations to the conference, clearly demonstrating to delegates complete lack of understanding.

**Lack of forethought wastes everybody's time**

This reveals the remarkable ineptitude of the account manager, but also raises serious questions about the overall processes for account management in this situation. The lack of control and requirement for proper justification of investment suggests that much of this organization's efforts in supporting key accounts might be misplaced. Tighter management controls were required to focus use of resources and to identify good and bad practice at account manager level. These have now been put in place in the organization concerned!

# SOME SAD STORIES

We have come across several examples in our research that are sad rather than bad, because they are about misjudgements and neglect rather than serious errors.

**Problems with data on end-customers**

One very sad story is of a Nordic pension provider that implemented mass communications programmes to address the end-consumers of group pension products, without sufficient testing or assessment of data quality. There were major errors in source data. This resulted in incorrect calculations of pension dates and personalized propositions. The volume and pervasiveness of the problem (covering multiple pension groups and unions) were quickly recognized by the media and highlighted on the front pages of major daily newspapers. As a result the reputation and brand of the company involved were severely damaged. It took considerable effort, time and cost to recover. This in turn had a detrimental effect on the company's relationships with the brokers and intermediaries who sell its products. This demonstrates a common problem for many FS companies dealing with end-customers through intermediaries. Many have greatly improved their KAM capabilities, but discover that final results are constrained by data quality.

**A customer's perspective on business banking**

This example concerns the customer perspective. It is based on the experience of the finance function in a large UK public sector institution. Our respondent, a finance manager, is generally happy with only limited contact with the banker on a day-to-day basis. He knows that when he has funds to invest, he can ring up the bank, get a view on whether it is a good time to invest and negotiate a decent deal if appropriate. He admits that he wouldn't be happy about the bank phoning him up every day. On the other hand there are circumstances where more proactive communication from the bank would be appropriate. An example cited by the finance manager was when there was a £300,000 drop in the value of funds invested because of a drop in government bond prices. This showed up on the regular weekly report from the bank. This report is basically just a figures report with no commentary. This is enough in normal circumstances, but requires more explanation when something exceptional happens. As the finance manager put it:

I thought it might have been sensible to send the reports in the post and phone me, saying 'The report is on the way; it doesn't look too good, but it's happened because of this, this and this. We expected it to happen. The reason why we bought the gilts in the first place was because they were under-priced and represented a good opportunity; we still think that is a good decision...', etc. A simple phone call like that. So when I have to do my own report which says our current balances have declined I can explain why.

The above example shows the importance of appropriate and proactive communications from the supplier. This can be challenging where it involves several different people in several different areas. A respondent from an insurance supplier related the problem where a key account is trying to get information from the insurer and the appropriate contact is not available. In this case the person may get put through to somebody else, who doesn't understand why that person is asking and gives the wrong information. As our respondent put it, 'I've had several phone conversations from directors and senior people within the key account who phoned me and said "I can't believe I've just had this conversation with one of your people."' This problem comes down to the member of staff involved not being fully aware of what's going on with the account. Ultimately it's down to communication.

**The importance of communication**

Another aspect of communication relates to the importance of managing expectations. The same respondent from an insurance company made the point that it is not always just about getting something done as quickly as possible: 'If you ask the right questions, you find out that they don't need it for a couple of weeks.' The difficulty occurs when your own people let you down and don't warn you until the last moment:

Despite checking and being told that everything is OK all the way along, two days before they say, 'We can't deliver.' That's when you have to take the bad part of the job; you have to make those phone calls and say 'We can't deliver', and you get it in the neck. It's not your fault, but you are representing the company, so you have to take it.

The other side of this is that the account manager also receives the praise when somebody else in the organization has done particularly well in delivering on time. In this case our insurance company respondent stressed the importance of passing this praise on: 'I always make a point of e-mailing their manager to say "I've had this said to me today", and they really appreciate it. They probably don't understand the benefit of it, but, in terms of relationship, maybe it's improved the relationship no end. Again, it's all down to communication.'

# SOME GOOD STORIES

**A focused and responsive service**

This story is about one highly successful lender to the UK university sector, as told to us by a decision maker on the customer side. It relates to a relatively small bank that had decided to target the sector because it thought that the customer wasn't getting the right rates and the right service, given its size. It put two senior managers on it and promoted the company strongly. It managed to get itself on some tenders and delivered very good prices. But it wasn't the price in that market that impressed, because this could change on a day-to-day basis. What impressed the buying organization was the after-sales service. In this sector, legislation surrounding the loans is complicated. Even after agreeing a rate for a loan, it can take some time to conclude the deal, with lawyers arguing over the small print. In the words of our respondent:

> This bank took the view that they should take decisions quickly, so they have a weekly banking meeting… Every Tuesday, the manager who we met actually went into his corporate team and gave a paper presenting our case and they said yes or no. Once they said yes, that then meant that within his discretion they could take decisions over the small print on the final contract. They didn't continually have to go back to their head office. So they devolved power to these people and once they had agreed a template for dealing with the people in this sector, they would then be able to roll that out.

This bank is reputed to be the most successful in the last two years in the university sector. It is building a reputation for closing deals effectively and quickly. In a market where there is limited rates differentiation between suppliers, it is getting repeat business because of its administration and speed of decision making.

**Strategic alliances to improve customer value**

A niche financial markets provider of investment services had been very focused on differentiating its 'unique' services to a major client over a long period. However, this extreme focus made it difficult for it to 'see the wood for the trees' or to see the buying issues from the purchaser's perspective. In one crucial review meeting it was advised that the purchaser's supplier list was being dramatically reduced to a few larger suppliers, to limit the costs and complexities of buying from too many niche providers (however good they each were). In this case the purchaser was a provider of consumer investment services, where there were increasingly severe constraints on the administration costs allowable for managed funds – costs had to be cut somehow.

Working with IBM, the financial markets provider considered alternative business strategies to maintain this key client relationship, without which the business would need to be dramatically cut in size. This started with a more complete exploration of the market issues faced by the client company, and consideration of how this supplier could assist. One obvious and eventually successful approach was to link with another top-three supplier that did a far greater volume of business with the key client but lacked the ability to offer differentiated and high-value service and products. By forming a small number of strategic alliances the financial markets supplier was able to meet the needs of this KAM relationship while offering entry opportunities to others.

# LEARNING THE LESSONS

The examples presented in this chapter demonstrate various aspects of KAM practice. An underlying theme in many of the bad and sad stories relates to poor communication. A central issue is lack of 'joined-up thinking' and breaking down the organizational silos that exist in many FS organizations today – which in most cases prevent the supplier from more fully addressing the needs of the buyer. Even where these needs seem to be addressed well, money is often 'left on the table' as other people in the supplier company are often unaware of the business opportunity and therefore unable to take advantage of the full opportunity.

For example, many relationships start with 'acquisition' products that a customer has a direct and immediate need for – a loan, for example. These are often commoditized products, usually poor use of business capital and poor generators of fees and profits. In a poorly planned and integrated organization, they are usually unable to exploit the newly acquired relationship to develop a key account where profit potential is maximized. Good planning helps to identify the full potential value of the new client, improving the understanding of the client's more complex needs and how to address them, and also identifying opportunities to propose value-added offerings that bring additional fees and profits. Poorly planned and integrated approaches are characterized by inability to:

- differentiate acquisition products and actions from up-sell;
- understand the full potential value of a new client;
- understand the full needs of the new client, beyond the most obvious;
- identify profitable development paths;
- maximize share of client spend, at acquisition and each development stage;
- mobilize internal resources effectively to maximize value offered to the client.

The attributes of a well-planned and integrated approach are:

- planned actions to move to up-selling;
- full evaluation of the full potential value of a new client;
- information and analysis used to understand the full needs of the new client;
- profitable development paths outlined;
- plans in place to maximize share of client spend, at acquisition and each development stage;
- effective client-focused processes in place.

# 7

# KAM profitability

In Chapter 4, we considered some 'sanity checks'. These ensure that our objectives are in line with the real world – the market opportunity and our business resources. Now we add a final, most important, 'sanity check': will KAM be profitable? Is it reasonable to expect that KAM will be more profitable than traditional selling? We are on potentially dangerous ground here. We might be considering a KAM strategy as a means to survival. To compare levels of profitability with 'what used to be' may be very misleading. What was is gone, and KAM is now a necessity. Without it, we die. Or we might consider that KAM offers a more efficient use of resources (and it almost certainly does), but does this inevitably lead to increased profits? Here's an example.

## The tale of the needy broker

A major insurance company decided that it needed to focus on a few key brokers. It presented its new strategy of KAM to these brokers. One of them, a complex network of many small, semi-independent members, loved the idea. It was very keen to work in closer partnership, developing integrated systems and benefiting from other support, such as training. Agreements were put in place at senior management level. A multi-functional task force of middle managers from both organizations was set up to 'make it all happen'. It was only then that the complexities and full cost of making the closer relationship work were uncovered. The broker was keen to work in closer partnership because it needed a lot of help. The resource implications for the insurer's systems, operations and training functions were significant enough to delay several other priority projects. In particular, it meant delaying a planned new product launch by four months. This example shows that pursuing a KAM strategy has considerable implications for the whole business. The diamond relationship, while improving the efficiency of relationships, will in itself demand many new actions. This is almost certainly 'a good thing' in as far as it cements the supplier–customer relationship, but does it increase costs and reduce profitability?

# WILL KAM BE PROFITABLE?

KAM can, of course, be profitable, provided that the following points are kept in mind:

- The costs of KAM *must* be understood and measured.
- Individual customer profitability *must* be measured, based on the above.
- Throwing resources at customers irrespective of their strategic intent is sure to reduce customer profitability.

**Three 'almost truths' of customer profitability in FS**

We consider this in the context of three 'almost truths' for FS (ie they are nearly always true):

1.  The cost of winning new customers, even in a high-growth environment, is usually higher than you think – retaining customers is usually more profitable.
2.  A business's largest customers by volume may not be its most profitable.
3.  Growth with retained customers increases profits over time.

All this relates to the relative value of retaining customers, smaller as well as larger, over time. KAM is as much about this as about the drive to win big new customers. Consider the 'future value' of customers – a concept that sadly rarely extends to how salespeople are measured. In a KAM environment, it should. The 'diamond relationship' or 'partnership KAM' almost always increases resources committed to a customer, but, most importantly, it also almost certainly increases your chances of retaining that customer. Even where the objectives of KAM are to secure growth through new entry, customer retention remains important. The alternative is to keep chasing new customers to replace those lost – expensive even in a growth environment, and in a mature market like FS, almost suicidal.

# WHY CUSTOMER RETENTION?

Which is worth more – customers kept or customers won? Finding competitive advantage, or gaining lead or key supplier status, is about security in a world of diminishing security. Several trends conspire to make this difficult.

## The strengthening of buying power resulting from customer amalgamation

Competition is becoming tougher, through the amalgamation of many FS suppliers. Buyers are often cutting the numbers of suppliers. In a mature market such as FS, customer retention is becoming a priority as competitors become stronger and more aggressive and the pool of new customers shrinks, with consolidation in many sectors. Mergers amongst customers tend to put the spotlight on existing suppliers, with subsequent rounds of rationalization. There is a general trend towards supplier rationalization. For whatever reasons it is practised – sometimes in pursuit of genuine efficiencies, sometimes as a cynical game of setting supplier against supplier – rationalization means that *customer retention* is now a vital sales objective. It is often argued that retaining a customer is more profitable than winning a new one. Certainly it is less costly in time and effort. But does it always apply to profit?

## The cost of winning new customers

The first point to recognize is that there are costs of winning new customers. In many FS markets, you need to invest much time and resources in understanding customer strategy, individual requirements and processes, just to be in a position to bid for their business. In intermediated situations, you need to work hard to understand the intermediary's end-customers. There are also the more obvious costs – any additional initial discounts given and the customer-imposed 'start-up costs'. The costs don't end at the pitch. Often a new customer will require you to integrate and customize aspects of your systems and processes. You may need to invest in training for your own and your customer's staff. You may have to set up new products, perhaps getting legal and compliance clearance, perhaps setting up new operating procedures. Changes to databases and promotional materials may be required. There is more. When you win a new customer, do you factor in the costs of people's time, the extra travel, the cost of presentations, meetings and entertainment? Do you also factor in the not-so-obvious cost of devoting less time to your other concerns? What if, while directing your best people to the new pursuit, you took your eye off the ball and lost an existing customer?… The story goes on.

# THE COSTS OF LARGE CUSTOMERS

In many industries, the largest customers are significantly less profitable for suppliers than the middle-ranking ones, despite their larger volumes. Not only are they costly to win but also, in an industry where economies of scale are suspect and perhaps margins are low, volume discounts can be damaging to profits. Such discounts can even result in a loss with very large customers. So why keep them? Often because their volume is what keeps your operation turning. This is OK provided everyone recognizes not only the reasons why but also the value of other, possibly more profitable, customers.

**Big isn't always beautiful, but it can be very useful!**   Big customers become aware of the prices offered to their competitors. They expect to see a differential for their greater size – a proposal hard to reject, but one that is often based less on logic than on ego. In demonstrating this, we recognize that gross margins in different FS markets vary widely from being calculated in basis points (100ths of 1 per cent) on large financial deals through to very high percentages where a high degree of risk is involved. Therefore the example in Table 7.1 demonstrates the general principle rather than applying to any particular financial service situation. For a supplier making a gross profit margin of 20 per cent, a discount in price of 5 per cent will require an extra 33 per cent volume *just to stand still* in profit terms. If the profit margin were less, say 15 per cent, the volume to make up for the same 5 per cent discount would be 50 per cent. Table 7.1 illustrates this relationship between margin, discounts and volume. The figures in the central boxes are the percentage increases in volume required for profits to stand still, if a discount is given as shown in the left-hand column, while the current profit margin is as shown along the top row.

**Table 7.1**   *Percentage volume increases required to maintain profit over percentage discounts given*

| Discount Given % | Current % Profit Margin | | | | | | | |
|---|---|---|---|---|---|---|---|---|
|  | 10 | 15 | 20 | 25 | 30 | 35 | 40 | 50 |
| 2 | 25 | 15 | 11 | 9 | 7 | 6 | 5 | 4 |
| 3 | 43 | 25 | 18 | 14 | 11 | 9 | 8 | 6 |
| 4 | 67 | 36 | 25 | 19 | 15 | 13 | 11 | 9 |
| 5 | 100 | 50 | 33 | 25 | 20 | 17 | 14 | 11 |
| 7.5 | 300 | 100 | 60 | 43 | 33 | 27 | 23 | 18 |
| 10 |  | 200 | 100 | 67 | 50 | 40 | 33 | 25 |
| 15 |  |  | 300 | 150 | 100 | 60 | 43 | 33 |
| 20 |  |  |  | 400 | 300 | 133 | 100 | 66 |

Consider this: a 43 per cent volume increase is required to stand still in profit terms, if a business making a 25 per cent profit margin reduces its price by 7.5 per cent. This doesn't take account of any resulting economies of scale, nor of the notion of marginal pricing and 'contribution to overheads', but even so the figures are arresting. Remember, this only refers to the cost of discounts – all the other costs of winning and servicing a major customer are on top of this. The largest customers expect the most attention, the best services, the best people, the most senior management time and the greatest number of concessions, *as well as* the best prices. You need to ask yourself some serious questions. For instance, do you know how much profit you get from your largest customers? Are you able to measure profit, after these sorts of costs, by customer? KAM, as a process of prioritizing effort, resources and commitments, requires that the answers to these questions be yes. The results of such measurement will often reveal much about the right candidates for KA status.

## KNOW YOUR MARGINS

There are two main reasons that people with customer responsibility don't know how much money they make from the customer: 1) their business systems are not able to measure with accuracy down to customer level; 2) the measurements are made, but the people are not trusted with the information for fear that they will tell the customer.

Whichever, it is clear by now that genuine KAM is not possible in such a circumstance.

The most common problem is the way businesses spread their overhead **Allocating the** costs across customers. They do the same when looking at product prof- **overheads** itability, even at different business units – a laziness equally damaging to decision making. Take the example shown in Table 7.2, of a company that talked itself out of business because of a lack of differentiation between customers in fully allocating costs. Again simple figures have been chosen to demonstrate the principle rather than relating to any particular situation in FS.

**Table 7.2**   *The problem of inaccurate cost allocation*

|              | Customer A | Customer B | Customer C | Customer D | Company Total |
|--------------|------------|------------|------------|------------|---------------|
| Gross profit | 100        | 80         | 60         | 50         | 290           |
| Overheads    | 60         | 60         | 60         | 60         | 240           |
| Net profit   | 40         | 20         | 0          | –10        | 50            |

The company has four customers and a profit in total, but the way that overheads are spread (because of the lack of accurate cost measurement systems) indicates a loss-making customer – customer D. The decision is taken to cease doing business with that customer. Unfortunately, overheads do not reduce immediately by the 60 units that had been allocated to customer D. But they do go down by 30 and people give themselves a slap on the back for a smart decision. The situation is now as shown in Table 7.3.

The company is still in profit, but customer C is now a loss-making customer and the troubled board meets to decide action. 'Concentrate on profitable customers', they say, and customer C is quietly dropped. But, unfortunately, the overheads do not reduce in line, as demonstrated in Table 7.4. You can guess what happens next.

The moral of the story is that decisions about customers cannot be taken without proper knowledge of their relative profitability. Perhaps customer D was profitable and it was customer A that was the problem (by sucking in resources). Perhaps if they had understood the principle of contribution… but perhaps is not enough. The answer lies in some form of activity-based costing, where the costs of activities, people, overheads, etc are allocated more precisely to individual customers. Our research suggests that most major FS companies involved in managing key account relationships recognize that being able to measure individual customer profitability is one of the most important requirements for a successful KAM strategy. However, within the FS sector the ability to do this effectively varies. The most sophisticated can combine information on costs by account with other dimensions

**Table 7.3**   *The problem of inaccurate cost allocation*

|  | Customer A | Customer B | Customer C | Customer D | Company Total |
|---|---|---|---|---|---|
| Gross Profit | 100 | 80 | 60 | xxxx | 240 |
| Overheads | 70 | 70 | 70 | xxxx | 210 |
| Net Profit | 30 | 10 | –10 | xxxx | 30 |

**Table 7.4**   *The problem of inaccurate cost allocation*

|  | Customer A | Customer B | Customer C | Customer D | Company Total |
|---|---|---|---|---|---|
| Gross Profit | 100 | 80 | xxxx | xxxx | 180 |
| Overheads | 90 | 90 | xxxx | xxxx | 180 |
| Net Profit | 10 | –10 | xxxx | xxxx | 0 |

such as the risk inherent in doing the business (for example, the risk of not being able to repay a loan). Others are still struggling with the basics.

# COST TO SERVE MODELS

One of the difficulties for FS stems from the challenges inherent in measuring what is often great complexity in customer relationships. Getting close to an understanding of cost to serve will often require a substantial audit of the nature of the relationship using assessment tools such as QCi's CMAT model (Starkey, Woodcock and Stone, 2002). Having done detailed analysis to break down the elements of customer service, there may then be a requirement to work closely with the finance function on imaginative solutions to providing effective ongoing measures of the most important elements. Once you can measure profitability in the way we have been suggesting, then you will be able to construct what we will call a 'cost to serve model'. An example is shown in Figure 7.1.

This shows each customer along the horizontal axis, from the most profitable through to the least, with the graph measuring the cumulative profit. Your business is likely to fit the 80:20 rule – a small number of customers account for most of the profit. You may have some customers where you make a loss. As ever with such a tool, the importance is what you do with it. Again there are choices.

What if the loss maker is a big customer, and they very often are? How dependent is your business on its volume – what would be the impact on covering your overheads of losing the customer? Even if the impact may be significant, is that a good excuse for losing money? Armed with the data, you are in a better position to consider the need for changing the customer's

**Cutting your losses…?**

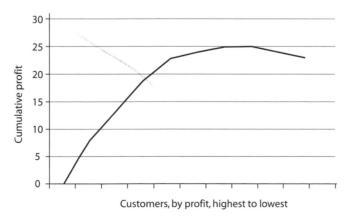

*Figure 7.1*   *The cost to serve model*

terms and calculating the impact on total profits. One option is to increase prices, knowing that you will lose half the business, but the remaining half will make real profit. Having shifted that customer leftwards on the cost to serve model, you may then discover that it is suddenly more attractive to chase this customer on new projects whereas before you may have seen such energy as throwing good money after bad – a happy ending may be in sight.

**Creating the model**     Creating such a model is no simple task. It involves the support and enthusiasm of finance and IT staff. Most importantly they will want to know why it is worth all the effort. Equally, those people that you start asking to keep some form of record on time spent or costs incurred with specific customers will want to know why – be sure you tell them. Some businesses will want and need to do this for all customers, some only for the largest, some only for those called 'key' – you make the rules. One option is to select a sample of customers, with very different profiles of scale and demands, and create the model on those. If nothing else, it tells you whether it is worth the effort to ask yet more questions.

# THE BENEFITS OF CUSTOMER RETENTION

Weighted against the costs of winning new customers and maintaining the big ones are the benefits of retaining customers over time. Many studies have shown that the longer the customer is retained, the more profitable it becomes. The reasons depend, of course, on the industry, but might include:

- gradual increases in volume of business over time;
- reduced operating costs as the supplier grows more experienced in servicing the customer;
- better forecasts bringing efficiencies in terms of providing support for the customer;
- better relationships resulting in a better level of understanding between supplier and customer;
- learning from this customer being of benefit in dealing with others;
- the customer bringing new business through referrals, or the evidence of its own success;
- in intermediary markets, with high levels of commission often paid up-front, product profitability building over time.

## Future value

If key accounts are investments, then their performance should be measured over the long term. It is the 'future value' of customers that is the true measure of their worth. Accepting that they were costly to win, we would like to see the paybacks increase with each year of retention. The higher the retention rate you achieve, the higher the future value, and, moreover, the costs of winning new customers reduce as you spend less time and effort fighting to get back into accounts lost in previous years. Winning new customers should be about genuinely new customers, not chasing up last year's defectors. It is easy to see how halving your customer defection rate can double the future value of your retained customers. Table 7.5 illustrates this point. This is, of course, an oversimplification. Perhaps your defecting customers were the least profitable – maybe that's why you let them go. Perhaps they are in any case the most promiscuous, but the principle is worth remembering: it is the future value of a customer that counts, not just this year's results.

**Table 7.5**  _Future value_

| Defection Rate (per year) | Average Life of Retained Customer | Profit Value (nominal) | 'Future Value' |
| --- | --- | --- | --- |
| 20% | 5 years | 1,000 | 5,000 |
| 10% | 10 years | 1,000 | 10,000 |

Do you measure sales performance on future value or this year's results? What is so special about 'this year'? Again we see KAM as a process that takes the long view – managing the future – a state of mind that can be difficult for those brought up in an environment of annual targets and budgets. Reichheld and Detrick (2003) estimate that in FS a 5 per cent increase in customer retention will produce more than a 25 per cent increase in profit because retained customers tend to buy more over time and the operating costs to serve them tend to decrease. They quote the example of Vanguard, the cost leader in the US mutual fund industry. They argue that the company's cost advantage is partly due to a commitment to customer retention – selecting the right kinds of customers and rejecting others such as the institutional investor that tried to invest $40 million in a fund, but was expected to churn the investment within a short period of time.

## Old or new, big or growing?

None of this is intended to dissuade you from winning new customers. If you are in a young, growth-orientated sector of FS, then this is, of course, vital. In such circumstances, it could be that any 'advice' to be concerned about reducing the 'acquisition costs' of winning new customers would be misplaced, or at least misinterpreted. But how many sectors of FS are in the rapid growth part of the cycle? Usually, most of the business for existing operators comes from established relationships. These comments on KAM profitability are intended to show that the costs and the benefits of KAM need to be viewed over the long term. Short-termism, where the 'high octane, supercharged atmosphere' of winning new accounts is allowed to dominate to the point that it chokes the nurturing, supportive kind of environment required for customer retention, can be a very expensive mistake. Remember the idea of KAM as an investment in the future. Then think of KAM as a means of balancing that investment portfolio, with the right balance of old and new, big and growing. Chapter 21 will look at this idea of a balanced portfolio in greater depth.

## Relationships, loyalty and customer retention

If established relationships are likely to be the biggest source of business for most FS suppliers, it is extremely important to understand why customers change suppliers. Research into why loyalty breaks down shows a common picture and, at first sight, a surprising one. Loyal customers don't 'snap' just because an alternative supplier arrives on the scene, even if it brings lower prices or better products. True loyalty, built over time through a breadth and depth in the relationship, can withstand such competition for a surprising amount of time. Customers 'snap' when the *relationship* breaks down; the result of arrogance, dishonesty or just plain indifference. Long-term customer retention relies on loyalty, which depends on strong, well-managed relationships – something beyond just winning the sale.

KAM is a process for managing those relationships. Before we do business with a customer, it is simply a *suspect* – a customer to be investigated. After some investigation, which proves its worth, the customer advances to being a *prospect* and we set off with the pre-KAM relationship. As we advance from pre-KAM to early KAM, the picture of the customer changes; it moves from being a *prospect* to a *customer*. Then, as the relationship develops through mid- and partnership KAM, the picture of the customer changes again, to *client*, *supporter*, *advocate* and on to *partner*. We are describing the theory of the 'relationship ladder', the idea that, as the relationship grows, so does customer loyalty and, hence, customer retention. Not only that, but we also reap the benefits of a customer that begins to act as a champion of our interests, even an advocate on our behalf. Certainly there are costs, but there are also cost reductions. Figure 7.2 shows how this might come about.

Let's just consider one circumstance, a bank that has a number of potential new business ideas that it wishes to trial with its corporate customers, only some of which will come to fruition. In a sales approach based on a series of bow-tie relationships with all customers, where it is difficult to distinguish between the likelihood or the value of one

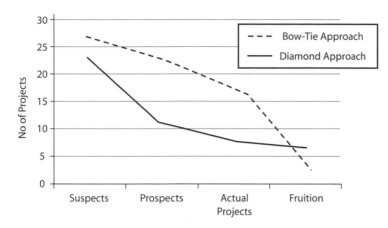

**Figure 7.2**   *The potential cost savings from diamond teams*

customer/project and another, there is a tendency to chase them all –
throwing a lot of mud at the wall and hoping some of it sticks. The costs of
this are high, particularly at the early stages. If the approach made more use
of diamond relationships with key customers, and those relationships gave
you the ability to judge a good customer/project from a bad one (based on
value and likelihood of fruition) then you might actually undertake far
fewer projects, at much lower cost. Add to this the fact that by taking on
fewer you do them better and you see the prospect of sharply declining costs
and rising profits.

# Part II

# The Customer's Perspective

# 8

# The buying process in financial services

The complexity of the FS industry is reflected in its buying process. The buyer needs specialist understanding. Buying decisions can have big implications for a business's overall performance and require board-level decisions. Research into the decision process for investment banking services by Turnbull and Moustakatos (1996) shows that the nature and level of the buying team vary according to the product purchased. The treasury department takes decisions on debt instruments, while, for equity instruments or advice-related services, decisions usually involve the chief executive/chairman and sometimes the board of directors. The purchase of an FS product in a business-to-business environment is rarely a one-off transaction, but usually one of several products supplied over time. Many of these products require ongoing servicing and support. So, the FS buying process is usually a product of a longer-term relationship between buyer and supplier or between supplier and intermediary.

## THE CORPORATE BUYING PROCESS

What is the range of needs for FS in the corporate market?

- To borrow money long- and short-term.
- To get a return on money long- and short-term.

- To move money.
- To insure against and manage risk.
- To provide benefits to employees, such as pensions.
- To receive information and advice across a wide range of related areas.

The list is long and the buying process varies greatly according to circumstances. Size of business may be an important factor. Small to medium businesses often focus on cash flow and managing liquidity, larger businesses on managing risk and the complexities of global expansion. The needs of small businesses may more closely resemble the retail market, involving personal FS, loans and money transmission. At the other end a multinational may require an integrated global capability from its suppliers.

## The spectrum of relationships

The closeness of the relationship between buyer and seller varies. It may be one-dimensional and arm's length, perhaps also tightly controlled by a formal supplier selection and purchasing process. Or it may involve a high degree of complex interrelations between two (or more) organizations, with considerable sharing of market knowledge and data in an effort to create innovative joint-value propositions. As discussed in Chapter 2, provision of FS in increasingly competitive markets often requires close collaboration between the supplier and the buyer. The customer often needs support in specifying requirements and providing feedback as the service is delivered. This requires the customer to be willing and able to be involved and to spend time and effort sharing plans and data. Success also depends on the skill and involvement of the supplier in helping the customer gain the proposed benefits. The supplier needs to understand in detail the needs of the client organization, and therefore the relationship necessarily needs to be close. A close relationship provides the opportunity to recognize new financial needs such as when the business is planning to expand production or distribution, to take on more staff or to acquire another business.

## Managing complexity

The complex buying process in complex inter-organizational relationships is demonstrated by investment banks in dealing with large corporations. Turnbull and Moustakatos's (1996) research found that this requires a multi-tier approach of contact at all decision-making levels, from assistant treasurer to the board of directors, but also involving the 'significant others' that might affect purchasing decisions or exploitation and assessment of service delivery in an unpredictable way. This requires assignment of different people from different levels in the investment bank to deal with their appropriate counterparts within the client organization. The overall relationship manager then needs to have some control over this, by having his or her own network within the investment bank. Clearly the implication of this is that the investment bank needs to be highly organized and aligned to serve the client in an integrated way, through sales and delivery KAM processes. Partnership-level KAM is required, operating the diamond model of relationships (see Chapter 5) in these circumstances.

## Dealing with corporate customers

Client coverage by personnel within the FS supplier is no longer simply an internal matter. A core provider must focus mainly on helping the client organization to achieve its strategic goals. This means maximizing the benefit from having enhanced access to the client by aligning product and coverage functions, defining overall objectives with the client, measuring performance against these objectives and continuously validating strategy with the client. It requires a joined-up view of relationships across products and geographies. In other words the corporate buying and exploitation process increasingly requires sophisticated KAM if opportunities are to be maximized.

# THE INTERMEDIATED BUYING PROCESS

Where an intermediary is involved, the product supplier is often distanced from the end-buyer and tends to focus its sales effort on the third-party broker or adviser. The buying process and closeness of relationship will vary very much according to the nature of the business and the size of the intermediary organization. Many suppliers lack internal clarity and agreement in defining the customer – the intermediary, the end-consumer or both. This makes successful KAM more difficult to achieve. In many countries, most intermediaries are small advisers and brokers, with limited relationships with FS suppliers. However, large intermediaries (often the result of mergers and acquisitions) and networks of brokers sharing support services have increased the need to manage relationships more closely.

### Levels of intermediary – an example

The relationship between a mortgage lender and a mortgage packaging company provides a good example of different levels of intermediated relationships in the home loans market. In this case the buying process is typically as follows. The aspiring borrower approaches a mortgage broker, who agrees to find the borrower a suitable loan. The broker deals with a packager, who sets up the loan, which is in turn funded by a bank. From the bank's point of view the packaging company may be seen as a key account, and the two organizations may work closely together so as to ensure an efficient service for the brokers and ultimately for the end-customer – the borrower. In some cases this may involve direct access to the bank's underwriting systems and even an underwriter from the lender being physically located in the packager's premises where the volume of business justifies it. At the same time the bank will probably be supplying promotional material direct to the consumer market and to the end-brokers in order to encourage sales of its product range, while these brokers may not be of sufficient size to merit any higher level of support or relationship activity.

## Dealing with intermediaries

In dealing effectively with intermediaries as key accounts, the supplier must understand the needs of the end-customers and support the intermediary in its sales and administration processes. Products may be developed specifically for the intermediary's end-customers, so research and development must be conducted in collaboration with the intermediary. Training and sales support material must be developed with full understanding of the sales and compliance processes and operational needs of the intermediary's staff. Multiple contacts and complex processes must be managed between the organizations to ensure good service to the end-customer. KAM is integral to the sales process to larger intermediary customers.

# CUSTOMER REQUIREMENTS IN BUYING FS

What are the most important requirements for business customers and intermediaries in buying FS? Obviously, many factors determine their needs, such as the size of company, their financial position, the nature of their business and style of management. The types of products required will also determine the choice of supplier. But there are a number of generic requirements that are of increasing importance in supplying FS, as detailed below.

## Value for money

This is not just about price. Value for money is more often about the buyer's perception of the overall package provided to the company. For some products, price is easy to compare. For highly tailor-made products, price comparisons are more difficult. For the latter, the buyer looks for transparency in pricing. Are all the charges clear? Is it clear what the supplier will provide? Which other aspects create value? Because product differentiation is difficult in FS, these other aspects such as reliability, responsiveness, accountability, empathy and trust, and proactiveness may be critical in creating a unique selling proposition.

# Reliability

This depends on the nature of the service provided. Where the service is highly transactional, there tends to be a premium on efficiency and consistency. Research on corporate banking by Tyler and Stanley (1999) found reliability to have four main aspects: minimal mistakes, efficient mistake handling, not needing to chase, and consistent service between all bank contacts. Where much administration is involved, mistakes can be expensive for the customer, in terms of staff and management time and resources required to resolve them. As the services of the supplier have an increasing effect on the value of the proposition to the end-consumer, reliability becomes more critical. Where the supplier's brand is known and valued by the consumer, joint branding is possible. In many other cases, only the brand of the organization directly dealing with end-customers would be used. In both cases poor reliability by the initial supplier can negatively affect the brand dealing directly with the end-consumer. Where the service provided is more concerned with risk and return, as in investment banking, the quality of advice given is clearly an important aspect of reliability. Here, regular reports and updates on performance may be crucial in managing the impression of service quality held by the client.

# Responsiveness

Business customers expect their suppliers to be responsive to their needs. How responsiveness is judged depends to a large extent on the particular priorities and comparison points (both other FS and non-FS providers) of the customer. Often the quality of the main contact person will have a very significant bearing on this, for example:

- How well has he or she explained the product features?
- Does he or she understand the customer's business?
- Is he or she available to answer questions?
- How quickly does the supplier make decisions?
- Can the supplier ensure operational delivery to support service commitments?

Responsiveness in dealing with operational issues as they arise is very important. Research on corporate banking found that while the concept of 'responsiveness' varied by customer and special customer requirements, there were some general views of what constituted responsiveness. Electronic payments should be dispatched within 10 minutes of receipt. For missing payments, the bank should provide initial feedback within an hour and resolution of the problem on the same day (Tyler and Stanley, 1999).

Suppliers are expected to be able to measure their achievements against committed service levels and to report this to the purchaser on a regular basis, with proposals and action plans for improvements in responsiveness where required.

## Accountability

The more important a supplier becomes to the client's business success, the more dependent the client is on delivery by the supplier. So, it becomes more important that customers are updated with any relevant changes in structure, processes or staff at the supplier. The better the customer understands the internal set-up and systems of the supplier, the easier it is to co-operate, to access quickly the right member of staff for advice or to resolve any problem. Supplier staff need a high level of technical knowledge to deal with queries. They must be empowered to act in resolving an issue on the client's behalf, or have quick access to appropriate specialist staff, if an issue is outside their area of expertise or knowledge. The accountability of staff in resolving issues is equally important in dealing directly with corporate customers and the intermediary environment. However, in the case of the intermediary, the issue may need to be resolved by the supplier on behalf of the end-customer. Problems in resolution directly affect the end-customer's perception of the service promised and provided by the intermediary.

## Empathy and trust

The concept of trust and commitment and its role in successful relationships are well established in the literature on relationship marketing (Morgan and Hunt, 1994). In a complex business such as FS, these components play a central role in maintaining the business relationship. Tyler and Stanley's research (1999) showed that corporate customers expected that bank staff should know not only about their own products, but also about the customer's business and banking needs. This has big implications for continuity and support of staff working on an account and for the training of new staff on the account. Another aspect of trust is the idea of a mutual understanding (or 'partnership') between the supplier and the buying organization that allows for open discussion and the flexibility to 'bend the rules' to create customized solutions.

## Proactiveness

It is not enough to be reliable, responsive and accountable within a trusting relationship. Because FS is usually a means to an end, business customers increasingly look to their providers for solutions to their problems or to help them exploit new business opportunities. Proactiveness might include improving processes and procedures to the benefit of the customer or coming up with new business ideas and innovations. This might require access to a wide range of market knowledge and expertise on the part of the supplier. In intermediary markets it demands a more detailed understanding of the needs of the end-customers and of how these needs are changing and developing.

# SUPPLIER CONSIDERATIONS IN SELLING FS

Suppliers also have criteria for selecting relationships to pursue and for managing them profitably.

## Achieving profitability

It is one thing to sell FS, another to sell FS profitably! The costs of developing and servicing a bespoke product for a customer may be considerable and hard to calculate up front. The costs of support, in terms of processes, regulatory compliance, product development and administrative support may change over time. Short-term losses on a business relationship may be acceptable in the expectation of longer-term business growth. At the same time relationships that were once profitable may cease to be so, with the cost of maintaining the business outweighing the rewards. Suppliers must be vigilant in understanding customer value and in determining strategic responses, as discussed in the next section.

## Customer value

The value of each customer to the FS supplier will vary and therefore it makes sense to concentrate resources on the customers that promise the greatest returns. KAM is a form of operational segmentation through which the skills and resources that could be employed across all clients are concentrated on the key accounts where the potential return is the greatest. Customer value varies. Larger customers may bring revenue but limited profit, owing to their negotiating power (see Chapter 7). Second-tier relationships can often prove more valued and profitable. Suppliers must identify the indicators of current and future profit and act accordingly. This requires a sophisticated understanding of profitability and the ability to measure and influence it. It also requires a segmentation policy backed up with the appropriate organization structure to deliver the value expected by the client.

## Segmentation

Traditional approaches to segmentation are based on factors such as geography, size of business, industry sector, etc. However, a true appraisal of customer value must also address the issues of the activities required in servicing the account and the future potential of developing the relationship. Research into segmentation by investment banks found some evidence of segmentation by size, value, complexity and difficulty of the transaction and the level of activity in buying investment banking services (Turnbull and Moustakatos, 1996). This research also reported that an appraisal of a client's business potential might have a significant impact on decisions about commitment of resources to that client. This appraisal sometimes used a formal methodology, but in many cases was informal or intuitive. Increasingly suppliers strive for more practical and actionable segmentations that can be used to apply appropriate efforts that result in an improvement in customer value. This may be achieved either by increasing revenues or by reducing costs, but while maintaining or improving service standards.

## Support supplied

The level of support needed to maintain the relationship and service the account is a major consideration. This depends partly on whether servicing the client requires costly systems or process development. It may also depend on how flexible the supplier is able to be in the creation and sharing of new value and joint benefits. How adaptable are its systems and processes? How flexible is its organizational structure? Is it focused on customer needs by segment or on the basis of its own functional departments? The ability of a KAM to respond effectively to client requirements depends largely on the answers to these questions. Committing to a key account approach means recognizing the need to cut across the organization to provide coordinated service to the client. It is necessary to recognize internal dependencies, align departmental objectives, improve measurement systems and related incentives, share client knowledge across the organization and incorporate and act on client feedback.

## MATCHING BUYER REQUIREMENTS EFFECTIVELY AND PROFITABLY

The business-to-business buying process for FS is rarely a single transaction. In this chapter we have shown how the requirements of the buying organization usually go far beyond the price and visible product characteristics. In turn the selling organization needs to be very clear in segmenting its customer base so as to manage the level of service in line with its perception of current and potential customer value. In this situation the relationship between the buying organization and the supplier may be the most important factor in meeting buyer needs. Tyler and Stanley's research in corporate banking (1999) suggests that relationships and perceptions of service are closely connected in the mind of the buyer. Service improvements accompanied by reduced relationship support (for example, a more automated approach) often result in reduced customer satisfaction. These reasons reinforce the importance of careful management of key relationships and key accounts in FS using integrated communications efforts.

# 9

# Supplier positioning – becoming a key supplier

The mutual dependence between buying and selling organizations in FS means that often the challenges facing the buyer and the seller are just two sides of the same coin. The buyer and seller may depend on each other, rather than having the adversarial stance of many other industries. The traditional 'milk round' approach to sales that views all customers as equal puts many pressures on the buying organization as well as the seller. A constant stream of suppliers, each needing attention, and an equally constant stream of requirements, each needing handling, will inundate a large buyer. So it is not surprising that organizations often seek to rationalize their supplier base.

## SUPPLIER POSITIONING MODELS

One aim of KAM is for sellers to make better use of time and effort. Many buyers seek the same, via supplier positioning models. A buying organization often finds that 80 per cent of its time and effort is spent on suppliers who constitute only 20 per cent of the total spend – yes, even buyers experience the 80/20 principle. The supplier positioning model attempts to redress this imbalance – it has four main aims:

- determining where to spend time and effort in sourcing new products and services;
- determining what sort of relationship should be established with different suppliers;
- determining what sort of activities should be worked on with different suppliers;
- identifying 'key suppliers'.

Any KAMs wanting to develop their relationship and expand on the range of activities with the customer must know how they themselves are seen. These next three chapters examine three different supplier positioning models: 1) the supplier power/buyer power model (this chapter); 2) the supplier power/value offered model (Chapter 10); 3) the supplier power/trust model (Chapter 11). Your customers might use any of these, or none. They might use them formally, perhaps sharing them with you, or not disclose them. The models may represent not a formal structure, but more 'gut feel'. Whichever it is, it is the KAM's job to understand how far such models are used, discussed or considered by the customer. Your customer might not use the words used here, but have similar thoughts with different terminology. From this point forward, use _the customer_'s words. Note that none of these models is easy for the customer to prepare in practice, using hard data. The information required, especially in large organizations, is hard to compile and much of it remains subjective, but the models provide valuable perspectives to view relationships from both the buyer's and supplier's points of view.

# THE SUPPLIER POWER/BUYER POWER MODEL

The matrix in Figure 9.1 can be used to 'position' suppliers, and categories or groups of suppliers, for the purpose of determining time spent, type of relationship required, activities undertaken and so on. We start by understanding the two axes and then examine the significance of the 'box' labels.

## Defining the axes

This model considers two broad issues:

- _Supplier power_ – how dependent are you on the supplier?
- _Buyer power_ – how important is your business to the supplier?

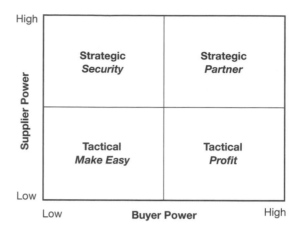

*Figure 9.1  Supplier positioning*

The two axes reflect the balance of power between supplier and customer. Supplier power depends on the significance of the product or service to the buyer's business and the risk if anything goes wrong. Buyer power is often about relative size of business. How would it affect the supplier if the buyer withdrew?

## Supplier power

This measure is common to all three models. In its broadest sense, it is a measure of how dependent the customer is on the suppliers. Suppose there is only one supplier for a particular product, or even category of product – perhaps because of a unique technology, or maybe it is a monopoly holder. The supplier is significant, so the risk for the purchaser is also high. Life without that supplier would be very difficult, perhaps inconceivable. Where there are many alternatives, the risk involved in losing a supplier is lower, so the significance of individual suppliers is also lower. This is simplistic, as in real life there are other factors to consider when defining supplier power. This is the challenge of the supplier power axis. By listing the factors that apply and prioritizing them, one can understand better the importance of a particular supplier to the purchasing organization. Below is a list of the types of factors that apply. The buying organization must identify ones relevant to it. The KAM has much to gain from understanding the selection:

- number of potential suppliers;
- technological/systems compatibility;
- level of technical support;
- level of operational support;
- range of capabilities and expertise;

- responsiveness;
- brand strength;
- geographic location;
- whether suppliers are also competitors;
- whether suppliers supply the customer's competitors;
- criticality of product;
- availability of substitutes;
- time required to switch suppliers;
- supplier's financial security;
- politics (the MD's favourite!).

### Buyer power

This depends greatly on the circumstances, but is often related to the value of business generated by the buying organization. All businesses from the smallest to the largest multinationals have banking needs, but they wield vastly different power. Intermediaries range from individual brokers through to retailing organizations with many millions of end-customers.

## Using the model

Increasingly those responsible for buying FS seek to manage their suppliers as much as sellers have managed customers. They have an advantage – they're the buyers! They want to determine:

- where to spend time and effort;
- what sort of relationship to establish with different suppliers;
- what sort of activities should be worked on with different suppliers;
- who should be their key suppliers.

Buyers expect to behave differently with suppliers in different boxes. Just consider your own buying. Would you buy a can of baked beans, home insurance, life insurance policy or a used car in the same way? Of course not. For most of us, the positioning of these four supply types would probably be as shown in Figure 9.2, and our buying behaviour would be appropriate to the positioning.

You will want to spend more time with the life insurance salesperson than you will scanning the supermarket shelves for beans. You don't mind putting a bit of effort into haggling over that used car, but you won't haggle so much over home insurance. You might go in for a scheme that pays for home insurance by a bank order, to be sure of having it, but you will buy beans when you see them. Of course, nothing is rigid in this model. For instance, there are differences of opinion or attitude among buyers. For someone, the

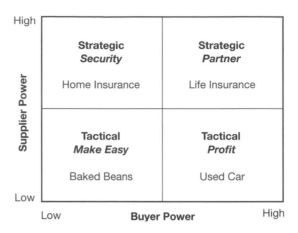

**Figure 9.2** *Supplier positioning example*

particular brand of beans, or make of car, might be so significant as to raise its positioning up the matrix. Or, seeing the tin of beans as a single product will place it in the bottom-left box. However, if you were to group together all similar purchases, you might find it heading towards the bottom-right box and you might then consider doing deals for bulk purchase.

## Time and effort in managing FS suppliers

How would the corporate FS customer use this model? At a high level, it can be used to position categories of suppliers: for instance, all suppliers of custom insurance services compared to transactional banking services. On a lower level, the matrix might encompass all suppliers from a particular category and then compare the individual suppliers against each other. In practice, the model is *best* suited to the higher-level analysis. The 80/20 rule applies to buyers just as much as sellers. Most time should be spent with suppliers in the top-right quadrant, the strategic partners – this is where you have a mutual interest. Developing your business is important to them and they are important to you in achieving your goals. However, many organizations find that they spend disproportionate time in the bottom-left quadrant, on simple transactional activities, on inevitable day-to-day problems and challenges. That is wrong. The model (Figure 9.3) helps managers reorientate their efforts on to suppliers away from the lower-left quadrant, the 'tactical make easy'. The label expresses the aims for this box: make things easy – often this involves working to make processes work efficiently with just a few suppliers.

What does the model mean for suppliers of FS? If you are top right, you might expect the customer to draw you in further – the 'diamond' of partnership KAM will be offered to you, even forced on you. If you are bottom left, then you might expect a tough set of standards to determine whether

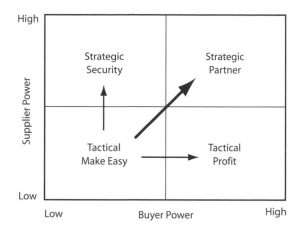

**Figure 9.3**  *Shift of time and effort*

you should be a supplier at all and, if you do survive, there may be very high demands made of you in terms of service efficiency levels. For the supplier assessed in this way, one implication is clear (and there is little point fighting it): to some extent you are being pigeonholed and so you will have to behave accordingly.

# WHAT RELATIONSHIPS, WHAT ACTIVITIES?

The implication for the KAM is that each quadrant of the matrix suggests a different relationship and a different focus of activities. Looking at each quadrant in turn, we will identify the different objectives being pursued by the customer and the implications this might have for the relationship. If you can identify how your customer positions you, you can assess the relevance of your current approach. Further, this understanding helps you judge the customer's strategic intent towards you and so maintain mutuality of intent (see Chapter 5).

## Strategic security – top left

This is where there is perhaps a relatively small choice of suppliers, or where the supplier provides a significant product or service but the buying organization has only limited power because it only delivers a low volume of business. Suppose a broker offers a specialist insurance product as part of its range. The broker doesn't sell many policies, but believes that it is an important part of offering a full service to clients. Here, buyer power is relatively low, while the fact that it is a specialist product may mean that there are few suppliers. In this quadrant suppliers expect to be treated with respect – they are, after all, quite important. The good news is that they shouldn't expect to be too pressed on price. The balance of power is with the supplier. You might also expect some buyer inertia when considering change of supplier, provided that the current suppliers behave adequately.

---

### Strategic security in specialist insurance advice

A university spends $2 million on its insurance policies, but doesn't employ anyone with insurance expertise. Its finance director must ensure that it has access to appropriate suppliers for its different insurance needs. The director uses a professional broker to help. The broker has access to suppliers of insurance services that the finance director may not know about, and can open up new markets and find new people interested in insuring the university. Here, outsourcing insurance advice and search gains the university professional expertise without having to take on additional specialists. The university only spends a minute proportion of its overall insurance budget on broker fees, and the type of service supplied by the broker ensures that it has few competitors. The broker's position is further strengthened by its intimate knowledge of the university's insurance needs.

---

## Strategic partners – top right

This is where financial service suppliers might expect to be welcomed in with open arms. They matter, and there is a mutual incentive to develop business opportunities, so the customer should be prepared to give them time. More than time, they should want to establish relationships on all levels – partnership KAM, perhaps even synergistic KAM for the most significant of all. The demand for more contact might come from the customer: a desire to meet senior management to discuss longer-term issues. The supplier should not of course expect an easy ride. The customer will make heavy demands. There is much money at stake, but rewards will be good for both parties. This is where hard-working suppliers can become very successful.

A large corporate organization wanting to expand its operation either through entering a new market or through acquisition will often need the resources and expertise of an investment bank to implement its strategy. This usually requires an intensive programme of work between the corporation and its banking partner over a long time period to realize the corporation's growth ambitions.

In the intermediary sector, non-FS organizations with strong consumer brands often partner strategically with traditional FS suppliers. The former provide access to a large customer base, while the latter provide the technical expertise and systems. This has happened extensively in the UK supermarket sector, as is demonstrated in the example of Sainsbury's Bank below.

Interestingly and perhaps uniquely in FS it is possible that part of the business of a corporate customer could be in this box, while at the same time other areas of business could be dealt with in a similar way to that in the 'tactical make easy' quadrant. Take the case of a bank dealing with a large corporate customer. Day-to-day transactional business is about 'tactical make easy': automating transactions and processes, and using standard products. Other aspects of banking related to business expansion involving loans, investment and advice need to be approached in a very different manner along 'strategic partner' lines. This is not a problem as long as both parties recognize this. The problem comes where the bank treats all business with the customer as 'tactical make easy', managing the relationship at 'arm's length', and then fails to win the strategic business because of lack of direct contact and understanding of the customer's business at this level.

## Partnering provides a new banking opportunity

In 1997 Sainsbury's was the first major supermarket in the UK to open a bank. It now has 2 million customer accounts on the books of its direct banking service, or roughly 1 in 10 UK households. How has it been able to achieve this significant share of a very traditional market? The answer lies in partnering. Sainsbury's Bank is a joint venture with Halifax Bank of Scotland (HBoS). Sainsbury's provides the brand image and distribution, using the bank to provide middle- and back-office expertise. By partnering with an established FS organization, Sainsbury's has bought in the needed FS capabilities. This has created a lean and flexible model, as the retailer needed no significant additional operational capacity. It gave it a financial model based entirely on variable costs – customers cost nothing until they buy a product. The success of this model so far is demonstrated by the development of banking by most other supermarkets in the UK.

Several factors account for the success of supermarkets like Sainsbury's in banking:

- the strength of their parent retail brands;
- the large number of loyal customers open to an FS offer;
- the knowledge that supermarkets have about their customers' lifestyles, needs and shopping habits;
- the frequency of shopping trips, each providing opportunities to promote the banking service;
- a low operational cost base (as little as 25 per cent of an average bank's), meaning they can undercut many of their competitors on a sustained basis and still deliver strong profits.

A key capability for success in supermarket banking is management of the partnership with the service provider. Supermarket banks must give customers the same service they expect from their brand without being burdened by the infrastructure themselves. Here, Sainsbury's Bank has a particular advantage in its strong alignment with its banking partner. Working closely in a strategic partnership provides Sainsbury's with a new business channel and HBoS with a means to diversify its business and economies of scale in covering its overheads.

(Adapted from IBM, 2003)

## Tactical make easy – bottom left

This is where much activity has been happening in FS, as suppliers use technology to cut costs of customer service. Banking for small to medium-size businesses often falls into this quadrant. In many countries, the number of suppliers offering services to this sector has declined with widespread consolidation of clearing banks. So small to medium businesses have limited choice of banks and are in a relatively weak position because their business is small from the point of view of the bank. Banking services are important to them in developing their business, but they may well have to settle for a lower level of support from their bank than they would like.

Today, the bottom two boxes are where the e-revolution is impacting most on supplier–customer relationships. The internet and call centres are used to replace local contact. Once buying organizations position suppliers in this bottom-left box, they find they have several suppliers of broadly similar products. For example, in the life insurance and investment sector, intermediaries often have a wide range of suppliers and products to choose. Grouping these suppliers and products together, through supplier base rationalization, brings savings in transaction costs, but the scale of buying from remaining suppliers increases to the point where time spent on negotiating a commission or discount is worth the effort. In other words, while individual suppliers might have been positioned bottom left, rationalization shifts a supply type to bottom right. An alternative outcome in moving towards the right might be to ask *more* from the supplier in terms of technical, systems, training or marketing support.

## Tactical profit – bottom right

This is where there are lots of fish in the sea and a lot of money at stake, so the buying organization can afford to negotiate hard. The provision of point-of-sale credit through a third party such as a car dealership might well fall into this box. It is a relatively simple product and there are a lot of suppliers. The third party has high buyer power because it will want only one preferred supplier for all its business. If suppliers find themselves in this quadrant, they can expect to be talking primarily about price and perhaps not much else.

# SO, WHO'S THE KEY SUPPLIER?

Don't leap to the assumption that only suppliers in the top-right quadrant can be viewed as key suppliers. They are certainly important, and perhaps have a head start, but there is more to this. So what is the requirement?

# Behave appropriately

This is another of those very simple concepts that doesn't take much to say, but if missed, you and your company can go through untold agonies of frustration and wasted time. So, don't skip past this next sentence too quickly. It's rather a 'Napoleon' of a sentence – short, but important:

> To be a key supplier, you must behave appropriately to your positioning in the eyes of the customer.

If the customer sees you in 'tactical make easy', be supremely easy to do business with. Make sure things flow readily through efficient processes – install efficient systems, communicate through e-mail, don't overburden the customer with your presence. Be there when required. Keep out of the way when not. Don't force complex relationships on the customer, unless they lead to easier transactions. Show willingness to set, and police, your own standards (but don't be too pushy!). Recognize that some aspects of FS will fall into this box, but that there may be other more strategic opportunities with the customer that need to be pursued differently.

If the customer sees you in 'tactical profit', be the sharpest on the block. Make sure your costs are the lowest in the business. Pass on efficiencies to the customer. Stay keen on prices. Keep close to movements in the market – you can put prices up when conditions allow. Of course, only do all of this if you really *do* want to be considered a key supplier by this customer. The alternative is to be more opportunistic with it and accept that it will be the same with you. Another alternative is to mark yourself out, finding differentiation that raises your significance to the customer. This will not be easy. Finding the differentiation is only half of the battle; communicating it convincingly to customers that have already positioned you as 'bottom right' will be tough.

If the customer sees you in 'strategic security', never let it down. Be top on reliability, or maintain your hold on the customer, whether through your brand name, your technology, your service or a long-term contract. Consider proposals that tie you in provided you *do* wish to be with this customer for the long term.

If the customer sees you in 'strategic partner', act like one. Spend lots of time with the customer. Establish all the relevant points of contact, particularly at senior level, and focus on the long term. Devote time and energy to understanding the customer's needs, issues and culture – and make sure that you continue to come up with the goods. Bring it your new ideas, first. Above all, get the relationship right. A 'tactical make easy' supplier that gets it wrong will be a nuisance, but a 'strategic partner' that gets it wrong will be a disaster.

# IS THERE ANY ESCAPE FOR SUPPLIERS?

Are you inevitably stuck with the customer's pigeonholing? In the short term, probably yes, but don't let that stop you planning to move. Three things should be remembered:

1.  The customer's perception of your position is more important than the fact. Work on the perceptions as much as trying to alter, or argue, the facts. Perhaps the customer places you in the bottom-left quadrant, whereas you know that the extent of service that you offer actually places you top left. Don't expect to be able just to tell it. Take every opportunity, and every potential contact, slowly to drip-feed the information required for it to change its view. Wait patiently for the opportunity to demonstrate your incomparability.
2.  Everything is relative. Your immediate contact might view you as bottom right, but the contact's boss watches a larger picture that might place you more towards the top left. You may have to demonstrate different behaviours at different levels of the customer. Take advantage of a more senior perspective, but don't expect the MD to take a great interest in your day-to-day meetings. Don't ever go behind your immediate contact's back!
3.  If you are not considered a strategic supplier but you provide superb value, then perhaps you need to persuade the customer to change its view of your potential. The 'value' model discussed in the next chapter would probably suit you better, but proceed with care. Remember, the customer chooses how to measure its suppliers, not you. The 'value, not price' argument is strong, but recognize that it is not always easy for customers to evaluate. They may be suspicious of your motives.

## Moving north...

Let's suppose that you are positioned in the bottom right-hand box but aspire to the top right. You are an insurance company with a small share of a broking network's overall business. You try to increase your significance to the broker by several means: you offer training support; special discounts on products not listed by the broker; point-of-sale promotional support; supporting seminars to end-customers; and so it goes on. Some of those grab the broker; some of them don't. The point-of-sale promotion is difficult to set up across the network, but the expert speakers you offer in support of the seminar programme just happens to be what the broker needs at the time. Slowly your relationship gets better and sales grow. What is happening here is that you are expanding your offer, sometimes through the product, more often in this case through the supporting services offered. Each time the offer is expanded, the competition catches up, of course, and so you must look for the next thing. It is rather like a series of concentric circles growing out from the original core product.

## Where does KAM come into this?

It is up to the KAM to be aware which of these various 'expansions' is doing the most for the customer's business, and then shout it out loud so that the customer has heard. But avoid overloading the customer with detail. The very practice of KAM is what helps suppliers identify these wider concentric circles in the first place. Use the KAM relationship to stimulate and develop the offer.

# 10

# Measuring value

## VALUE FOR MONEY IN FS

A useful model in thinking about the customer's perspective in buying FS relates to how value for money is perceived and rated by buyers. In Chapter 8 we explained that as FS products are hard to differentiate, other aspects of the offer or relationship are often crucial in creating a unique selling proposition. We identified several factors that create value for the buying organization. These are: reliability, responsiveness, accountability, empathy and trust, and proactiveness. But how far and how frequently does a buying organization measure performance on these factors and recognize the value created for it? More often than not it will be up to the seller to provide the evidence. We call this 'the problem of hidden value'. This chapter is about how this value is made explicit to customers, so that it is accepted as part of the total offer and relationship.

**Uncovering hidden value**

Where the relationship between an FS supplier and its customer has been going for years, it is easy for the customer to take the supplier's expertise for granted. Consider a global manufacturing company that has maintained relationships with its suppliers over years (indeed some relationships have lasted up to 50 years). The overall inter-organizational relationships are made up of relationships between individuals. Over the years, suppliers' employees, especially those of one FS supplier, have acquired enormous knowledge and experience specific to the customer. The FS supplier has been involved in many high-level strategic decisions by the customer and has employees who have worked closely with the customer for many years. However, changes in the customer's senior management team threaten the supplier's position. A new finance director wants to cut finance costs. Many other potential suppliers are knocking on the door. The incumbent supplier is in a strong position because of its intimate customer knowledge, but knows the true costs of dealing effectively with this very demanding customer and does not believe that the low cost of service being offered by some of its competitors would be feasible. Here, it is imperative that the supplier makes explicit the value that it has contributed and that it has the potential to contribute going forward. For example, the tax-saving proposal that it developed without being asked two years ago was subsequently adopted saving many millions of dollars. The supplier needs to quantify all such contributions and make sure that the finance director knows about them. It also needs to use its intimate customer knowledge to develop ideas of how the savings required by the finance director might be achieved. By demonstrating the value that has been partly taken for granted and by showing a willingness to help the finance director achieve the cost-cutting objective going forward, the supplier is giving itself a fair chance of keeping this key account.

# SUMMARIZING VALUE

The customer will see value in terms of what the supplier, the product or the service can do for its business. This is easier to judge in some circumstances than others. For example, in providing consultative services, the proof of quality may take years to come through. Getting value is, in this sense, rather like buying insurance – you don't realize its worth until you need it. We know how easy it is to ignore the arguments of 'future value' we hear from those 'silver-tongued' salespeople. 'Value in use' is a result of experience. For a few FS products (eg non-life products) there is often a shorter experience and learning process, facilitating quick assessment of 'value in use'. Other products may be long-term (eg reinsurance) or even lifetime (eg pension schemes), where there is little opportunity to experience value in use before deciding.

For both supplier and buyer, trial and error usually forms part of the measurement process. As a supplier, stay patient; wait for the opportunity. As a customer, look for suppliers that will help you take the risk out of trialling. However, no matter how the customer measures – price, cost or value – the supplier has a key role in presenting the case, not only in the sales process but as a proof point or reminder throughout the relationship and use of products. Some customers need to be 'helped' towards this more complicated measure of supplier performance. The seller has to juggle the needs of the customer with what the customer is prepared to pay for the service. This is usually easier where the customer already uses something like the value-based supplier positioning model.

# THE SUPPLIER POWER/VALUE MODEL

This is the hardest model for any business to prepare. Not surprisingly, given the effort, few use it. This is a pity, for both supplier and buyer have much to gain from it. The model is illustrated in Figure 10.1. The vertical axis of the first supplier positioning model remains the same; we have replaced 'buyer power' with 'total value', as defined in the preceding section.

## Managed supplier

Suppliers will be under close scrutiny, 'managed' to deliver more value. Access to contacts in the customer organization will be controlled; information will flow as demands rather than as shared insights, so it may be hard to make progress or to make progress quickly. The supplier must realize what is at issue and start working on value propositions. Slowly, the effort *will* be appreciated, even if at first it misses the target. Patience is required.

## Partnered supplier

This suggests open doors, perhaps even open books if value really is the issue at stake, and not costs and prices (see below). As ever, the warning to suppliers is not to become complacent, as the customer will be working with market demands that create pressure to find new and improved value propositions.

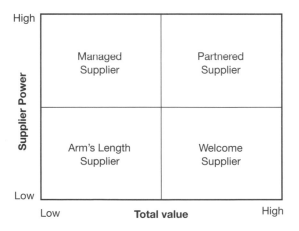

*Figure 10.1*   *The supplier power/value model*

## Welcome supplier

This suggests that there is an opportunity for the supplier to win more business, to become a larger supplier with greater significance, and so develop into a partnered supplier. The door is always open, but learn how to use this privilege to the *customer*'s benefit – don't abuse it.

## Arm's length supplier

Here, you will only be called upon in times of great need. Not a good starting point, but times of need are when you can prove yourself by demonstrating how you can get the customer out of a hole – a high-value outcome.

# OPEN-BOOK TRADING

Buyers across many business-to-business markets have always tried to get cost breakdowns from their suppliers. This is an old-fashioned but effective way of getting price reductions. The trick is to get the supplier, often through an indiscretion, to disclose the costs of various parts of its package – perhaps the delivery costs, the packaging costs or even the costs of the salespeople. Then, choose part of the product or service that you can do without and demand a discount for this new, stripped-down package. Here is an example.

---

### The tale of the sales force

An insurance product supplier found its back against the wall with its largest customer, a national broker. The supplier was told that it was not doing as much as its main competitors to help the customer. It was about time things changed. Being in a corner, the account manager 'broke' and said, 'But that's not true; just the support from our sales team costs us at least £100,000 a year.' Indeed, the sales team was of high value to the customer – they undertook training, advised on compliance issues, dealt with administration issues and handled complaints. But that was not the point.

A few weeks later, the account manager was summoned to a meeting with the broker's sales director. 'We have been considering your services to us,' the director began, 'and we have decided that we no longer require your sales team support at branch level. We will do it ourselves, starting next month, and we would like you to compensate us for our extra work, from the £100,000 that we will be saving you.'

This was not strictly true as the sales team covered other customers as well. Rather than saving £100,000, costs might actually increase, compared to sales achieved. But that was not the point. The sales team was removed and a substantial payment made to the broker.

The story gets worse. After a few months, it was clear to the insurance supplier that sales were declining. The lack of local support had taken the focus away from the supplier's products at the branch level. The account manager was forced to go back to the sales director. 'Can we put our sales team back in?' was the plea. 'Of course, they can start tomorrow,' came the answer, 'but don't expect your money back...'

---

**Trick or treat?** So, where does this leave FS suppliers asked to give full breakdowns of costs in order to demonstrate the value delivered? Is this open-book trading a new term for an old trick, or is it a genuine attempt to secure greater value from the combined supply chains? Suppliers with the most to fear from open-book trading are those with activities or costs that do not give value. It is their own fault if they are caught out. Suppliers in the top-left quadrant of the value model might experience the worst of this new demand and should fear meeting it. It does not make for good relations and the whole thing could end in ruin. Much better to start working on improving the value delivered and ironing out the 'wrinkles' of activities that only add cost. Suppliers in the top-right quadrant might even welcome the request. They have little to fear and much to learn of the customer's own chain.

Of course in FS the portfolio of products and services offered may bridge quadrants, and create cross-subsidization. Loans may be commodities and low-profit items, but act as an acquisition product (to acquire a new customer relationship) that can be developed over time through the provision of more profitable, perhaps fee-based, services. In this case a breakdown of costs could show some very profitable products. There would be inevitable pressure to reduce these profits, even if they are an essential part of a balanced business. Suppliers must use their judgement. Full sharing of information is appropriate sometimes, such as in a joint business venture. We are dealing here in the realms of trust, one of the components of value in FS identified in Chapter 8. This is particularly important for FS where there is often an element of risk or where privileged access is granted to information. The third supplier positioning model, based on trust rather than buyer power or value, is useful in considering this question, and will be examined in the next chapter.

# DEMONSTRATING VALUE

Negotiation on pricing in FS often revolves around different understandings of the costs involved in servicing the customer. Providing a bespoke product may involve servicing costs that are hard to calculate up front. The costs may not be explicit and may change over time. Or the expected volume or value of business may not be achieved through this KAM relationship or across others. So, try to allow room for renegotiation of terms on the basis of experience. Suppliers should continue to demonstrate value for money to the customer and make explicit the hidden value in the service offered.

## Reliability

In highly transactional situations, process efficiency and consistency are important. Mistakes on either side can be expensive in terms of staff and management time. When things go well, we take things for granted. It is only when things go wrong that we focus on the service offered. Can you measure the reliability of your service and the benefits that this is giving to the customer? When things have gone wrong, how quickly and effectively have you rectified the situation? Is it clear where the fault lies and what should be done on both sides to correct it? In situations where you are one of a number of suppliers, for instance in selling through an intermediary, do you know how your service compares with the competition?

## Responsiveness

Customers judge responsiveness in a variety of ways. Do you understand what your customer expects in this respect? Expectations vary between functions and departments. In the case of an intermediary, an operational function may define service in terms of efficient processes, while the human resources function may be mainly concerned with training support. This is a good reason for penetrating the customer's snail in order to understand the varying requirements based on which different parties may judge your service. Responsiveness expectations are rising in FS, as more business is contracted and delivered within short timescales.

## Accountability

What added value do your managers and staff provide via their knowledge of the customer's business? It is easy to take this for granted particularly in long-term relationships where knowledge and experience have accumulated over a long time, as in the example at the beginning of this chapter. This value will become more apparent if your customer moves the business to an alternative supplier. Then both must go through the learning process again. However, by that stage it would be too late from your point of view, as your only opportunity then is to win back! What can you do to demonstrate this value while you still have the business? Perhaps better reporting on problems resolved or a regular summary of support given might help.

## Proactiveness

Complacency can creep into long-term relationships. Competitors trying to win the business may work harder to come up with new ideas than the incumbent supplier. Having a regular forum with the customer to work on new ideas or improvements to processes may help make a proactive approach more routine and a key part of relationship value. It may also maintain the relationship at different levels of communication and acceptance and also keep the supplier up to date with the customer's strategies and plans.

## Steps to demonstrating value

Demonstrating value means taking a number of steps as summarized below:

1.   Understand the customer's needs.
2.   Identify what matters most to the customer right now – what are its challenges and headaches?
3.   Understand its definitions of value received.
4.   Understand its cost structures and financial performance measurements.
5.   Construct your value proposition based on the above.
6.   Find the people who benefit most from your proposal.
7.   Sell to the 'snail', not just the buyer.

Of course, underlying the perception of value provided is the concept of trust on which the relationship is based. In FS, this is critical. The wrong decisions may have great implications for the financial health of the buyer. The third model based on trust is useful in considering this.

# 11

# Measuring trust

Your customer may not be able or willing to make the effort to measure either the balance of supplier/buyer power or value. Perhaps it 'positions' suppliers of FS in a far more subjective way – a *feeling*…

The trust model is therefore far more subjective. It considers hard-to-quantify factors – trust and confidence. As a result, it is a more 'seat of the pants' model. So the title of this chapter is rather misleading. The model does not try to 'measure' trust, but rather to recognize its importance in the relationship. Even thinking of this as a formal model can be misleading. While the previous two models may get put on to paper, this one usually stays in the head or the heart. This does not make it any less important. Intangible elements such as empathy and trust are at the heart of the relationship between the supplier and customer in FS.

In most sales situations, 'rapport' between those involved is very important (see Chapter 29, 'Selling to the individual'). It is difficult to *measure* such things accurately and quantifiably, but this doesn't mean they don't count. Just because you can measure some things does not mean that they must be important. Answering the telephone before the fourth ring has become a customer service mantra. It has certainly gone a long way to improving customer relations, but how much more important are the voice that answers the call, the tone, the words used and the actual help given? The number of rings is measurable, the rest is much harder to turn into statistics; yet which is more important in building trust?

# TRUST MATTERS MORE THAN YOU WILL EVER BE ABLE TO MEASURE

The level of trust and confidence in the supplier is often underestimated by salespeople, perhaps because of the sometimes theatrically contrived postures taken up by people on the buying side. Who could believe that they actually cared about such stuff? But they *do* care, very much indeed. Independent surveys of what customers want from suppliers regularly place 'honesty' or 'reliability' at the top of the list – so why don't they say this to the seller's face? There are many reasons, ranging from 'It's not an easy conversation to have' through to 'This is my perception, not a judgement based on facts.' As any experienced salesperson will say, the customer's perceptions almost always count for more than any evidence or facts that might argue against them. Let's not forget that we are selling to human beings. Customers assess suppliers on a combination of factors, from a proven track record, honesty, reliability, a sense of substance, to judgement on ethical standards and matching of moral and brand values. These are not easy to quantify and any attempt to measure trust is best left, in the end, to an understanding of the power of *feelings*.

### Establishing trust at the beginning

Successful insurance salespeople recognize the importance of a thorough approach to establishing trust at the beginning of a customer relationship. Sid Friedman, President and Chairman of Corporate FS, and featured as a top earner in *Forbes*, had the following philosophy in selling insurance to a new customer:

> I don't have anything to sell unless I know what is wrong. Just like a doctor. He'll take blood pressure, look in my eyes, ears, and take some blood and an electrocardiogram. He wants to find out what's going on in my body. By the time I tell him what's wrong and he looks over the tests, he'll tell me what to do next. Now if he doesn't do all that and still recommends a cure? I'll go somewhere else.

(*Direct Marketing*, 1994)

# THE SUPPLIER POWER/TRUST MODEL

Figure 11.1 depicts the trust model. The labels on the boxes may not seem very different from the value model, but what is more interesting here is the sort of relationship you might expect as a supplier viewed in each of these four ways.

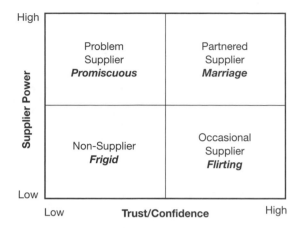

**Figure 11.1**  *The supplier power/trust model*

## Partnered supplier

This is like a marriage, and so has its ups and downs. The relationship needs continual effort and attention from both parties to maintain sufficient trust and confidence. The real test, as with a marriage, is how it stands up to hard times. The best marriages have ways of building strength and cohesion through adversity and external challenges, while in others these put the relationship under increasing stress.

## Problem supplier

This is like promiscuity. The customer is ever on the lookout for alternatives. Despite your obvious attractions, there is something not quite right about you, at least not to warrant full commitment. Without proper attention, an apparently loyal customer will 'snap' when a better offer comes along (see Chapter 3).

## Occasional supplier

Be prepared for 'flirtatious' or dating buying behaviour. The customer may give you time and 'pick your brains' for ideas, sometimes taking up a lot of your time, but rarely proceeding to use your services or your products. As in life, this is a position full of frustrations.

## Non-supplier

Plain and simple, a 'frigid' buying behaviour.

# WINNING TRUST

Without trust and with no reason to recognize a supplier's significance, the relationship is cold. If the customer is new and you are an untried supplier, you begin here. If you aspire to partnered supplier status, aim to win trust and confidence before trying to prove your significance. But how do you win trust and confidence if the customer doesn't do business with you? It won't do business with you unless it recognizes your significance to it. It is reluctant to see that significance if it doesn't have trust and confidence. A vicious circle of doubt? No, because patience pays. Recognize that it is the small things that win the customer's confidence. The way you behave, the way you keep your promises: to send a brochure by the next available post or to call back within the committed week with the expected figures – these are the most important things at the outset of any relationship. Persistence, balanced by large doses of empathy, is the best approach. Don't talk about what you want or what you need; talk about what the customer might want and need. Once you have won these early confidences then, and only then, will customers listen to your proposals. Go in too early with assertions of what you can do for them and they will simply not be listening, possibly because they may not believe you.

# THE REWARDS OF TRUST

The pursuit of a customer's trust and confidence is not just a question of business ethics or morality – it is the pursuit of competitive advantage. Trust is like a reservoir of good will from which both sides can take, provided it is topped up regularly. But trust does not happen instantly; it needs to be built up over time. In many instances in FS, long-standing personal relationships are eroded through frequent reorganizations and a consequent lack of continuity and consistency of contact.

### The breakdown of personal contact

Changes in the banking sector have had significant implications for relationships at a local level. A customer perspective from a large regional organization is revealing. In the view of the finance director, the banking sector has changed beyond all recognition. Ten years ago, the relationship with the organization's main bank was at local director level. Since then there have been so many reorganizations that personal relationships have not been maintained, to the point that the finance director doesn't now know the names of any contacts within the bank:

Because of how they were organized within the bank, for the local bank manager, lending us a few million dollars was big business, so he would pass it up to his director and they would all work together. There simply aren't enough people in the bank to give us the same level of advice any more. So you get side-tracked to the expert arm of the bank, which purely deals with corporate finance. This area was originally geographically based; now they have cut the cake a different way again. It's very difficult for us to know who our contact is because they have reorganized so many times and I think they concentrate on core business and have left the borrowing to a different area. But now nobody knows our business.

The degree of personal contact is limited at lower levels between banks and their corporate customers. As a finance manager puts it:

I don't think we are being treated less favourably than other customers of theirs, but I have noticed the tendency towards service centres. It is a bad one. You certainly don't get anything like the level of service we would have had on a day-to-day basis... If we are looking to borrow $50 million, then I am sure the service we get today will be as good as it was 5, 10, 15 years ago. But for the day-to-day management of accounts, the simple things like resolving statement queries, then the level of service is nowhere near what it was a while ago.

The perspective of the finance manager is that dealing through an impersonal service centre does not work as well as a local contact who understands your business and has local ownership of problems.

# WHEN TRUST GOES OUT THE WINDOW

In situations such as the above, the drive towards centralization and service efficiency is at the expense of the loss of personal relationships and consequent lack of understanding and insight in relation to the customer. We have heard plenty of stories of sellers of FS crying 'foul' over customers they thought were 'tame' who then suddenly turned on them. Their use of language suggests that there may be something less than two-way trust. Such appeals often show a level of innocence that we must not permit, as innocence breeds all sorts of relationship problems. Trust breeds complacency, and complacency blinds us to the real world.

## Complacency

Selling is sometimes like dating. It all begins with a view from afar, and then moves slowly towards contact, at which point the pace quickens amid treats, gifts and armloads of flowers. Then comes the engagement, marriage and the honeymoon and slowly the flowers start to drop off. The months and the

**You don't bring me flowers any more...**

years pass and suddenly someone comes home with a bunch of flowers – and the response? OK, so what have you done?

## The real world carries on...

So you appear to have perfect trust and openness and suddenly the customer demands a price cut or else you will be out. Salespeople can react to such things with all the surprise of a jilted lover, which suggests that they have not been paying attention. Such sudden demands usually result from something – poor trading conditions for the customer, pressure on the customer's margins, a review of costs, new initiatives from the competition – the very sort of things the KAM should anticipate. The skilled KAM knows when to speak to customers about what help they might need – the perfect timing being just before they speak to you! That way changes to arrangements don't lead to breaches of trust; indeed, they work to strengthen it all the more.

# 12

# Managing financial services suppliers

The previous three chapters have focused on tools that customers can use to analyse their suppliers' relative position and the value that they get from the relationship. The result of all this mapping and analysis of supplier positioning is the customer's general desire to 'manage' its suppliers more effectively. The idea of supplier optimization has been applied in many business-to-business products and services. FS suppliers are not immune from this trend. In managing suppliers, buying companies are broadly seeking answers to two questions: 1) Which suppliers will best help us? 2) How must we help them? This might involve reducing numbers, finding new suppliers or resurrecting sleeping ones. It might even involve actively developing the capabilities of some suppliers.

The applicability of this approach in FS varies according to the circumstances and nature of the product. In commodity markets involving simple transactions, there may be little incentive to reduce supplier numbers or to develop the relationship. Indeed, customers may want a large number of suppliers so as to maximize choice and negotiating position. However, in other situations it is more relevant. Intermediaries may want to reduce their supplier base to enable them to rationalize their processes and simplify staff training. With consolidation and rationalization taking place in many industries, FS suppliers are often under scrutiny as reorganization and centralization take place amongst customers. Moves towards efficient working practices, using the latest technology, mean that customers will continue to put pressure on FS suppliers to work closely in developing a service tailored to their needs.

This chapter will look at these areas:

1.   reductions in supplier numbers;
2.   rationalization and centralization; and
3.   tailoring the service to the customer's needs.

# REDUCING SUPPLIER NUMBERS

'Supplier rationalization' strikes terror into the hearts of many suppliers. Of course, if you are on the list of survivors, it is good news, but that hardly makes you feel good while the process is under way. Done badly, rationalization creates havoc for both suppliers and customers. Confidence is blown and performance suffers. A nervous supplier is not the best supplier. Doing it 'badly' might mean any number of things: in a hurry, without warning, without supplier consultation, without defining the rules or, worst, to a hidden agenda. However, done well, the outcome can be good for all, even for the non-selected suppliers, who at least now understand what it takes to be selected. There is an analogy with 'downsizing', the trend of the 1980s and 1990s where staff levels were radically reduced, particularly at middle-management levels. We all know of situations where key people were removed, essential expertise lost and basics like customer service began to crumble. There are also cases where businesses were transformed from near-death to prosperity. The difference usually lay in how the exercise was carried out. Doing it 'well' might mean: planned, with clear objectives, communicated to all involved, with the support of suppliers and for the benefit of the whole supply chain. For the supplier faced with rationalization, the most important thing is to talk, early, to the customer concerned and to ask some crucial questions:

**Don't fight it. Seek to understand the rules and play to win**

- Why is the buyer reducing supplier numbers? To achieve greater efficiency, for performance improvement, to lower transaction costs, to form closer alliances?
- What are the target outcomes? Final numbers, specific performance measures, lower costs, better value?
- What standards will they apply?
- What are the givens and what are the differentiators? What must any supplier do – what might make a supplier stand out from the crowd?
- Will they be 'selecting out' or 'selecting in'? Removing the chaff, picking the winners?

- How do we stand right now?
- What must we do to meet your standards?
- How long do we have?
- What can we expect in return for meeting your standards?
- Who are the decision makers?

The earlier you talk and the broader your contacts (remember, the 'diamond' relationship is about ensuring long-term security and customer retention), the more likely you are to survive rationalization. With appropriate skill and subtlety, perhaps you can even influence the setting of standards and performance measures by which the decisions will be taken, to suit, of course, your own performance advantages. The worst thing to do would be just to await your sentence, good or bad. Rationalization can be as daunting for the customer as for suppliers. Suppliers that can actively help with the process have a greater chance of surviving.

## Potential downsides

Be aware of the objectives and also be aware of some of the potential downsides of rationalization. These might be useful, not to use as arguments *against* the customer's intentions, but to demonstrate your concern to help the customer get the best outcome:

- Is it just considered a fashion, possibly to be reversed in a few years' time?
- Where will all the 'rationalized-out' suppliers go – the competition?
- What if a supplier is killed?
- What if, as times change, suppliers are needed back?
- With the advance of e-commerce, is there still a need to rationalize?
- Will the remaining suppliers be as capable as they claim?
- Is risk exposure increasing?

## Is the trend waning?

Downsizing was a trend a few years ago, but we have seen evidence of its reversal recently. Is optimizing suppliers the same? If we remember the objectives of reducing supplier numbers – efficiency, leverage, control and value – then, if other ways of achieving this appear, we might expect the trend to weaken or even reverse. One such alternative is the use of e-commerce to reduce costs (see Chapter 27). When considering your own future with a customer that has a supplier optimization programme, you need to walk carefully between two principles. In theory, the ends and not the means should determine the outcome; if you can offer greater efficiency through e-commerce, why should the customer de-list you merely in pursuit of a numbers game? But, in practice, you must also adhere to its current thinking, which may have more regard for the immediate means – the programme itself.

# RATIONALIZATION AND CENTRALIZATION

Changes in the shape of your customer's organization, whether through merger or internal initiatives to make it more effective, can pose a threat to incumbent suppliers of FS. Established relationships cultivated over many years may be ended. The question – is this type of rationalization good for a supplier? – seems to depend rather on the supplier's starting point. If you are one of the remaining suppliers, perhaps that's OK, but what if it costs you weaker margins? Or is this the wrong sort of question? If the customer is centralizing and rationalizing, then you only have one choice – to help. Consider how difficult it is for the customer. It has its own internal problems to cope with – the last thing it wants is an uncooperative supplier. What it really wants is someone who will help it succeed in what is a tough challenge.

## The benefits of a proactive approach...

Here is a life assurance example that shows the benefit of a key account approach to supplying resources to help an intermediary centralize and increase the cost-effectiveness of its business. A major insurance provider was in the middle of reorganizing its own business, having identified a small number of strategic accounts, while continuing to support the rest of its business through a local sales force. Hearing about this, a significant regional advisory firm, not nominated as a strategic account, approached the insurer asking for strategic account status. The advisory firm recognized the limitations of doing business at the local level and wanted to do something about growing its business strategically with the insurer. In taking a more centralized approach, the firm would remove much of the local decision making on recommended products and so would focus on fewer suppliers, with subsequent sales increases for those involved. The insurer considered that this firm had the potential to develop into a major player in the market and allocated it strategic account status. This would entitle the firm to considerable support from the insurer in developing strategic marketing plans, in training, merchandising and systems. Because the insurer had already set in motion a KAM approach with other accounts it was in a position to offer this package and to secure the position it wanted in relation to this firm. The moral of the story? The key supplier is the one that helps the customer achieve what it wants, in an intelligent and economical way. Don't fight supplier reduction; make it work for you by using your knowledge and expertise to the customer's benefit.

# TAILORING THE SERVICE TO THE CUSTOMER'S NEEDS

An outcome of the general trend towards supplier management may be a more proactive stance on the buying side. This may involve working with key suppliers to improve their ability to offer a service tailored to the needs of the customer. For some suppliers, this might result in a different kind of relationship, where they are managed *by* the customer. This is particularly common when supplying an own-label FS product through an intermediary such as a retailer. The retail customer might set the standards and the specification; it may well initiate new product developments; and, most importantly, pricing may be set on the basis of an agreed margin. The style and resulting activities of such a relationship might depend on the box occupied in the supplier positioning model. Let us go back to the supplier power/buyer power model from Chapter 9.

## Bottom left – tactical make easy

This is where buyer power is relatively low, but the suppliers are generally undifferentiated. Processes must be integrated to provide efficient and effective support for the customer, particularly using e-commerce. There will be limited individual customer tailor-making in this quadrant, but it may be worth developing service packages targeted at groups of customers in order to meet the needs of particular segments.

## Top left – strategic security

The customer will be concerned about ensuring that its needs continue to be catered for despite the fact that it has limited buying power. The supplier may be unwilling to provide tailored service, preferring to focus on its bigger customers. Again a segmented strategy may be appropriate here. The supplier might provide a small support unit to cater for customers in this category, providing support for this segment as a whole.

## Top right – strategic partner

Strategic partnership comes with potentially huge benefits in terms of the access allowed to the FS supplier. But it also has its downsides. This gets to the very nub of relationships in this box: the supplier has undoubted privileges, but they come with attendant responsibilities. The customer may let you get very close, provided you agree not to supply its competitors.

---

### Exclusivity – the price of maintaining the business

Take the example of a global food company. This company seeks to cultivate long-term relationships with its employees and with those suppliers that are similarly organized and have a similar culture to itself. Many of its employees have grown up with the company, as have many of the employees in its FS suppliers. The advantage of this is that the company as dealing 'like with like' with people who understand intimately the business strategies needed to run this global company successfully. However, a problem has arisen because of consolidation amongst FS suppliers and their customers. As our respondent put it:

> We had to say to at least one supplier of FS that 'we really can't deal with you because you act for one of our major competitors', so we've had to ask them to take a decision. We've had to say to them either you want to stay with us and drop the other people or are you going to drop us and stay with the others? It's a simple choice.

This shows that a successful relationship in this box requires a very long-term commitment and may have strategic implications for both partners that will not always be apparent at the beginning of the relationship.

---

## Bottom right – tactical profit

In this box there are typically many suppliers vying for one piece of business, and discussions on price often predominate. In some cases this situation may reflect a commodity market and there may be little return from trying to tailor the service. But in other cases there may be benefit in the supplier investigating how it can add value, for instance by providing support through integration of processes and administrative procedures. This could create a degree of customer dependence on the supplier and move the relationship upwards towards the more strategic end.

# 13

# Understanding business strategy, culture and values – becoming a strategic supplier

The example from Chapter 12 of the global food company and how it works with its FS suppliers involved two elements to do with value, one obvious and the other subtler. The obvious measure of value involves tangible servicing costs and costs of products. The more subtle sense of value relates to the depth of the relationship between the company and its suppliers. This developed from a complex web of relationships between employees from both parties who worked together over many years, and from a common understanding and culture, and a belief that their core FS suppliers understood their business intimately.

The more subtle, or broader, sense of value used to assess a supplier often relates to the broader aspirations of the business – the *business strategy*. A supplier may be seen as a key supplier because it behaves appropriately against the expectations of the customer – KAMs certainly need to identify the 'obvious' measures of value. To become a strategic supplier, KAMs must identify with the subtle measures as well. To do this they must understand the customer's culture and the values that drive it. More than this, KAMs must orientate their own business so that their operations in front of the customer match the customer's values. If we see the achievement of strategic supplier status as a development beyond key supplier status, then ignorance of the more subtle sense of values will do most to deny the supplier the accolade.

### Key, strategic, preferred, honoured… what's in a word?

Maybe nothing. Your customer may use entirely different words, or none at all. No matter, the definition of 'strategic supplier' as used here is simply a supplier that manages to have a positive impact on the very heart of its customer's business. This chapter gives a very short summary of some foundations of business strategy and how they might reflect in the values held by the business. The purpose is to help KAMs from FS suppliers identify the values driving *their* customers, and be better placed to match them.

### What are they up against?

In Chapter 3 we looked at Porter's (1980) model for assessing the competitive forces on a business in order to understand our own competitive position. We might attempt to do the same for our customers: what forces are they trying to resist, what barriers might they raise or what obstacles do they seek to overcome in order to achieve their strategy? The supplier that understands the customer's competitive position, and acts to enhance it, advances itself several places in the queue for 'strategic supplier' status. To do this, the supplier must first be able to identify the customer's business strategy, a task not as easy as it may sound. How often have you complained of not knowing your *own* company's strategy? Then why should your customer's staff be any better informed? Such understanding will require a breadth of contacts, particularly at a senior level.

# BUSINESS STRATEGY

Business strategy is a vast subject. Countless textbooks explain its intricacies. Much time is spent on its development. Here, the focus is on identifying with your customer's business strategy and its implications for your key account planning. Put simply, business strategy, at the level we wish to understand it, might be said to be the outcome of three questions, each with its own issues and each with its own simple model to aid understanding (see Table 13.1). The result is a set of specific aspirations, values and approaches that define the activities of the business. The more that can be understood of the customer's wider aspirations and strategy and how these are manifested in the business's culture and values, the better. The rest of this chapter takes each of these three questions in turn, using the appropriate model as a guide to uncovering the answers and illustrating how those answers might impact on a supplier.

**Table 13.1**  *Business strategy questions*

| Questions | Issues | Model |
|---|---|---|
| What to sell and where? | Products, markets and risk | The Ansoff matrix The product life cycle |
| Why will people buy? | Competitive advantage | Michael Porter's competitive advantage |
| What makes your business hum? | Leading business system or driver | Treacy and Weirsema's value drivers |

# WHAT TO SELL AND WHERE? THE ANSOFF MATRIX AND RISK

For any business wishing to grow, there are four choices with regard to what it sells and where, expressed by the four boxes in the Ansoff matrix (Figure 13.1), named after its developer (1957):

- Sell more of existing products into existing markets – *market penetration*.
- Sell existing products into new markets – *market extension*.
- Sell new products into existing markets – *new product development*.
- Sell new products into new markets – *diversification*.

## Market penetration

Provided that there is more business to be had in your existing market (you do not already 'own' 100 per cent), then market penetration is usually the

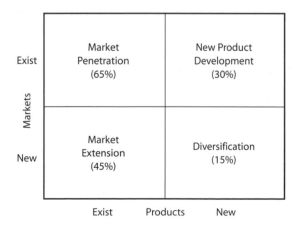

***Figure 13.1***  *The Ansoff matrix (likelihood of success in pursuing alternative strategies)*

safest strategy. You already have a presence, you know the requirements and you can measure your activities with some confidence. As your chosen growth strategy moves around the matrix, from penetration to extension, to new product development (NPD) and, finally, to diversification, the risk of failure increases. Why does risk increase? With each step away from your existing market and your existing products you are moving further into the unknown. Of course, some risk is necessary if you wish to grow, but any sensible business will always seek to manage or contain that risk as far as it can. There are many things that can be done to manage risk:

- market research;
- market testing;
- joint ventures with experienced partners;
- taking on experienced staff, or undertaking training;
- seeking help from the suppliers with specialist expertise.

If the customer's business strategy involves market extension, NPD or diversification, one can help reduce risk or manage the increased risk. FS suppliers, particularly in banking, have the expertise needed to support their customers in pursuing growth and managing risk. Risk may provide a number of opportunities from the supplier's point of view, if they can help the customer with it.

## Market extension

Companies seeking new markets may need information and expertise in relation to a new or unfamiliar area. As an FS supplier, you may have relevant contacts or access to useful information and expertise. The opportunity to be more involved with the customer's market place is almost always welcomed by a supplier. The more involved the supplier becomes, the more likely it will be viewed as a strategic supplier.

## New product development

Here the main issue may be sharing of risk. Nine out of ten new products fail. While a staged process may be used to cut out potential failures prior to launch, there will always be some uncertainty of outcome until the new product is proven in the market. Large sums of money are often involved in developing and launching new products and they represent an investment in the future of the business. Reducing your own risk depends on your ability to assess your customer's level of risk.

# Diversification

The risks are so great here (eg a record producer that enters the airline business, a cigarette manufacturer that enters the fashion market) that most businesses seek help and support from suppliers. An investment bank may be involved in advising on various aspects of entering the new market, for instance providing tax advice or advice on mergers and acquisitions and funding instruments. Certain types of diversification may involve an FS supplier as a partner. When a brand in an established market chooses to offer FS to its customers, it will often seek to develop a capability in partnership with an existing FS operator.

For example, the Virgin formula (record producer, to airline, to hotelier, to soft drinks, to railways, to investment manager – diversification with a vengeance!) is to minimize risk through close partnerships with key suppliers. Virgin brings the brand name; the supplier brings the market expertise. The supplier is expected to take some or most of the risk. Should it fail in any way, then Virgin retains the right to step in. In 1995 Virgin entered the UK FS market in a shared venture with Norwich Union. Following the success of direct (over-the-telephone) operators First Direct and Direct Line, Virgin's owner Richard Branson aimed to cut prices by selling direct to customers and cutting out expensive intermediaries. The philosophy of the business was to offer simple, high-quality, low-priced products through the telephone. Applying the Virgin formula supported by the administrative and investment expertise of a long-established FS operation resulted in the launch of a UK index tracker trust fund. The attraction of the product was its simple proposition and low upfront and annual charges. This formula proved successful in what was at the time a buoyant stock market and has been emulated by a number of competitors.

Success stories in diversification become legends, but there are many failures. The challenge for the KAM is in knowing when to back and when to back off. The judgement requires an intimate knowledge of the customer and its capabilities, and should you decide to proceed, the closeness of the working relationship will require a close mirroring of culture and values.

## WHAT TO SELL AND WHERE? THE PRODUCT LIFE CYCLE

For companies with a range of products, understanding of their business strategy can be aided by the application of the product life cycle (PLC) – an idea from classic marketing theory. Figure 13.2 shows a standard PLC, with the introduction followed by growth, moving into maturity and then into saturation and decline.

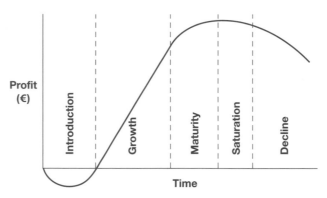

**Figure 13.2**   *The product life cycle*

The implications for FS suppliers of where their customers' products are on the PLC vary greatly according to the type of financial service supplied. The PLC helps explain the context for business decisions and therefore may be an aid to analysis and understanding. Figure 13.3 suggests some typical concerns for the customer at each stage of its own product's life cycle.

## The stages of the product life cycle

### Introduction

Understanding where the customer is on its product life cycle gives big clues as to what it might expect from its suppliers. We have seen from the Ansoff matrix (Figure 13.1) the high risks of new product development, and it is at this early stage of life that most flops occur. Suppliers are targeted for all kinds of help before the introduction to maximize the chance of success, but at the critical moment of launch one requirement stands out above all others – timeliness. Speed to market is critical in competitive markets. Days can

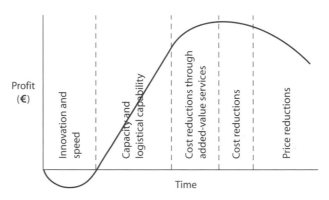

**Figure 13.3**   *Customer concerns during the life cycle*

make the difference between exclusivity and 'me too', between success and failure. A supplier that misses deadlines here is signing its own death warrant, but sometimes being too early is as bad as too late. The target is: on time and in full.

### Growth

When a product moves into the growth phase, the biggest problem is often dealing with its success. Forecasting is one thing, but nobody wants to hold back a runaway success just because the forecast was for less. Funding may need to be extended to support cash flow in the short to medium term, as the company seeks to establish a prime position in the market. It cannot afford to lose out to competitors at this vital stage in market development.

### Maturity

If the marketers are unable to ward off maturity, then the customer will turn to a different kind of remedy – the search for increased efficiency and cost control. The company looks for all opportunities to receive greater value. For the supplier, this might mean developing a service offer that reduces costs for the customer. Added-value services are at their most popular at this stage and, if they can help the customer to revive the product into a new period of growth, then they will be welcomed at a premium.

### Saturation

Here, the buyer will seek to cut costs in the simplest way – price. The future value in the product is not sufficient to justify more complex solutions that might involve new investment.

### Decline

The product is on its way out, but the customer must still keep it going with minimal effort. A successful company will have other products at earlier stages in the PLC through its programme of new product development. The company that has not invested in bringing through new products will probably itself go into terminal decline.

## Observation and identification in the real world

Understanding the issue of the customer's PLC is one thing, but being able to spot what stage a product is at is quite another. We are right back to the discussion in Chapter 3 about understanding the customer's market. Only through such an understanding can we hope to be able to identify a product's position in its life cycle.

# WHY WILL PEOPLE BUY? PORTER AND COMPETITIVE ADVANTAGE

Michael Porter, in his *Competitive Strategy* (1980), outlines the competitive forces that act on a business (see Chapter 3). He argues that competitive advantage – the reason people buy from you – comes from one of two sources: being the lowest-cost supplier; or being a differentiated supplier. Success comes from focusing the whole business on the chosen route. Failure results from vacillation between the two, or from functions or departments that argue with each other as to the right choice. The implications on suppliers and their activities are clear, but only if they understand what their customer is trying to achieve.

## Lowest-cost suppliers

This does not mean low quality, nor selling at the lowest price, though they will be able to do this should the need arise. A successful practitioner of this strategy once said to us, 'The trick is to be the lowest-cost supplier, but not let the customer know that!' It means aiming to supply at a lower cost than competitors. Lowest-cost suppliers examine the total costs of supply, purchasing, manufacture, distribution – the total supply chain – and take appropriate actions in each case. The answer may be investing in state-of-the-art production facilities or management systems. Wal-Mart, the huge US retailer, has invested more than any other retailer in information systems, and the result has been hugely reduced operating costs. It might result from buying cheaper raw materials, but it could also result from buying higher-quality materials that reduce wastage, prevent recalls and speed the production process.

For the supplier, the *value in use* argument is vital. Often, the easiest, and the laziest, way to cut costs is to get the supplier to reduce price. Poor suppliers succumb to such pressure. A good supplier, a key supplier, perhaps even a strategic supplier, seeks to reduce its customers' costs by more creative means, by changes to specifications, improvements to quality, changes to service, more technical support and, maybe, just maybe, a *higher* price.

## Differentiation

The customer that sees its route to success through building points of difference from its competitors will be seeking suppliers that can help it achieve this. It will be important for suppliers to understand what differentiation their customers are seeking to bring to the market, to enable them to make an appropriate offer.

## Different sectors/different needs amongst intermediaries

A major life company recognized different competitive approaches in the advisory sector when it reorganized its operation away from a geographical basis to focus on strategic accounts. For example, a banking strategic account team was set up in recognition that the banking model for distribution of life and investment products has particular characteristics. In the banking context, individual advisers are working in a tightly controlled corporate environment, where the major sales opportunities may come from encouraging unqualified staff (such as tellers) to recognize customer needs and to pass on leads to qualified advisers. A separate strategic account team deals with major advisory networks. In the network context, individual advisers are separate businesses and therefore operate very differently from those in a corporate context. They will tend to be far less closely managed and more entrepreneurial in their approach, depending on their local reputation for their sales leads. As a strategic account manager at the insurer puts it: 'Different sectors have different needs. If you look at a network and you look at the bank sector, they are poles apart in what products they buy, what's important to them, in terms of their choice, in terms of buying and in how we would need to interact with them.'

# WHAT MAKES YOUR CUSTOMERS' BUSINESSES HUM? TREACY AND WEIRSEMA'S BUSINESS VALUE DRIVERS

What makes your customers' businesses hum? In other words, what values distinguish them and drive them? How do their staff know what to do each day – what values drive them and their decisions? What aspect of each business leads to its success – general all-round ability, or is there something more specific? Treacy and Weirsema, in their book _The Discipline of Market Leaders_ (1995), identify three key business drivers. All may be present in any successful business, but in _really_ successful businesses one or other of these drivers tends to stands out, distinguishing the business for their staff and for their customers. Some examples are illustrated in Table 13.2.

**Table 13.2** _Examples of companies demonstrating Treacy and Weirsema's value drivers_

| Driver | Examples |
| --- | --- |
| Operational excellence | Federal Express, McDonald's, IKEA, Wal-Mart |
| Product leadership | 3M, Merck, Intel, Nike |
| Customer intimacy | Kraft, Quest International, Airborne Express, IBM* |

\* For more on how IBM and many other companies achieve this in business solutions, see Cerasale and Stone (2004).

*Operational excellence* is about doing what you do, well. It is about effective processes, smooth mechanics and the efficiency with which products or services are brought to market. Efficiencies of production, economies of scale, uniformity and conformance, accurate forecasting, slick distribution, fast response – these are the sorts of things that might be important to a business seeking operational excellence. Such 'excellence' can bring significant competitive advantage in a market where reliability is important or price is competitive. In the main, businesses in the mass market – the no-frills, low-hassle, low-price arena – will be driven by this value.

## One size fits all

IKEA achieves efficiencies through logistics, from manufacture to store, and self-selection and self-collection in-store complete the operational excellence of the supply chain, reflected in excellent value for customers. International uniformity (Swedish product names like *Gutvik* and *Sprallig* make it all the way to Australia), modular ranges and a carefully honed (limited, but it doesn't seem so) offer are some of the watchwords.

*Product leadership* is about producing the best, leading-edge or market-dominant products. Businesses with high rates of innovation and patent application often have this value at their heart. It is hard to imagine a successful pharmaceuticals company not driven by this. Investment in successful NPD is key to success. The market for 'nearly there' or 'almost as good as the best one' drugs is poor. A threat for businesses driven by this value is falling behind. They need to push the boundaries of performance – and be *seen* to be doing so.

*Customer intimacy* is the ability to identify with specific customer needs and match products and services accordingly. What distinguishes the customer-intimate business is its stated determination to develop close customer relationships and to act on the resultant knowledge at all levels of the operation. It will probably have a wide menu of products and services and the ability to mix and match these to suit individual customer requirements – or perhaps it will go further than this and offer a totally bespoke service. There is a limit to how many customers this can be done for, and a customer-intimate business will think carefully about segmentation and key account identification. Something else that often distinguishes a business driven by customer intimacy is willingness to share risks with customers and to expect a concomitant share of the rewards.

Quest International (part of ICI) supplies fragrances to the perfume industry. Each of its customers' products is unique and the fragrance is equally unique – there are few off-the-shelf solutions. The perfumer's art is as much one of black magic as chemistry, and Quest must be able to identify with this. Customer intimacy is essential for success:

absolute identification with the customer's needs and the ability to focus the whole organization on meeting them. Many of Quest's customers are driven by product leadership – branding is all – and Quest must be intimate with *that* value driver in order to be regarded as a key supplier. Its success is evidence of a broader observation: truly customer-intimate suppliers must be able to identify with value drivers in their customers that are quite different from their own.

## Implications for your customer's overall business operation

Those businesses with clear business strategies will probably also exhibit a clear preference for one of these values or drivers. Businesses less able to define where they are headed and how they will get there might exhibit a vague mixture of these values, often to their cost. It will be clear that the drivers could be in conflict with each other, particularly if different functions adhere to different values. A customer-intimate sales force promising product and service variations may be in open conflict with its own production and distribution departments if those functions are driven by operational excellence. If a successful business makes clear its leading business driver, then it is easy for the functions in that business to focus their activities. If customer intimacy is the goal, then that doesn't mean the factory should throw operational excellence out of the window. What it *does* mean is that the business should seek to identify *appropriate* operational excellence – perhaps measured by customer satisfaction rather than occupacity (the efficiency with which plant is used to ensure maximum output).

## Business value drivers in FS organizations

While the focus in this chapter has been on identifying the business strategy of your corporate customers, it is relevant here to reflect on the business value drivers that predominate in FS. This is of obvious relevance for suppliers selling through the FS intermediary sector and also for you to reflect on the value drivers for your own organization. You may find that you need to adapt Treacy and Weirsema's drivers somewhat for analysing FS. Product leadership is rare as a key value driver in this sector because of the ease of copying products. Instead, there are two additional value drivers – distribution reach, and risk and capital management – to add to customer intimacy and operational excellence. Distribution and risk management were identified in Chapter 1 as factors that are special features of KAM in FS, and both can be seen to provide competitive advantage and drive the business for a number of FS suppliers.

Table 13.3 illustrates the value drivers for US FS suppliers. The segmentation in Table 13.3 using the value drivers of distribution reach, risk and

**Table 13.3** *Segmentation of US FS by value drivers*

| Distribution Reach | Risk and Capital Management | Customer Intimacy | Operational Excellence |
|---|---|---|---|
| **Universal Banks** | **Integrated Capital Markets Firms** | **Integrated Monolines** | **Hybrid Manufacturers and Processors** |
| Bank of America<br>Citigroup<br>Deutsche Bank<br>HSBC<br>JP Morgan Chase<br>UBS | Goldman Sachs<br>Bear Sterns<br>Merrill Lynch<br>Morgan Stanley | Fidelity<br>Janus Capital<br>T. Rowe Price<br>Vanguard<br>American Express<br>Capital One<br>MBNA<br>USA Capital | Federated<br>Investors<br>Putnam<br>State Street<br>ING Direct<br>Amresco<br>CIT Group<br>GE Capital<br>GMAC<br>AIB Capital |
| **National and Regional Banks** | **Risk Specialists** | **Cross Product Distributors** | **Niche Manufacturers** |
| Bank One<br>CIBC<br>Comerica<br>Fleet Bank<br>National City<br>Washington Mutual<br>Wells Fargo<br>Compass<br>Huntington | Factors<br>Fannie Mae<br>Farmer Mac<br>Freddie Mac<br>Sallie Mae | Ameritrade<br>Charles Schwab<br>E*Trade<br>TD Waterhouse<br>Ditech<br>eLoan<br>Intuit<br>Lending Tree | Mellon Global Cash<br>Gabelli Asset<br>MFS<br>Ford Credit<br>Household<br>IBM Global Finance |
| **Community Banks** | | **Niche Distributors** | **Processing Specialists** |
| Chittenden<br>Hibernia<br>Provident<br>Financial<br>Silicon Valley Bank<br>West America | | First Direct<br>Futures<br>Insweb<br>Multex<br>Access Group<br>AmeriCredit<br>Apex | ACE<br>Baker Hill<br>Bisys<br>Certegy<br>First Data<br>Resources<br>Global Payments |
| | | **Insight Specialists** | **Networks** |
| | | Acxiom<br>Financial Engines<br>First Call<br>Dunn & Bradstreet<br>Equifax<br>Experian | Concord EFS<br>Fed check system<br>Fed Wire<br>Island<br>Cirrus<br>MasterCard<br>Visa |

Copyright IBM Corporation, 2004

capital management, customer intimacy and operational excellence is one way to consider the US market, showing how value drivers can be applied. It provides food for thought in considering the value drivers for your own organization.

## Implications for KAM

If you can identify your customer's business strategy in terms of its value drivers, then you might be able to predict what issues are important. By acting positively on these issues, you may increase your chance of being viewed as a strategic supplier. FS suppliers that show an interest in understanding such things about their customer will usually be regarded in a good light. Asking the right questions, of the right people, brings valuable information. This is a task for the KA team, gleaning snippets of information at every point of contact and piecing those snippets together for an *intimate* understanding of the customer and its market.

## Does it matter what *you* are?

This chapter has been about understanding what makes the customer tick and how identification with that will enhance your ability to become a strategic supplier. The very same questions – what to sell, why will people buy and what makes your business hum – can, of course, be asked of your own business. In particular, the understanding of value drivers is important to any business embarking on a KAM strategy. While the principles and disciplines of KAM suggest that a KAM strategy requires a customer-intimate driver, it is possible for KAM to exist and thrive in a business driven by operational excellence or product leadership.

## The supplier's own value drivers will influence the way that KAM is practised

The customer relationship can be 'intimate' in any scenario; it is how that intimacy is turned into actions and commitments that may vary. A supplier driven by operational excellence seeks activities that both meet customers' needs and suit its own strengths and abilities – matching market opportunity with business resources. The same can be said of the business driven by product leadership. Even a business with a brilliant list of product innovations can rarely survive without nurturing its customer relationships. Indeed, in many business-to-business markets, success comes from developing products based on ideas from customers. Still, a customer intimacy culture and a KAM culture have much in common. Both recognize customer relationships as the foundation of knowledge and so competitive advantage.

Both recognize the need to focus the whole business on to the customer. Both customer intimacy and KAM, to be fully effective, must become cross-business processes.

In Chapter 4, we identified what KAM might actually feel like, with two features standing out:

- KAM will change the nature of the relationship with customers, both in its complexity and in its purpose.
- KAMs and their teams will take on a much greater responsibility for the impact of their activities on their own business and must aim to align their business colleagues behind those activities.

In a customer intimacy-led business, both of these features have full rein. Indeed, they need to if the business is to be true to its values. In an operational excellence-led business, there may be restrictions on the scope of these two features. There may be little point establishing complex in-depth relationships with a customer (at least to the same extent as with the customer-intimate business) if operational excellence depends on an entirely standardized offer. Indeed, you may frustrate customers if all you do is raise expectations for change.

# THE CULTURAL MATCH

To be regarded as a strategic supplier, must the supplier be so similar to the customer? Must they be alike on a cultural level as suggested in the global food company example from Chapter 12? Not necessarily! Many successful relationships exist between absolute opposites, particularly on the global stage. However, such relationships sometimes have their moments of doubt, when both sides desire something more than that tangible demonstration of business value, when the customer wants to feel it is working with 'like souls'. A preference to work with suppliers from the customer's home country rather than from abroad is often more than a simple matter of the efficiencies of geographic proximity. So, to be considered a truly strategic supplier, you may need some level of 'cultural mirroring'. If this is not possible or desirable on the supplier's part, then it may be necessary to review how far this particular relationship can develop. By understanding the customer's business strategy and trying to make a positive impact on it, the supplier will in some way develop a closer 'cultural match' with the customer. That cultural match might be observed on several levels, from things as simple and as observable as dress codes through to the complexity of organizational culture. Some factors are easier to match than others, and some are more deserving of the attempt than others.

Remembering to dress up or down when visiting the customer is simple enough (and the way to avoid much discomfort), while changing your organization's structure to mirror the customer's is a much bigger throw (and may not even be necessary).

Table 13.4 is a list of the kind of areas that you might need to examine (with some inevitably vague definitions against a notional spectrum in each case), first to understand the customer's culture and then to assess the likelihood or desirability of a match. How far you go will be entirely down to your own circumstances, capabilities and ambitions. There is no golden rule, other than to observe and understand – once that is done, the necessary actions become much clearer.

**Table 13.4** _Some factors to consider when looking at 'cultural matching'_

| | | | |
|---|---|---|---|
| **Dress code** | Informal | Formal | Uniform |
| **'Entertainment'** | None | Internal only | From suppliers |
| **Meeting venues** | Customer's | Neutral | Supplier's |
| **Meeting style** | One to one | Ad hoc | Teams |
| **Organizational structure** | Hierarchies | Teams | Flat |
| **Management control** | Open | Federal | Centralized |
| **Management style** | Empowered | Process led | Individualistic |
| **Internal communications** | Informal | Ad hoc | Formal |
| **Career development** | Ad hoc | Fluid | Structured |
| **Time horizons** | Short | Medium | Long |
| **Attitude to risk** | Averse | 'Shared' | Entrepreneurial |
| **Growth aspirations** | Low | Medium | High |
| **Growth methodology** | Organic | Mixed | Acquisition |
| **Growth strategy (Ansoff)** | Penetration | Market extension/ NPD | Diversification |
| **Competitive edge (Porter)** | Lowest cost | Mixed | Differentiated |
| **Value drivers (Weirsema)** | Operational excellence | Product leadership | Customer intimacy |

# Part III

# Preparing for Key Account Management

# 14

# What will it take? Goals and obstacles

There will be a list of issues that confront you, depending on how far your business is oriented towards KAM:

1. Where do you want to get to? What are your goals?
2. What obstacles stand in the way?
3. What new attitudes, behaviours, skills, systems, organization and resources will be required?
4. What changes, activities and commitments will be critical to your success?
5. How will you manage the change required?

## GOALS

The KAM and key supplier status models (see Chapters 5, 9, 10 and 11) should help you and your team identify current positions and articulate goals. They provide a common language. Remember, *everyone* in your organization must be able to identify with these goals – everyone must speak the same language. The models also describe and guide the journey involved, providing important signposts and comforting milestones of progress made. It may seem obvious, but it is very important to start with an assessment of where you think you are – not everyone may agree.

## Goal 'hierarchies'

There are KAM goals for individual accounts, but also KAM goals for the whole business. Is the business using KAM simply to identify the most important customers, or is a 'KAM culture' being sought – perhaps a process for driving and directing the business? The wider the scope of the goals, the more radical their impact on the business and the greater the need for change, then the greater the obstacles and opposition that might be expected. The following chapters attempt to outline those obstacles and indicate what skills, systems, organization, resources and change management will be required to overcome them. Part IV then looks at definitions for key accounts and others that are needed to align the whole business behind the KAM concept.

# OBSTACLES

The obstacles to KAM do not come from the market, from customers or competitors, but from your own organization. Table 14.1 covers those most frequently found together with some short examples. Of course your own list will be unique to you – please don't be nervous about adding some more! We have not listed them in any order of severity (they are in fact in the order in which we address them in the following chapters), and in different circumstances what constitutes the 'worst sin' may vary considerably. Some are encountered once the journey is under way – KAM as bureaucracy, for instance – while others will stop it even starting – complacency and inertia being particular killers. The list is daunting. Even the most successful applications of KAM contain some of them. Perhaps your task at this stage is to determine exactly what does stand in the way (are you starting, or are things in progress?), and which need to be tackled earlier and which can be left for the moment.

**Table 14.1**   *Obstacles to KAM*

| Obstacles within the Organization | Short Examples |
| --- | --- |
| **Poor skills:**<br>– Resistance from the sales team (eg due to fear of change).<br>– Inappropriate skills.<br>– Inappropriate people or skills (eg a non-'streetwise' supporting team). | – Previous training and experience focuses on selling particular products or services.<br>– Staff and managers recruited for administration or compliance expertise, but lacking 'customer-facing' experience. |

**Poor systems and processes:**
- Failure to measure the impact.
- Poor measurements of account profitability.
- Conflicting measure of performance across departments/regions.
- Clashes of objectives and priorities across functions, eg inappropriate operational excellence.
- KAM as bureaucracy, eg telephone directory account plans, too many meetings.
- Poor disciplines for internal communication.
- Systems and processes designed to support sales of particular products or services.
- Systems and processes purely designed to meet legal and compliance requirements.
- Lack of coordinated strategic planning in specifying systems.
- Wrongly assuming that technology alone will provide a solution to customer relationship management challenges.
- Paying lip-service to KAM without a full commitment at the highest levels within the organization to the changes required.

**Inappropriate organization or structure:**
- The silo mentality: functional managers as 'barons'.
- Multiple or competing supplier business units (competing for customer ownership).
- Strong focus on individual products, reinforced by performance targets: particularly common in financial markets between those specializing in different categories of funding, eg bonds, shares.

**Failure to make it happen:**
- Top-management 'cop-outs', eg short-termism, failure to respect the need for investment, to identify the key accounts, to align the business, to empower the key account teams or to stick to the concept in times of crisis.
- Complacency and inertia, eg no dissatisfaction with the status quo, existing processes no longer appropriate but too deeply embedded.
- Senior management talks the language of KAM but in fact still gives greatest attention to those who perform well for individual products, and takes their objections to KAM too seriously.
- Mergers and acquisitions cut across key account strategy.
- Those wedded to the past stall progress in implementing KAM through lack of commitment or even employing 'spoiling tactics'.

**Failure to make the hard choices:**
- Too many key accounts.
- No plan for servicing the non-key accounts, eg failing to free up the energy required, service creep (every customer gets the package designed for the key accounts).
- Unwillingness to commit to changing channel strategy, so prefer to give poor direct sales attention to all clients.
- Senior management not prepared to give sufficient priority to KAM over other projects.

# 15

# What will it take? Skills

## THE CHANGING REQUIREMENT

Sales professionals are often the worst judges of the skills needed by a KAM! Why? Because their view usually differs so much from what the customer thinks is needed. Cranfield Business School has researched a number of industries to find what customers seek in a KAM. The answers are surprising (at least for KAMs!). Instead of selling skills, negotiation skills, presentation skills and the like, the customer values integrity, trust, the keeping of promises and an ability to get things done in the KAM's own organization. The supplier really must leave behind some beliefs and attitudes that may have served it well in the past, perhaps very well! Figure 15.1 shows the skills needed in traditional sales, compared with KAM. It is possible to find the skills for the traditional sales task all in one person. Indeed, absence of any one of these skills is usually quite apparent from the person's performance. How about the skills for the KAM task?

### KAMs and the obstacles

**Man or Superman?** Chapter 14 laid out the deadly sins. What is the expectation on the KAM's skills with regard to handling those sins? Some human resource functions insist that all KAMs must be top-level influencers, able to remove any internal obstacles. Others think it best to remove the internal obstacles first, or to provide support to achieve this as and when required, accepting that KAMs are mere mortals after all. We leave you to make the choice.

- **Traditional Sales Task**
  - Product knowledge
  - Interpersonal skills
  - Presentation skills
  - Negotiation skills
  - Self-organization
  - Time management
  - Territory management
  - Independence

  **Possible in a
  top-class salesperson**

- **The Key Account Task**
  - Strategic planning
  - Business management
  - Project management
  - Team leadership
  - Strategic influencing
  - Innovation and creativity
  - Managing diversity
  - Coordination

  **Possible in a
  well-formed KA team**

_Figure 15.1   Skills needed_

If the absence of a particular skill in the traditional sales representative is easy to spot from the person's performance, how much more serious is the absence of any particular capability listed under the KAM task (Figure 15.1)?

Do you know anyone who meets all these requirements? They are broader than most individuals can manage, hence the importance of the key account team. Provided that the team has these skills and abilities (eg product managers might supply project management skills, and market research or strategic planning departments might supply information and support in strategic planning), the KAM does not need to be a super-being. This is a relief to all involved in KAM, and not least to the HR department that despairs of finding such rare creatures. This doesn't mean that sales professionals can just carry on as before. Instead it raises perhaps the biggest change that salespeople will be asked to make on becoming KAMs. To use a musical analogy, they must be able to put down their violin – whatever their virtuoso ability – and pick up the conductor's baton. Their role is to conduct the orchestra. Their ability to motivate others, to delegate tasks and to co-ordinate a team becomes paramount.

**KAMs are important people, but their team is even more important**

## The key competencies

Many organizations work with competency models, and there are many such models. What follows is our view of the main competencies required by FS KAMs:

1. The ability to coordinate, motivate and direct the team that supports and services the customer. These people probably do not work directly for them (in a line management sense); some of them may well be very senior and are almost certainly more expert in their own areas.
2. A focus on creating value for the customer. This involves seeing opportunities, marshalling internal resources to meet them and presenting powerful propositions.

3.  The ability to build long-term relationships based on trust. This involves an ability to assess complex decision-making processes, the ability to network and the ability to work in a cooperative and consultative way.
4.  The ability to enhance profitability by planning the development of the business relationship with the customer in the light of understanding what drives profit for the supplier.

## THE TEAM'S SKILLS AND ABILITIES

The need for new skills and abilities does not stop with the KAM. KA team members have their own challenges. If people from 'back-room' functions are involved with customers, they need new skills and abilities, such as:

- commercial understanding – a 'streetwise' appreciation of their environment and responsibilities, particularly in front of the customer;
- interpersonal skills;
- persuasion and influencing skills;
- presentation and negotiation skills.

In the KAM approach, people from 'back-room' functions must become more customer focused and commercially aware. This is just as important as getting the skills of the KAM up to scratch. Behind this challenge lie many obstacles. For one, these people might not want to – plenty of people go into administration, process, compliance or IT roles just because they *want* a so-called 'back-room job'. Equally, KAMs may have sales backgrounds because they wanted jobs with 'independence', away from head office responsibilities and politics. They might view their new role with apprehension or distaste. We are dealing not only with skills, but with people's attitudes and behaviours.

## ATTITUDES AND BEHAVIOURS

New skills do not appear just because job responsibilities change or because people are sent on training courses. Skills do not develop in a vacuum. Before new skills can be taken on, those involved need to understand what is required of them, why it matters and how they might benefit from the change. A man who has spent a lifetime in the role of family breadwinner does not become an ideal househusband just because he loses his job. Almost certainly, those asked to adopt new skills will also need to adopt new attitudes and behaviours. Attitudes and behaviours are deeply entrenched. They rarely respond to simple exhortations to change. A skill can be learnt, but will not be applied unless there is a desire to do so.

Attitudes are the most deeply entrenched, and take longest to change. Behaviours result from attitudes. Although we can all 'play-act' to some extent, our true colours eventually show. Skills are the tip of the iceberg. Consider this example, from a salesperson's perspective.

## Selling versus collaborating

A traditional salesperson might have been used, over the years, to receiving annual sales targets, regular updates to products and instructions to go out and sell these. In order to succeed (and survive), the following attitudes and behaviours (good and bad) might have been in evidence:

- 'My job is to make the customer want what we have.'
- 'I work in my own best interests and, if that doesn't suit the customer, I will let my company know through periodic sales reports.'
- 'Achieving my sales target is my number one objective.'
- 'I will aim to do this with minimum disruption to my own organization.'
- 'I will do this single-handed (because I have to!).'
- 'If I encounter internal opposition, who am I to argue?'
- 'If I encounter customer opposition, I need to sell harder.'
- 'Success will result from my own energy and my ability to present and negotiate.'

It may be very different for KAMs. To begin with, they may set their own targets. Also, any new products they have to offer may have emerged as much as a result of their own lobbying as of any marketing department's say-so. For them, the word 'sell' has a different ring. Success depends on a different set of attitudes and behaviours:

- Not: 'My job is to make the customer want what we have', but: _'Our KA team's job is to develop an intimacy of relationship that allows us fully to understand our KA customer's needs.'_
- Not: 'I work in my own best interests and, if that doesn't suit the customer, I will let my company know through periodic sales reports', but: _'It is the KA team's responsibility to seek alignment between our and the customer's interests (where this is not possible, perhaps the customer cannot be a KA).'_
- Not: 'Achieving my sales target is my number one objective', but: _'Satisfying the customer in a profitable manner is our number one objective.'_
- Not: 'I will aim to do this with minimum disruption to my own organization', but: _'We will aim to do this by involving and directing the organization as appropriate.'_
- Not: 'I will do this single-handed (because I have to!)', but: _'The KA team will achieve this, with my leadership where required.'_

**New ways of thinking – not easy, but essential for success**

- Not: 'If I encounter internal opposition, who am I to argue?', but: *'If we encounter internal opposition, we must understand why and seek a way forward (perhaps using our executive sponsorship of KAM strategies), continually aiming to align the business behind our KA objectives.'*
- Not: 'If I encounter customer opposition, I need to sell harder', but: *'If we encounter customer opposition, we may well be doing the wrong thing.'*
- Not: 'Success will result from my own energy and my ability to present and negotiate', but: *'Success will result from our ability to work in collaboration with the customer and to harness the resources of our own organization.'*

If traditional salespeople see themselves solely as messengers, with perhaps occasional lobbying on behalf of their customers, then KAMs must take on the role of 'champion' for their customers. Moreover, they must become the responsible managers of the total relationship between the two organizations. This sort of change cannot be expected to occur overnight, because:

- It *will* take time.
- It *will* require the support of senior management – particularly when there are setbacks.
- The *whole* business must be aligned behind the goals and concepts of KAM.
- Such change has to be managed – *someone has to be responsible*.

## And the KAMs themselves?

The main skills KAMs require are:

- leadership skills and, in particular, the ability to coordinate, direct and motivate a cross-functional team, few if any of whom report directly to the KAM, many of whom are senior to the KAM and most of whom will be more expert in their particular area;
- influencing skills, with the customer and within their own organization, so demonstrating to the customer that they have the ability to make things happen;
- strategic vision – the ability to see opportunities in complex circumstances and to direct a team of experts in matching those opportunities with solutions;
- a focus on the reward for their team's brilliance.

Chapter 17 asks the difficult question– are our existing salespeople the right ones for the KAM job? Chapter 18 explores the principles behind managing change of this nature; and in Part VII we offer a timetable and development track for KAMs and their teams.

# 16

# What will it take? Processes and systems

Trying to get all the systems and processes required for KAM in place before the journey starts is not sensible. The nature of the requirement will be determined to a large degree by the nature of your own particular journey and experience. There is a lot to be said for learning and building as you go in this regard, but with a long-term plan and architecture in mind of course. However, there are some things that almost all businesses involved in FS need to consider at an early stage in developing a KAM approach. The first half of this chapter discusses these more general systems and process requirements (or will refer to other chapters where they are tackled in more detail). In the second half of this chapter we then look in more detail at system design and the challenges of developing a KAM system in the context of pre-existing systems architecture.

## MAKING IT EASY TO DO BUSINESS WITH YOU

In vendor ratings and in customer satisfaction surveys, the issue that emerges most often is 'making it easy for customers to do business with you'. So, if you want to be a key FS supplier, then you must be easy to do business with. This simple notion should be shouted loud and clear every time that you consider a system or a process – *will it make us easier to do business with?* The following analysis examines five broad categories of systems and processes:

- *Customer classification:*
    - identifying key accounts;
    - customer distinction;
    - offer development and management.
- *Information:*
    - measuring key account profitability (including risk and cost to serve models);
    - customer information (CRM – customer relationship management);
    - knowledge management.
- *Communication:*
    - e-mail and more (internal/external).
- *Operational:*
    - forecasting and operational support;
    - managing customers across multiple channels (consistent sales and service processes);
    - e-commerce;
    - key account plans.
- *Performance measurement:*
    - incentive management;
    - the performance map (performance scorecards).

# CUSTOMER CLASSIFICATION AND CUSTOMER DISTINCTION

This will be dealt with in detail in Chapters 21 and 22. You need to identify who the key accounts are and how much profit you make from them, and segment or classify customers by criteria that help you create unique offers and service packages for each category. The process used for this classification must be understood by everyone involved with KAM, across all functions – it needs to be simple and transparent.

# INFORMATION SYSTEMS

## Measuring profitability

In Chapter 7 we stressed the need to measure account profitability. This is not easy for many FS organizations. Traditional accounting systems are not designed on an account-by-account basis. It may also be hard to record the costs involved in every aspect of servicing each account. Even if you can measure today's profitability, you may wish to view the customer on a longer-term basis by trying to estimate future customer value. In FS, this often includes risk measures. You certainly need to engage the support of your business accountants and IT people if profitability is to be measured successfully. Make them part of the team and ensure they understand the importance of what you are asking them to do. Don't expect just to hand them a brief – or, if you do, don't be surprised when nothing happens or an inappropriate result appears. Measuring profit by customer may require a substantial overhaul of current sales and profit reporting systems – perhaps a substantial investment of time and money – and almost certainly a change to some accepted wisdoms and conventions. The reasons for doing so will have to be very clear before you are allowed to proceed.

### The risk of losing profitable customers

An FS company that provided credit and debit card authorization equipment to retailers, and provided the network and transaction processing capabilities, was surprised to see the results of a simple segmentation of its customer base. It had already realized that a certain amount of business was lapsing on a regular basis, but considered that this was replaced by similar levels of new business. A first-level analysis of current customer value (profitability) enabled it to see that high-value customers were being lost; yet the replacement new customers won were of far lower value. As soon as this was identified, a targeted retention programme was put in place with excellent short-term results. In subsequent development stages, a specialist support and negotiation unit was set up to assist in the management of key accounts through critical relationship stages (eg contract renegotiation), enabling the most profitable relationships to be retained more frequently.

## Customer information

If a true 'team sell' is to be achieved, then many people need to know about the customer and have access to the increasing wealth of knowledge about that customer. Old-style visit reports are unlikely to be sufficient; indeed, they are likely to become a bureaucratic nightmare. The KA team will need access to a more ambitious customer information database. There are many such systems on the market. You may need or want to develop your own.

## CRM – customer relationship management systems

The salesperson is trained to be on the lookout for a range of information – customer needs, buying criteria, perceptions – and to feed this back to those who can do something with it – product departments, administration, distribution, marketing. Such is the theory, but often such knowledge stays locked in the salesperson's head, or is lost in a string of miscommunications, or is simply ignored by the head office folk who clearly know better. CRM uses various systems and software packages to harvest this kind of information from the host of electronic interactions with customers, whether these are visits to the supplier's website or the transactions of e-commerce. Every interaction with the customer has the potential to provide information about its needs, its buying behaviour, its perceptions, its concerns and its frustrations.

The internet allows other techniques to be used. Analysis of customers' clickstreams as they navigate your site can reveal how they go about making their choices. Do they look for information first? Do they check for alternatives? How do these internet channel interactions complement what we know about the other channels they use? The self-service 'virtual sales assistant' is a technique that allows customers to ask questions, and in so doing reveal much about their interests, their certainties, their doubts and their priorities. Some internet sites allow customers to interrogate 'virtual customers', to seek 'opinions' of the product or service, and through this interaction the customer will display a whole range of concerns, attitudes and perceptions. This is no different in principle to utilizing the traditional skills of the salesperson. We might equate the analysis of the clickstream with the salesperson's ability to read body language, only now we see the potential for harvesting these observations on a massive scale and using them to modify the proposition. (It is an irony that marketers will now happily listen to what the salespeople have to say, provided that those salespeople remain reliably virtual!)

Such information is kept in a *data warehouse*. Without sophisticated analysis techniques such as *data mining* we would soon be pining for the 'old-fashioned' market researcher. Data mining involves a range of techniques for identifying patterns of behaviour from sales information and other transactional histories. The concept of 'signalling' is one such, trying to recognize customers' intentions from their transactional behaviour – perhaps a willingness to pay more for speed, or a desire to set a specification.

**And in practice...?**    That's the theory, but what about the practice? Simply installing a new system will do nothing for the supplier or the customer. This mode of doing business requires trained staff, clear objectives and genuine value for the customer – elements of the equation all too often ignored by companies that think they can hand the responsibility of all this over to the IT experts. The answer of course is to integrate these IT experts into the key account teams hoping to use these new systems. The M for 'management' in CRM is perhaps misleading. People will still manage the relationship; the system will provide the information. That is true at least for key accounts. Chapter 21 looks at other classifications of accounts, and CRM may have a very different role to play in the more active management of what we will be calling *maintenance* and *opportunistic* accounts.

# Knowledge management

Capturing information is one thing; turning it into knowledge and using it to enhance performance is quite another. What many organizations are calling 'knowledge management' is becoming a source of competitive advantage – those companies that can not only 'discover' valuable information, but also disseminate it to those that need to know, *and put it to positive use*, have a significant advantage – knowledge is indeed power. The challenge is to find the combination of systems, discipline and skills that will form the core of a knowledge management culture (Figure 16.1). Knowledge may be power, but power for the organization, not the individual. That is the main cultural challenge. The organization must develop a means of capturing information and ideas, editing those ideas, sharing them with the right people and putting them into action. The KA team is the means of capture, and it is also responsible for ensuring that the rest of this challenge is met, as shown in Figure 16.2.

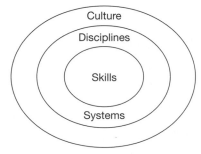

*Figure 16.1*   *The core of a knowledge management culture*

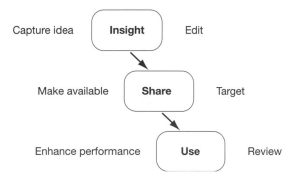

*Figure 16.2*   *Knowledge management in practice*

---

### Knowledge management in a bank

Effective knowledge management at a major bank comes from using technology effectively in the context of regional, but specialized, teams. It manages its regional key accounts on a local basis with teams that are dedicated to particular sectors. The result of this is that although this is a very large bank, the local team is typically focused on a limited number of key accounts. Two main systems, the performance management system and the client record, support knowledge management in this bank. The performance management system records earnings and expenditure by account based on the products supplied and including risk factors. The client record is updated with all the main contacts and resulting actions relating to the customer. Anyone contacting the customer can first have a quick look at the record to see what has been going on. This is very important, as relationships are developed at different levels within the team and all members are encouraged to use the client record to ensure they are up to date. However, the bank also stresses that it is important to meet up with other members of the support team to understand fully what is happening with the client. The client record only gives a partial picture of the state of the relationship and is no substitute for regular face-to-face discussions with those dealing with the customer daily. So, effective knowledge management in this bank is not just about having efficient systems. It is about using those systems in the context of localized teams that can share knowledge formally and informally.

---

# COMMUNICATION

As the KAM relationship approaches anything that looks like the 'diamond' of partnership KAM, the KA team, or indeed the business, can suffer a breakdown through a communications overload. As more people talk to each other, and more meeting reports flow, and more data are gathered and shared, then KAM can become a monstrous bureaucracy. There will be a need for new systems and new disciplines to manage communications. Some systems support distribution of information (eg e-mail systems), while others provide access to information (for example, real-time customer or product data) 'on demand'. A real-time customer information file (CIF) supported by core system access (legacy systems) and intranet facilities is an ideal combination for this purpose.

## Making remote communications work

You have spent a lot of money on getting the systems in place, but how much have you spent on training people to use them? The technology exists; that is not the issue. It is how the technology is deployed and used that matters. Whether e-mail helps or hinders is down to the users. How many messages do you have when you return from a week away? It wasn't the system that sent you this headache – it was people. Call centres and the internet have taken over as major channels of communication in FS. A proper and disciplined use of these media is more important than ever. In managing global key accounts, or accounts with a wide geographic spread, your own team may itself be based in several different locations. It must be able to work as a _virtual team_ with remote communication the norm and physical get-togethers the exception. Continuing improvements to video-conferencing technology make this ever more easy (though by no means simple), but there is still no replacement for a physical meeting of the team, as often as is possible, and certainly once a year. The social element of the team is very important, and the simple fact of putting faces and personalities to names is hugely beneficial. Any new members of the team tend to remain outsiders until such time as they meet their colleagues face to face. However, for most of the time the discussions will be at a distance, and e-mail will be the vital link. It will be as well then to understand some of the pros and cons of this medium, and to agree some team 'rules' on its use.

## E-mail – the pros and cons

The advantages of e-mail are many, ranging from its low cost to its immediacy, and including its ability to make time zone differences of little significance, the fact that a written record is kept of all discussions, and the ability to include the customer in the net. The downsides must be recognized and faced up to. It is relatively impersonal. It is easy to cause offence or confusion. Most of us do not write as clearly as we think we do and, worse, we tend to express our written feelings with greater bluntness than we would dream of doing face to face. Quite simply, if there is any chance of upsetting folk in your team, then e-mail is the surest way to ensure that you do! E-mail is great for detail, but not yet ideal for complex debates or for negotiation or persuasion. Unless you have some special extenuating circumstance, never try to negotiate a price increase with a key account by e-mail and never ask a question by e-mail where the answer 'no' will be unacceptable but all too likely. Finally, if yours is a global team, don't forget the language issue. Face to face we realize the limitations of each other's understanding, but when separated we too easily take it for granted that everyone understands all that is said. So it is a good idea to agree as a team what we might call a 'communications charter' – a rulebook of guidelines on how to behave. This is something that you might tackle at your first physical gathering.

## The 'communications charter'

The issues to agree on might include:

- _Address groups_ – do we want all communications shared across the whole team or will the unthinking use of address groups lead to overload? Start a campaign within your team against the receipt and the sending of junk mail.

- *Confirmations* – when someone asks for something to be done, must recipients reply to say they are doing it, or can it be taken as read?
- *E-mail or telephone* – what sort of conversations should we try to have by telephone, or video-conferencing, rather than e-mail?
- *Attachments* – take note of the fact that mobile users based at home or in hotel rooms can have their line occupied for huge chunks of time with complex PowerPoint presentations and the like as attachments – be sensitive to their different working norms.
- *Length of messages* – messages should be edited ruthlessly: don't send long rambling 'streams of consciousness'.

# OPERATIONAL SYSTEMS AND PROCESSES

## Forecasting and operational support

The implications for the business of full KAM are sometimes daunting. The impact on lead times, the demands for flexibility, the impact of 'bespoke' offers: all of this could turn a business from profit to loss if the right operational processes and systems are not in place. At the top of most lists will be a system giving accurate, updatable forecasting. Of course, the best forecasting systems are ones that involve the customer. The more intimate the customer relationship, the closer you get to accurate information. The closer you work together, the more you know of the customer's *doubts*, the key to *real, long-term* forecasting, rather than relying on its public pronouncements – usually of enormous growth. A forecasting system that allows an element of judgement, a percentage certainty of a particular order, for instance, is one that will suit the intimacy of a KAM environment.

Consider who forecasts are for. Usually they are important for the support functions, so that they can plan their activities and staff up to the degree required. But if they are to base their operational decisions on those forecasts, they need faith and trust in them. There is nothing worse for the relationship with an intermediary partner than when a big deal is set up and the partner puts an enormous effort into selling, but then finds that the supplier cannot service the agreed volume efficiently because operational and support units did not believe the forecasts. At the same time, having support units sitting idle because the intermediary came nowhere near meeting inflated forecasts is not good for the supplier's profitability. Another example is where forecasts may be crucial for the treasury or finance functions in hedging funds or securing tranches of funding behind a product. Because of the size of the deals involved, lack of accuracy or lack of trust in forecasts can have a massive impact on the profit on the deal. Forecasts must be 'owned' by all, and they must be continually reviewed and updated. Whatever system is adopted, it must allow for that joint ownership and flexibility.

## Managing customers across channels

With the proliferation of channels for customer service using the internet and call centres, in addition to traditional face-to-face methods, the question of consistency of service provision has come to the fore. The problem is often that separate operating systems provide the platform for each channel and that in developing your KAM system you are not starting from a clean sheet of paper. The second half of this chapter provides a model for tackling KAM systems design within existing systems architecture.

## E-commerce

Chapter 27 goes into detail on this increasingly important aspect of conducting FS business. E-commerce provides opportunities to improve business processes, particularly those between supplier and customer, to a degree thought impossible only a few years ago. E-commerce speeds transactions, and captures information in a way that allows both supplier and customer to work together in improving those transactions.

## Key account plans

Chapter 31 looks at the process for turning the theory of KAM into practice. Key account plans must above all else be practical documents – short and to the point. There is no room for 'telephone directory'-sized documents filled with diagrams that simply show you have read a textbook!

# PERFORMANCE MEASUREMENT

Of course, just as new skills (discussed in Chapter 15) are insufficient without the right attitudes and behaviours, so will new systems fail if there is not a wider understanding of their aims and purpose. Installing a system to measure profit is one thing but, without an agreed definition, across the business, of what profit *means* and how this information will be used, the system is all but useless. We are beset by conventions in measuring and reporting performance, but there are two common conventions, or limitations, that can be particularly damaging to the implementation of KAM: firstly, what we call the 'burden of the year'; and secondly, the clash of competing measurements, as is often seen between functions.

## The burden of the year

KAM can be a long-term process. Developing a particularly complex customer relationship may take time, the benefits may not accrue immediately, and performance after a year may look fairly dull. It would be tragic if annual requirements caused you to pull back at this point, simply because you were not able to measure performance over a longer period. Remember the notion of 'future value' (Chapter 7). At the same time you will need to be mindful of your customer's criteria in judging performance and the phasing of its sales periods and financial year. You may well also need to be able to view your performance with the customer according to its preferred timescales. Whichever the need, longer or shorter periods of measurement, your accountants and IT people will doubtless relish the challenge, *and* rise to it, if you involve them in the team.

## Competing performance measures

A common obstacle to KAM is the existence of performance measures that work against a customer orientation. These measures often reside in the functions that support the KAM effort. Consider two examples.

### Production measures

An administration manager might be measured on 'productivity' – the efficiency with which he or she uses resources to ensure maximum throughput. A KAM might approach that manager with a 'customer-focused' request – to produce a modified offer or service. Let's say that this might involve halting the current processes, a redesign, a relatively short trial, another halt, another change and then back to where we were previously. Should the KAM be surprised if the administration manager sends him or her away?

### Changing requirements

Administration functions crave regularity and order – 'operational excellence'. 'Customer-intimate' KAMs with short-notice requests to help customers get out of a hole are not welcomed. Suppose a mortgage lender has an understanding with its intermediaries that it will set up new own-branded mortgage products for them within six weeks. Perhaps this 'understanding' has worked well in the past. Times change, and customers change. Newer customers demand shorter lead times. It is the trend in the market. They need to get new products on to the market within four weeks. The competitive environment is changing. The KAM, intimate not only with the customer but with the customer's market, is keen to meet the new demands. But administration feels no obligation to meet them. They were not part of the original 'understanding'. Administration's performance measures focus on administrative efficiency. The result is chaos. Some salespeople are better than others at getting their 'rush orders' accepted, but in doing so put at risk the company's ability to meet the established service standards for others. The result? Nobody is happy.

## Incentive management

A concerted approach is needed by sales and administration to understand what is required to develop the required forecasting systems and processes, and to agree performance measurements to monitor the system. Administration will still aim for 'operational excellence', but in a customer-focused context, not in a vacuum – what we might call 'appropriate operational excellence'. The answer to the problem lies in how that administration manager is measured, which brings us to the tale of the basketball player. In professional basketball, there is a measure for everything. Two measures stand out – 'baskets', and 'assists', that is, how many times players put the ball through the hoop, and how many times their 'play' helped _another_ player put the ball through the hoop. Couldn't some KAM functions be measured on 'assists' as well?

## The performance map

There is a lot to making KAM work, and so there is much to measure and to monitor. We need a map showing where we have to go, where we are now, how far we have to go and the best direction to take. This is the performance map (Figure 16.3). The map uses software to lay out the elements on the KAM journey that are important to you. The steps relate to each other in logical sequences – for instance, two specific requirements might be a key account plan and an analysis of the customer's decision-making process (Chapters 23 and 24), but it is unlikely that you will have prepared a decent plan without first having done that piece of analysis. A questionnaire is used to assess your capability at each step, and the results plotted on the map using green and red lines to indicate good and bad performance. The result is a picture of where you have strengths – the way you have come – but also where you need to improve performance – the map for the way ahead.

# DESIGNING THE SYSTEM

One of the main problems in implementing KAM systems is we rarely start with a clean sheet of paper. There are always existing systems in place, although they may not support desired KAM capabilities. In the rest of this chapter, we consider an approach to KAM system design, taking advantage of

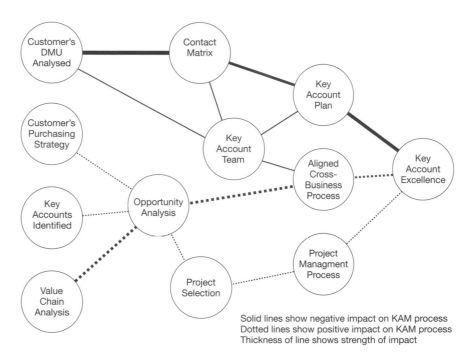

Solid lines show negative impact on KAM process
Dotted lines show positive impact on KAM process
Thickness of line shows strength of impact

**Figure 16.3**  *The performance map*

existing systems investments where possible. To avoid reinventing the wheel and incurring additional cost, it is important to use a comprehensive, proven industry model for the KAM systems and data environment. The model helps achieve goals, by encouraging formation of a detailed, prioritized plan covering every relevant aspect of IT. This plan is the overall systems architecture. The main elements of an IT architecture are described in Table 16.1.

## The KAM ecosystem

There are three elements of a 'closed-loop' KAM ecosystem, which allows key account salespeople to manage customers professionally while supporting marketers, finance people and others in their work in analysis, planning and operations:

- *Collaborative KAM* – where channels or touch points share and use information about customers, whether serviced or self-service.
- *Operational KAM* – where each person in contact with customers, or the customer directly, accesses the organization's back-office systems for straight-through processing.
- *Analytical KAM* – where the integration of customer, financial, risk and marketing information allows more focused, effective and profitable information analysis and directed activity across the organization.

**Table 16.1** _Components of an IT architecture_

| Component | Description |
| --- | --- |
| Context | A plan that conveys basic requirements, guidelines and constraints. It may itself be an output of a higher-level architecture such as a business plan, so there is input here from the business vision statement. |
| Frameworks | A multi-layered approach to developing the architecture in stages. Typical frameworks consist of a series of elements and levels that can be envisaged as a grid. Elements include computing systems, communications systems, data management and applications software. These are then specified with increasing degrees of precision as initial parameters are translated into policies, models, plans and procedures. This is how integration is achieved – by ensuring that each part of this 'grid' fits to the next part. For example, the area of data management might proceed from defining data assets, through to requirements for use, access control and storage. It would not be possible to use, say, data warehousing or data mining without thinking through the implications for other elements. |
| Components | Commonly accepted objects that make up building blocks. The purpose of architecture is to define and arrange these. Within these the architect will define hardware, software, people, and decisions processes. |
| Interrelationships | Relationships between objects are based on some sort of modelling. The purpose is to evaluate the effect of varying relationships between components so as to maximize synergy and interaction. We look at customer-to-customer links (processes), the flow of decisions, the proximity of functions, data dictionaries and indexing (of databases). |
| Models | There is a need for standard components or interfaces to act as guidelines for developers and for aesthetics. If people do not like the look and feel of software, they might not use it. |
| Architects | The people who turn visions into reality and provide the link between concept and implementation. They must identify and meet the needs of users so as to produce executable plans. Users are often not directly involved in systems development, so architects must link information services (IS) with business managers. A data warehouse is an expensive waste of money if nobody wants to use it because it is too complicated, slow or unwieldy. In this example, the architect would be the KAM project manager. |

The result of applying and integrating collaborative, operational and analytical KAM is *closed-loop KAM*. This is when a continuing learning loop – a virtuous circle – is created that delivers increasingly effective activity in each area. Additional customer information is acquired and stored at every interaction, while the organization's customer knowledge is deployed and redeployed to optimize the value of each relationship. The common enabling factor in all these forms of KAM is integration, which we deal with later in this chapter.

A key element in systems models for KAM is whether the data can be traced from business requirements to source and to other uses of the same data. Systems models should therefore provide for easy integration of best-practice one-off applications into an integrated systems approach. For example, a new profitability reporting application can identify and share data from earlier projects, requiring only previously unused data to be added. Even staged project change costs can be reduced as additional databases may be modelled and mapped with overall consistency.

The complete full-cycle architecture produces an operational business system. Once, decision support systems were considered as non-operational IT, with the only outputs being printed reports. Only transaction systems, eg sales force management systems, were seen as operational. Production of reports for decision making was seen as having only a loose or indirect connection with day-to-day operations. The feedback loop through decision, action and measurement was usually not fully implemented. Modern closed-loop systems implementations allow us to customize complex FS products rapidly and to improve yield management (product repricing based on demand management) through feedback and learning. These features depend on constant market intelligence and rapid decision making, affecting both operational and non-operational systems.

## Building a 'full-cycle' system

The complete data cycle is complex, but it can be developed in stages that exploit the systems you already have in place. A business assessment (eg CMAT) will direct prioritization of development and funding for business benefit. If the start point is sources of data arising mainly from customer interactions (for example, as an input to analysis of customer needs and behaviours), we need to manipulate these data in various ways. They must be combined from different originating points, transformed and analysed before using them for business decisions. Once implemented, decisions produce propositions (eg account development) and further customer interactions that have to be measured. The cycle is illustrated in Figure 16.4:

● Data are sourced from customer or partner contacts, legacy systems and external data sources.

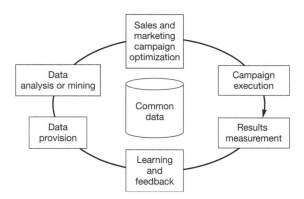

**Figure 16.4**  *The learning and development cycle*

- A common data store such as a data warehouse or data mart is designed and built for all selected, cleaned and structured data.
- Customer data are then analysed using online analytical processing (OLAP) and data-mining tools. These produce customer scores that classify customers and may help us forecast, for example, the receptiveness of customers to particular products or services.
- Planned customer dialogues and contacts are then optimized for maximum return – even in the world of KAM, salesforce intervention is more effective if backed by an appropriate offer and structured marketing dialogue.
- Marketing and sales initiatives (eg seminars) are designed and executed based on these plans, with contact follow-up activities.
- These initiatives are evaluated individually, against each other and against revenue and profit plans.
- Learning and new knowledge are internalized into processes and campaign improvements.

This does not imply that the systems solution should be defined in detail at the start, nor that the whole system must be built before benefits are obtained. It is designed and built in stages. Focus on developing a specific capability usually provides a basic definition of systems and data needs. With this focused approach, the IT implications of the early stages are often much smaller than expected as they can exploit previous investments. For example, not all legacy system data need to be extracted, cleansed, structured and analysed. A narrow focus on business requirements normally delimits a small subset of data that reduce timescales, effort, cost and risk. As an example, a project that aims to cross-sell (for example, to turn corporate customers for equities into customers for bonds) may only require details of past purchases, specific buying indicators, potential profitability and risk.

Quite often a subsequent project phase will then need only small additions to the data already available and in use. Much customer information will prove to be common to many new capabilities. Even in the worst case, it is usual for only limited additional data to be required. It is not necessary to build a broad cycle of systems and data, with all feedback mechanisms, to create the first learning loop; a simple loop can be rapidly developed and then broadened later. Interim feedback mechanisms can be created to enable rapid learning capability, for example manual analysis processes that can be auto-mated later when proven. A good KA system architecture and approach will draw on many years of previous implementation experience whilst retaining the flexibility to customize the approach in each project.

The planning approach or architecture should not determine pre-set business or data cycle times. Rather it should enable incremental improvements in cycle times as KA capabilities develop. As experience and understanding of managing customers improve, it becomes more practical to make just-in-time (even real-time) responses to individual clients, which should result in an improved return from each systems project. The systems solution will evolve. Different data items will be identified as key at different stages. Significant differences may be identified either within small customer segments or across large customer groups. The basic architecture should however enable planned, continual systems changes in response to both trials and operational use.

## The main requirements for success

*A sound system architecture for the complete solution set*

This includes development and management of linkages and feedback loops to ensure a seamless systems and data transition between and in support of business processes.

### The use of an existing industry data model

This can save substantial time and cost in both the short and long term. A fairly complete, well-tried model will have been applied many times in different projects, gaining content and rigour from each application. Such a model can underpin the 'build in stages, use in stages' systems approach, as the required data for each stage have an integrated structure. Even when additional data items are identified such as new customer attributes, there is normally an obvious place for them to be added within a proven model.

### A common language

The data that support customer and product profitability management tend to be unique to each company. The management of customer risk plays a large role. The data model often introduces a common, agreed business language for the first time. For example, the terms 'lapsed customer', 'product' or even 'customer profitability' may well have been in general usage within departments previously but they will need to be defined exactly if they are to be employed consistently across the enterprise through processes supported by a computer-based system. While these definitions may appear 'obvious' to different managers, big differences often emerge between and within business departments, between business managers and IT managers, and between merged or international companies. A common language is important to successful KAM, as this requires the business to act in a consistent manner. There may also be legal or cultural implications for the use of terms in the data model. These are important to a company when implementing a global programme. It is easy to underestimate the in-house build cost of such models. They can often be bought for much less.

## A common view of relationships

It is crucial to be able to view all data by customer and by contact. In a KAM environment the customer is usually a company or division of a company, or a group of several companies. Such groups and the individuals within them are the basis of what we call a 'party database'. A party database seeks to capture and represent data about all relationships relevant to the contact life cycle (prior and planned contacts). It is equally important to retain views of data by product, channel or intermediary. This is sometimes forgotten in the rush for a 'customer' database. A practical system enables any or all relationship views to be exploited as required. Much learning and expertise of this sort can be imported via a bought-in system, operational data store (ODS) or customer information file (CIF).

## Accept the unexpected

When system and data models are designed and built in-house, a step at a time, you may need to restructure periodically for unforeseen requirements. For example, in one project it was unclear at the early stages where profit data should reside within the database. Using an established system helps avoid the costs associated with unnecessary data complexity introduced insidiously as a result of gradual learning. In another project the importance of the group was not documented in the initial systems requirements. It was identified and added to the model much later. Because of this late, major change the database survived only a few years before yet more unexpected changes required a fresh start to control unnecessary complexity and cost. The impact on the business project timescale, delayed development of KAM capability and eventual return on investment (ROI) was substantial.

# UPDATING CURRENT IT SYSTEMS

## Extending the role of transaction databases

The move from a product to a product and customer focus has usually led to the development of a common customer database in front of or alongside legacy transaction systems. This customer (or party) database is transactional, as it supports contact with the customer in daily business operations, for example in the contact centre or behind the website or other electronic channels. The implementation of a separate front-end customer database enables new contact management capabilities to be implemented without replacing other administrative systems in the short term. Some early implementations of this sort of front-end database are little more than indexes, pointing to customer data held within multiple legacy systems. With only a customer index and a unique customer reference such as a product reference number, contact name or primary address, it is usually possible to identify whether the customer has an existing relationship with a company. The purchases of that customer can then be found even though the details may be spread across a number of legacy transaction systems.

Over time, developments of the transaction database allow for consolidation of common customer data so that each record is held only once. Common data can then be removed from the legacy systems or updated as a shadow or copy of the single customer view database. Other data relevant to the management of the customer may then be added, for example customer value or potential value indicators. A contact log is especially important as this is required to manage the customer across many contacts and channels, by different salespeople, senior managers, product managers, customer service staff and so on. Otherwise, each contact is made without reference to the others. Both customer and company expect all relevant contacts to be taken into account in the relationship, whichever channels they take place through.

The customer database is designed for rapid access to support individual customer contact. For example, immediate and simultaneous access may be required for salesforce, internet and customer service centre enquiries, as a transaction may start in one channel and move to another. So it would not be appropriate to use the same database for analysis. The operational data structures would be designed for performance, rather than for ease of use for report production. For technical reasons, the performance of the operational database is likely to be poor when used for analysis. Performing analysis would degrade daily operational response rates, which must usually be sub-second to support a serviced or self-service conversation. In addition there is a need for more historic and supplementary data for analysis. So, it makes sense to have some separation of data structures, storage and use between the operational (or transaction) and information (or analytic) systems. However, enormous improvements can be made to customer contact systems such as those in customer service centres or KAM support systems without major changes to the underlying legacy systems. Once a transaction customer database is in place, legacy systems can be updated or replaced over time, as illustrated by Figure 16.5.

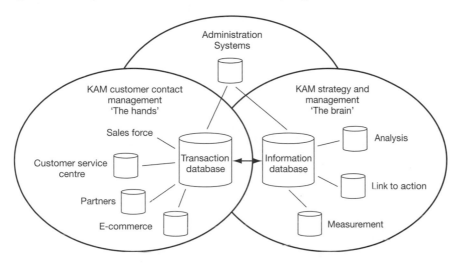

**Figure 16.5**   *Relationship between transaction and information databases*

Integrated contact systems and needed support data are the 'hands' of the organization, where analytics are the 'brain'. Channels include any or all direct (self-service) or indirect (serviced and/or intermediated) contact methods based on different technologies. The transaction database is used directly or indirectly to support and coordinate all customer contacts dynamically. The brain represents integrated decision and learning systems, sometimes called 'business intelligence systems'. It draws on current and historical data. Analysis includes segmentation management; sales campaign planning; contact management; profitability management; proposition development; knowledge management; and other applications. The link to action may include direct customer contact, agent management or product development. Administration represents product support, administration and legacy systems. In the KAM ecosystem the hands provide collaborative KAM; the brain is the analytical aspect of KAM. Integrating these together and with the administrative and transactional systems (sometimes called 'legacy') creates the closed loop that completes the ecosystem.

## Supporting hybrid channel management

This architectural approach is becoming common to KAM systems in many industries, but especially FS industries, where multiple contact channels are now commonplace. Many projects now use channels cooperatively (or in collaboration) to achieve higher revenues via a hybrid sales and marketing approach. Customers can review or amend their business arrangements electronically as they decide. However, although some product purchases can be arranged over the internet, personal contact may be required by the client during the process, for assistance or even just for reassurance. This hybrid channel approach requires a common service centre to coordinate prescriptive (outbound to customer) and responsive (inbound initiated by customer) contacts.

The contact log provides a record of all outbound and inbound customer contacts, through any contact method including sales force, internet, e-mail, mail and phone. It can be part of the transaction database or held alongside. It will also be duplicated in the information database or data warehouse, for mining or analysis.

The costs and complexity of such systems are usually high owing to links with many product administration systems and customer contact channels. The business case will only succeed if strong sales sponsorship exists, or if customer service managers have substantial budgets and power. The financial benefit of improved customer service is hard to justify unless as part of a full-cycle project. Financial benefits are usually in terms of revenue increases from vague cross-selling opportunities. Without sales involvement it is hard to establish the value of these revenues in the short term, so a focus on retention efforts is sometimes a stronger base for development and learning through KAM. As a result, projects usually start with stand-alone systems in campaign management or in the call centre. Inevitably these need to be integrated with other systems eventually, or they will be considered as of marginal impact. The transaction database then becomes a key component in that integration. If it is overlooked, problems may occur in contact coordination that are only too evident to the customer.

These systems investments concentrate on the ability to act. They are developing the hands, arms and legs of the organization. However, we cannot manage customers effectively without a brain. Integration of the controlling and learning brain with the hands' ability to act is key.

## BUILDING THE BRAIN

To support the development of KAM strategies, we need to understand customers. The capability to do this goes under many labels, including 'decision support system' (DSS), 'market intelligence system' (MIS) and the more recent 'business intelligence' (BI) or analytical systems. These systems support the organizational decision making and learning. Information produced by transaction systems must be interpreted by business managers in some way to direct future efforts towards KAM goals. Without effective intelligence, the business's capacity to act is greatly reduced or wasted. The company may end up trying to sell unprofitable products to unprofitable customers, or acquiring and retaining bad customers. Transaction systems with the capability to implement new products rapidly, or to customize existing products, cannot be exploited without understanding what customers will respond to. This understanding emerges from the BI brain.

## The role of the data warehouse

The brain is built on the customer database, the data warehouse. This is the partner of the transaction database and exchanges data with it. A data warehouse is structured for analytic performance, in terms of ease of regular data load or update, ease of access, fast analysis of large data sets and efficient report generation. Comprehensive historic data are important so that the past can be used to predict the future (which is not always possible if sudden changes in trends occur or where customer behaviour is very erratic). Nevertheless, past responses to sales and marketing campaigns are often used as an indicator of future behaviour. What level of historic data needs to be held becomes clearer over time and depends on the nature of the data and the volatility of the market. Accurate data time-stamping in the transaction database is central to the reliability of the data warehouse, as this forms the basis of sales and other time-based reports. The data warehouse holds much more information than other databases, even the transaction database. For global customers, the data are needed not only to understand performance in each country, but increasingly for regulatory compliance and governance reasons. The data warehouse may even hold potential prospects and will grow over time as relationship priorities develop. Many large companies are building and using these strategic data warehouses to provide the BI to drive marketing strategies.

As customer information is acquired and the data warehouse develops, it makes no sense to hide this valuable information away within a few internal departments. New PC-based tools and other workplace technologies are making ready exploitation of the data more viable. Most PCs now have standard web browsers readily available as the primary user interface. These tools enable easy database access from almost any PC. Appropriate data can then be made available from the data warehouse to branches, business partners and even customers. Regular reports, for example by sales territory, can be distributed automatically, enabling security-protected 'drill-down' by authorized users so they can better understand the reason for out-of-line business indicators. It is this technology that underpins the use of key performance indicators (KPIs).

Reporting tools can then work on an exception basis, identifying and broadcasting reports only when KPIs are out of line. This push technology enables broadcast data to be sent to almost any device, including a website, an e-mail address, a laptop computer, a mobile phone, a pager or a PDA. Such data services are becoming recognized for their value in managing business relationships.

## Combining analysis and action

There are big differences in the way operational or transaction data and information or decision support data are managed. If these differences are ignored in the basic architecture and in feedback mechanisms, then major problems occur for large-scale usage. Today, systems-automated or direct linkages are being created from information to transaction systems (from the brain to the hands). For example, the actual mailing of targeted propositions derived from scoring by the data warehouse, perhaps using data drawn from analysis of customers browsing your website, can be distributed over the internet to sales agents.

Meanwhile, the contact and transaction systems add more information to the data warehouse about customer responses and purchases, thereby improving the knowledge-handling algorithm even further. In other words, more iterations yield more data, which improves relationship handling, which produces more interactions, and so on, exploiting the closed loop as a learning loop. However, integrating these feedback links into a complete system design is not easy, even with a proven architectural approach. Systems complexity quickly escalates. This is not only expensive but can become a major constraint on further development work. While a number of companies have developed integrated KAM system strategies, there are very few examples of companies that have achieved more than the first few stages of implementation successfully.

Route maps or IT cookbooks are emerging that encapsulate the experience from successful and failed projects and especially the role of pilots, prototypes, staged build and outsourcing. As more fast-start assets of this sort become available, the cost, timescales and risk of large KAM project implementation will reduce. Experienced KAM skills are in short supply. The use of an agreed architecture and project method can help ensure that available skills are used to best effect. In addition it becomes practical to use other, less experienced developers as part of the project. A broad mix of many different technical skills will be required but there is a tendency at the moment to specialize on one topic such as change management, data quality, salesforce operations and so on. As there are few hybrid skills available, architecture and method assume greater importance in terms of leveraging and coordinating expertise to best effect.

# THE IMPACT OF MERGERS AND ACQUISITIONS

Companies recently merged, or with merger strategies, may encounter special systems and data challenges, not just in creating a strong strategy but in ensuring practical implementation. Mergers within a country or market can often delay evolving KAM programmes by two to three years. This is due to the increased complexity of integrating marketing and sales strategies; differences in the operational management of different marketing and sales units; or the added complexity of integrating IT systems and databases. The most valuable asset of a modern enterprise is the knowledge (in the form of expertise) and the information (in the form of databases) that it owns. If this is to be recognized, the 'predator' company's first steps when considering a merger or acquisition should be to devise ways of retaining key personnel in the target company and ensuring that the information services of the two enterprises can be combined at reasonable cost.

The merger objective is often market share and cost reduction, so that immediately after the fusion of the two companies there is a flurry of cost reductions. Product rationalization is often the basis of the cost reduction exercise so as to enable processes and systems to be simplified. However, this can quickly backfire. Indeed, it has been known to result in almost the complete loss of customers from the target company, as products and services that attracted and retained them are removed.

An alternative approach is to analyse the two sets of databases for common customers and for differences. Building a strategy for the management, retention and growth of the merged customer base is a better starting point for positive rationalization of channels and products. In practice, there are very few examples of mergers being tackled in this manner. Many companies miss this one-time opportunity and can take years to recover. They may even claim that merger activities have made them too busy to consider KAM issues.

Global or cross-market mergers often aim to increase market access. This is still the most usual approach to becoming a more global player. In this scenario the challenge is to gain benefit in other ways from the merged company. For example, a global FS company may intend to replicate its KAM projects between markets, so as to leverage its marketing capabilities through parallel learning. Alternatively or additionally central resources may be shared to reduce operating costs. If financial responsibilities are then delegated to country or market level, the KAM programme will only be able to benefit where there is a cooperative management structure and a strong project champion at the highest level. So, while the rewards of integration may be high for merged companies, the execution of strategy is often difficult.

# INTEGRATING KAM SYSTEMS

The benefits – to companies and customers – of KAM are fairly clear, particularly when strategy is based on a well-thought-out model of KAM and when the implementation programme is carefully planned and managed. However, few companies anywhere have overcome the technical barriers to achieving the full potential of KAM. From a systems point of view, the key is integration of the many systems that a company uses to manage different aspects of its relationship with customers (and increasingly that customers use to manage their relationships with the company). Integration allows data arising and used in many different types of interaction, in many channels and for different products and services to be brought together and transformed into valuable and accessible customer information. The reason for this is that many companies develop their IT infrastructures organically over decades, adding systems to meet particular business needs as they arise. This means that many companies have systems that were conceived during the 1980s or even earlier, running alongside ones implemented in the 21st century. The older ones are usually referred to as 'legacy systems', although in many cases they are critical operational systems without which the business would collapse. The technologies and computer languages that these use are completely different, and there are formidable obstacles that make it very difficult for these systems to communicate with each other.

To improve the consistency, productivity and benefit of KAM, data must be derived from many incompatible systems and turned into useful information that can be used to build a complete picture of each customer. It requires specialist knowledge, combined with experience of previous projects, to transform data resident in many systems into actionable information that can be used when managing a particular customer. The information is used to ensure that:

- The right product is offered to the right customer at the right time.
- Where the product can be customized in any way (eg features, pricing), it is done in such a way as to optimize the customer's lifetime value and profitability to the company.
- The business has the resources, at that moment, to close and fulfil all the deals that will flow from the offer.
- Customers are managed in a way that optimizes the cost-effectiveness of each channel.
- Senior and middle managers always have what they need to make the best-informed strategic decisions more quickly than their competitors.
- In its most advanced form, that customer knowledge is used by every layer of management, from the CEO for strategy development, across sales, marketing, operations and financial management, uniquely

providing an integrated approach to KAM from the CEO right through to the database administrators who enable all the above to work.

● Collaborative working takes place across departments and channels, especially in areas such as customer retention and new product development.

**Data where it's needed... when it's needed**

Integration involves more than unlocking data imprisoned in many legacy systems. Just as important is the ability to move current data around the business. Particularly now, with customers being offered and choosing to use a variety of touch points, it is important that some forms of data are updated instantly. Of course, not all areas of business are time-critical, requiring immediate access to up-to-the-minute information. For example, data can be batch-processed using traditional ETL (extract, transform and load) techniques. But where KAM requires a customer view that is correct up to the minute, it is important to make sure that, say, the sales office, the call centre and the website all show the same information at any given moment.

**When theory meets practice**

The process of migrating, integrating and consolidating data is littered with obstacles. It often causes serious slippage in project timetables – and equally harmful budget overspend. Frequently, projects fail to deliver the anticipated business benefits, simply because the quality of the data they produce is too suspect to be useful. Worse, some projects are never completed at all. The reason for much of this is unpredictability of the integration process. Until recently, the investment in time and money required to assess the issues involved has been so great that it has been unfeasible to gain a full understanding of a project's scope and scale until the migration and integration team is well into its work. Even then, there was no guarantee that unwelcome difficulties would not arise unexpectedly. What is certain is that often up to 50 per cent of a project's cost and time can be taken up by the data migration and integration effort.

**When you can't start from scratch**

A primary objective of a KAM systems initiative is to build as clear a picture as possible of each customer (including customer value) through a continuing process of acquiring and using information. For most projects, the richest source of start-up information is the historical data stored in the company's legacy systems. These databases may contain transaction histories for different sorts of products or services (including ones for which the customer is no longer active), responses to various marketing offers, customer service queries (complaints, requests for information), core customer data, product holding / purchase records, and so forth. Generally speaking, all of the different sources of data are likely to have been constructed at different times, for different purposes, and often using different technologies. The challenges of transforming such varied data into usable and valuable information are formidable. Conflicts can be as basic as having the same data presented in different-length fields in different databases. More seriously, data with the same meaning may be recorded differently in various systems, resulting in varying degrees of reliability. Some data may not even match their original document description. When such 'semantic drift' and 'data mutation' arise, assessing the value to be placed on each source takes on a central significance.

Integrated systems are required to support integrated business capabilities for KAM. New capabilities can be added alongside existing systems and integrated to provide improved ability to gain return on investments. These developments can be prioritized and carried out in stages if a consistent approach is deployed that reuses skills, methods and tools against a common architecture and roadmap. A closed-loop operation can be developed in one business area or for one KAM objective and extended to others. Over time the KAM ecosystem is developed by combining collaborative (multi-channel) and analytical capabilities through operational integration.

# What will it take? Organization and resources

After several years of working with a range of businesses seeking to implement KAM, one thing has become abundantly clear: the need to secure senior management commitment and support. Without this, the effort will become a sales initiative, successful in forging enhanced customer relationships, but doomed to failure once it takes on the challenge of making it work within the supplier's own organization. This is probably the formula for the greatest disaster of all: building customers' expectations and then cheating them of any action.

Senior management must take on board a series of issues:

- the need for new organizational structures;
- the selection of appropriate KAMs;
- the management, development, reward and retention of these 'rare beasts'.

## ORGANIZATION

The impact of KAM on the way your operation is organized might be quite profound, especially if you intend it to be! If the implementation of KAM is intended to establish a customer-focused business, without 'silo mentality', with performance measures relating to the customer's satisfaction and with the business decisions driven increasingly by key account needs, then expect the organization to be turned upside down.

## Turn the organization upside down

Take one requirement – all functions must share the same values of customer focus and customer satisfaction. How can they do this if the business is still organized in traditional hierarchies and silo-like functions? One option, if you intend turning it upside down anyway, is to start that way on paper – turn the organization upside down, quite literally, as in Figure 17.1. In traditional hierarchies, management sits at the top and those with customer contact sit lower down, often at the bottom. In a KAM hierarchy, those with customer contact (whether salespeople, customer service, operations or whoever) are right at the top, with management beneath.

**If you can't be rid of silos, at least turn them in the direction of the customer**

So what? The message was well expressed by a manager when he took over a company that he felt was arrogant and distant from its customers. This was how he addressed his first meeting with the senior management team: 'If in your job you don't actually meet with customers, then you had better make damned sure you support someone who does.' The KAM team should be empowered to act on behalf of the customer. The point of the upside-down structure charts (or perhaps we should start to call them right-way-up charts) is that the management structure should exist to service those who service the customers. The same point can be made for the functions: they exist for the customers, not for their own definitions of opera-

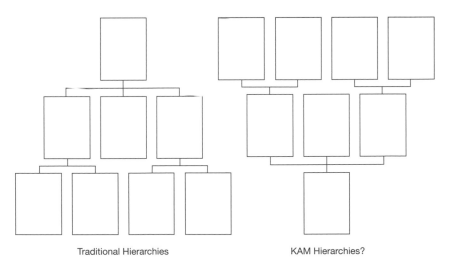

Traditional Hierarchies          KAM Hierarchies?

*Figure 17.1*   *Turning the organization upside down*

tional excellence. Customers have little understanding of or sympathy for suppliers' structures or for organizations that might mean something to the supplier but have no positive impact on the customer or, worse, seem to operate as obstacles to progress. Whereas in the past a good supplier would try to secure an organization or structure chart of its customer, it is now quite normal for customers to ask suppliers to provide details _and explanations_ of _their_ structures. This is seen as something that a good supply-side manager should aim to influence in managing a supplier.

Suppliers operating several different business streams (often so after mergers between FS suppliers) might find some sense in having separate sales teams for the same customer, but often the customer does not see things the same way. Duplication of contacts is bad enough, but if this complexity leads to different terms, conditions and service levels, then the customer is likely to be dissatisfied. The pressure will be on to change the organization in response to customer demand – not a bad motivation, but it is always best if the organization can pre-empt such demands and look at its own organization from the customer's perspective first.

## Letting the customer determine your structure

Many FS sectors have become near-commodity markets in recent years with competitive pressures leading to lower margins and prices. If your products and services fall into this category and the customers in your market want lower prices, then a structure allowing a focus on reducing the costs of supply will probably have formed. If the route to lower prices is through operational efficiency, then operations and IT will perhaps take a lead role, driving the business through the standardization and automation of processes. The sales function might be subservient, focused on volume-related issues with big customers. We might expect a business driven by operational excellence and structured accordingly. However, if your products or services are complex with a high degree of 'added value', a different structure will have formed, perhaps allowing a focus on 'staying ahead of the field'. We might expect to find a far more flexible operational capability with marketing or a business development function in a prominent position in such an organization. We might expect a business driven by product leadership or product tailoring and structured accordingly. This relates to two of Treacy and Weirsema's (1995) three business drivers (as discussed in Chapter 13), as well as to the fundamental choice facing a business seeking competitive advantage, as described by Porter (1980) (also Chapter 13) – lowest-cost supply or differentiation. This one decision, if you have taken it, will already have determined much of your structure and organization.

## Avoiding meltdown

Should KAM be allowed to take it still further? Should the business be driven by the demands of key accounts? Should cross-functional key account teams determine the objectives and activities of the functions they represent?

This is perhaps the biggest 'it depends' question of the lot, and few generalizations are likely to be relevant to your own circumstances. The complexity of the situation may well depend on whether your organization deals only with corporate customers or intermediaries or whether it serves a mass market of retail customers as well. Many FS organizations serve many markets in this way. Clearly the needs of the mass market may be very different from those of a limited number of key accounts. In turn, the organizational structure needed to deal with these different types of markets will be different. If you have applied the thinking suggested by this book to your market and your customers, then you will be in the best position to judge!

**Your own structure will never be perfect, but if you wish to practise KAM, then you will consider your customers' organizations as much as your own**

If your business success comes from high market share for a standard product, uniformity, economies of scale and standardized operations (operational excellence – see Chapter 13), then accommodating too many individual customer demands can put it at risk. That is not to say that we should not practise KAM, but rather that the emphasis is on the 'relationship management' side, not on the 'committing the business' side. If your business success comes from bespoke offers for precisely articulated needs (customer intimacy – see Chapter 13), then both sides of the KAM story come into play – intimate relationships and a committed organization. Whichever the case, the selection of key accounts is vital. In the former, we can only spread our team resources so far; in the latter, we can only work on so many different activities at a time. We can perhaps console ourselves that we rarely need to decide, in full, one way or the other. The challenge of management is to cope with perpetual change – nothing is for ever. We cannot afford to drift, but we *can* consider such decisions as a development over time.

Let's take an insurance company that operates in three countries and has three separate business operations (life assurance, general insurance and a specialist medical insurance business) operating in each. For good reasons, historically, it has chosen to organize geographically, by countries. Local relationships are important and local variation and flavour of greater significance to success than any 'global' standardization. But this structure has started to give problems. The needs of customers have become more specific, more challenging, and they have caused a rise in business operation-specific activities. Each business operation is starting to take on its own approach and values. With a country-based structure this gives some problems. There is duplication of effort and dilution of impact. So, the organization is changed – three business units overlying country structures and perhaps, in time, replacing them. Now there is more scope for developing efficient operational and support processes based on the different business types and for developing a KAM strategy (see Figure 17.2).

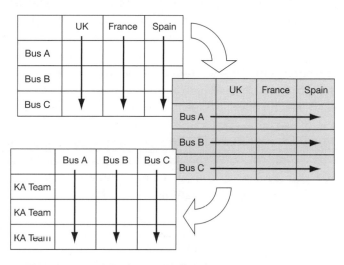

**Figure 17.2**   _Moving towards a business-specific focus_

How far you go towards the KAM teams directing your focus will depend, but they provide a bridge through any transitional phase. As time goes by, different strains are felt in the new structure. The development of KAM practice has raised the level of customer intimacy in the businesses and there is a need to review the structure in order to meet new goals. Perhaps the global customer has become a reality and some of these are supplied by more than one of the business units. KA teams become the route to KAM as a cross-business process, perhaps even a cross-company process. In time, it may be the KAM process that emerges as the most significant structural device for managing the customer – a truly customer-intimate development.

Avoid revolution! It rarely works, being either too hard to instigate or too difficult to control. Avoid black and white too. The complexity of working in a matrix of reporting lines may seem crazy at times, but the days of simple straight lines are long gone. In Chapter 15, we identified 'the ability to co-ordinate, motivate and direct the team' as one of the skills required by a KAM. Making significant structural changes to a business can be traumatic. Merging different business units that might occupy different sites, or have very different cultures, perhaps even see each other as competitors, can take years. The KAM process can act as a bridge between units in such circumstances. Whatever the resultant organization, the important thing is to give KAM some teeth.

## From silos to customer focus

Figure 17.3 shows a traditional silo structure for an FS company with all the problems of aligning internally focused functions and activities towards the customer. The right structure depends on circumstances. There is no precise blueprint. One thing is certain – your structure will never be perfect. Suppose an organization has only two customers. One of those customers has a highly centralized organization, while the other customer is a loose federation of regional sites. Unless the supplier organization divides into two businesses, however it is structured it is likely to be wrong at least half of the time! Most FS suppliers deal with many different types of customer organizations, and many suppliers also serve mass-market end-customers too!

Figure 17.4 shows not so much a structure as an aspiration, with service functions providing the core, operating in support of those parts of the business with direct customer contact, whether they are key account teams, sales teams, call centres, retail operations, central operations or marketing.

***Figure 17.3***   *The silo structure*

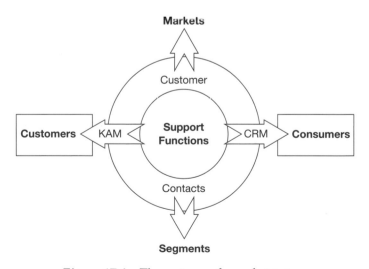

***Figure 17.4***   *The customer-focused structure*

## Key account selection

If the business organization and structure *is* determined by the demands of key accounts, then the *selection* of accounts is critical, as is selection into categories or segments with common needs – it allows a business to be customer intimate, while retaining critical mass. Part IV explores the relationship between market segmentation and identification of key accounts, and how to avoid a business pulled too many ways by its customers.

# HUMAN RESOURCES

Chapter 15 made it clear that a good KAM is rare and valuable. Many businesses have looked at their existing sales force and found it wanting, turning instead to outside recruitment. While this secures the needed skills, it doesn't always make for an easy initiation for the new recruit. Existing salespeople may see the role of KAM as their natural next step and may be less than cooperative with anyone moving them off the promotion track. FS KAMs recruited from outside the sector may have to work hard to get the specialist expertise and credibility necessary to operate in this area.

## Death of the salesperson?

Does the ideal KAM have to come from a sales background at all? This is not meant to frighten salespeople or suggest that they cannot handle this job, but many companies find that the 'traditional' sales representative, employed for independence and one-to-one skills, may not be best for the KAM job. Recalling Chapter 15's music analogy, the KAM from the sales team must put down the violin and pick up the conductor's baton, but the best violinists don't always make the best conductors. The need for planning, coordination, and project management skills, and for influence within the business, may lead you towards people who already have those skills and abilities. Perhaps they come not from the sales team but from a support function. If so, training plays its part in adding the selling skills, or perhaps the obvious sales activities can be performed by a salesperson within the team. Certainly, in the 'diamond' partnership KAM relationship, if a particular function holds the key to building that relationship, then it is more common for the KAM to come from that function.

### Building on existing relationships

A major international insurer had a small number of very long-standing relationships with key distributors, in some cases going back as far as the birth of both companies. More recently there had been increased competitive pressure to provide added value through the relationship, or lose these key accounts to innovators with new capabilities and KAM techniques that delivered the added value required. While the KA managers were very experienced and capable executives, their backgrounds were generally administrative and service oriented, managing the very large support teams required. It was important to provide additional sales and KAM skills very rapidly. This was achieved using the well-recognized IBM internal KAM sales training school. Of course a few could not make the change and were reassigned to more suitable roles, for their own benefit as much as the insurer's. As a result these major relationships were retained and developed. Remember, the KAM is not a 'super-salesperson', but a coordinator of the team's capabilities. Selling skills must exist in the team, but they don't have to be the sole preserve of the KAM; indeed, it is much better if they are not.

# How senior?

As each year passes, the seniority of KAMs increases. In many KAM implementations, the KAM is taken from a level of management senior to the existing sales team, perhaps even senior to the sales managers. Indeed, the role of the traditional sales manager is as much in question here as that of the traditional sales representative. A KAM in many cases reports directly to the business management team, not through a 'sales silo'. This is most evident where the objectives for KAM cut across business and functional lines – perhaps an intention to establish 'global key accounts' in a multinational, multi-business environment. In such a case, the KAM needs the credibility and authority that comes with his or her seniority and experience.

### Sometimes it starts at the very top

A former senior manager at an international reinsurer has strong views about the benefit of involving senior people in managing the relationship with key accounts. This reinsurer gave much attention to getting the relationship right at all levels, making sure that contact points were established all the way through, from the chief executive down to the people who were processing the business. The KAM would typically be someone who was 'two-thirds up the tree'. As our respondent puts it:

> I think this is an important point; if you have accounts managed at too junior a level, a) they don't appreciate the strategic issues very often, and b) it's very hard for them to engage with the decision makers at the company on things. I think it needs to be a fairly senior process – I think people are also flattered if you have senior people that they know are senior managing their accounts because it looks as though you're taking the account seriously.

## Sponsors in the boardroom

The challenge of the internal role – aligning the business to respond to the enhanced understanding of customers' needs – has led many businesses to appoint senior managers, perhaps even from board level, as key account 'sponsors'. They don't manage the account day to day, and do not interfere with the activities and decisions of the KAM. Their role is to facilitate the internal changes required with regard to issues such as organization, resources and any clashes of priorities. Such appointments are also symbolic, expressing the commitment to KAM at a senior level. If the senior manager is also head of a support function or a business unit, and he or she signs on to the principles of KAM, that is one less 'baron' with a 'silo mentality' to worry about!

## Directors as KAMs?

Sometimes it's more than being a sponsor, and a senior manager will take on actual responsibility for a specific key account. The senior manager will retain the services of a KAM, but take on a more active directing and supervisory role. This is common when accounts are global and the supplier works in a number of different territories. There are of course plenty of pros and cons to such a move. The disadvantages include the danger of becoming sucked into the daily detail, becoming a 'super-rep', confusing the KAM over who is responsible for what and confusing the customer with the same, and perhaps worst of all demotivating the KAM. The advantages are simple, but significant – the manager's seniority and clout help to make it happen! You might be worried that the appointment of a non-salesperson as KAM only risks losing accumulated skills of the sales force and ignores the continuing need for top-flight selling skills in front of the customer. However, in many cases, dealing with large accounts requires setting up several points of contact within the KAM team. Salespeople may be ideal to take on these roles. The growth of global accounts in many FS markets provides an example of this.

## Global accounts

In a global key account, there will almost certainly be a need for regional account managers with regional sales responsibilities, or there may be sales professionals in their own regional teams. Global account managers may also have a global sales role, but it is often better if they remove themselves from the nitty-gritty of the negotiations and raise the nature of their customer relationship to a more strategic level. The supplier side of the diamond might look something like that shown in Figure 17.5.

**Figure 17.5** *The global key account team*

There is sometimes confusion about points of contact in global accounts. Figure 17.5 should resolve this. A truly global customer (ie not just situated globally but also operating globally) can be frustrated by regional operating differences of a global supplier. Its protests may be misinterpreted as a request for 'one point of contact rather than all this diversity'. It is unlikely to request this. If this approach were to be tried, the person holding the post would probably collapse under the strain (although he or she would do well in frequent-flyer programmes). What the customer may be trying to say is that it wants one point of control or coordination, and that is the global KAM. It is the KAM's task to gather the global team, including regional salespeople, and direct these multiple points of contact along some uniform processes.

So, KAM is certainly not the death of the salesperson, but for some it asks for a marked change of direction.

## New lines of reporting and responsibility

As KA teams begin to establish themselves, people from the functions find new calls on their time. As well as their functional responsibilities, as KA team members they also have customer-specific responsibilities. What about time management and priorities? What about objective setting and annual reviews? It becomes normal for people to have objectives for their jobs that come from more than one point – their function and their customer. In time, not having a customer objective, whatever your role, becomes so unusual as to be cause for concern! In the long run, the customer part of the job might grow to become dominant or even full time. In some cases, formal KA teams with their own reporting lines will be the solution, while in others the ambiguity of *matrix management* will rule. There is no one way to handle the complex reporting lines, the *solid* and the *dotted lines*, the matrix management. The right answer is what works in practice. Whatever the outcome, the change requires constant attention in the human resources area. HR people have a key role – welcome them to the team!

# KAM and downsizing?

KAM may result in fewer salespeople – but don't let cost cutting become the sole basis for this vital business decision. Some businesses see KAM as a way to cut their sales force – replacing regional structures of field-based reps with a small team of KAMs supported by a customer service office of telesales people. This may be a possible outcome, but, as an objective for KAM, care should be taken that objectives, resources and opportunity (see Chapter 3) are not out of balance – is it really possible to service your customers that way?

## A carefully managed approach to working more efficiently

A major UK life company has taken a proactive stance to KAM, partly in response to changes in legislation that allow multi-tying with intermediaries, which puts further pressure on already thin supplier margins. The company had operated with a traditional branch-based geographic face-to-face sales force that had evolved over years. However, it has recognized that structural changes were taking place in the industry, with new intermediary market segments emerging. The new structure is based on key account teams supported by a communications–sales–contact centre, combining desk-based sales support and e-based support to intermediaries, segments and distribution groups. The number of face-to-face salespeople has been reduced to be replaced by a smaller number of better-qualified, better-able local account managers to support the KAMs. The emerging structure cuts the cost of doing business. However, it is recognized that the strategy will only be effective if the new technology works well, if the right support teams can be put in place and if it is set up flexibly to allow it to adapt to the needs of the market. Central to the strategy is the cost-effective use of desk-based sales consultants supported by readily available account information at the touch of a button. This shows a highly planned and carefully phased approach to changing the sales structure. The KAM-oriented FS business must look with great care at how to service its customers and assess the impact on its salesforce requirement. While in many cases technology has been used to reduce servicing costs, there is also much evidence that customers prefer personal interaction. Consult with customers to find out what they want!

# KAM and reward and recognition

Much time and thought have been given by sales managers to the reward and recognition of their salespeople, using every kind of package from straight salary to 100 per cent commission and all stops in between. KAM reward requires a new creativity. The solutions must be designed to suit your own circumstances, and must above all be designed to support business objectives. These four questions might stimulate your own debate:

1. On what criteria should reward be based?
2. Do you reward the KAM or the team?
3. If the KAM is a senior salesperson, how should his or her reward compare to that of other senior managers?
4. Given the rarity of good KAMs, how do you keep them without promoting them beyond the job?

## Reward criteria

Short-term sales volume and value are unlikely to be the best measures, although they are certainly the easiest. Better measures will be those that emphasize the key account as an investment. Profitability is therefore to be preferred, but is harder to measure. Future value, as described in Chapter 7, is even better. There should also be measures that relate to the nature of the task, such as building a customer relationship. Customer satisfaction ratings might form a part of such measures. Finally, probably the best measure of all is what progress is made towards the objectives set down in the KA plan. Linking reward to objective setting, planning and successful implementation also helps establish the responsibilities of KAM on the same kind of level as business management, which is precisely where they should be.

## The manager or the team?

The team, of course. So this requires formal definition of a team with clear goals, roles, obligations and work plans for each member and for the team as a whole. Until such a team exists, reward might be related in part to the KAM's ability to form the team, this being one of the objectives of the KA plan.

## The dual ladder

Military and research organizations need to retain people who want to stay in front-line or research roles rather than move to staff or management roles. They have a professional ladder, allowing these people to progress without moving to management or staff. A 'sales ladder' can do the same for KAMs, as it has in some FS companies as the business value of KAM executives becomes recognized.

## Sales awards

Don't be surprised if your sales awards find their way to salespeople who win the most exciting piece of new business of the year. In the KAM environment, you might like to consider three changes. Give awards to teams, not individuals. Give an award to the account team that has retained the most business in difficult circumstances – a real test of KAM skills in a mature market. As KAM matures, use 'balanced scorecards' and customized incentives that reflect the unique objectives of different key accounts at any one time.

# 18

# What will it take? Making it happen

By now, you know what is required. You know what skills, attitudes and behaviours must be developed. You have planned for new systems and a new organization. Now you just have to make it happen! You have some choices, including:

1. Jump in and get going with incremental activities – perhaps a training course in project management, perhaps a new e-mail system – depending on priorities.
2. Be a little more structured and focus on one major thing at a time – perhaps a full-scale overhaul of the cost reporting system.
3. Proceed by stages from assessment and perhaps benchmarking (to know your starting point and to identify the highest priority efforts as a roadmap for change), through alignment and change management to the implementation of some first practical steps of a longer-term change programme.

Hopefully, the folly of options one and two is clear. The activities in themselves may be done well, but were they really the right things to be doing first or at all? Perhaps nobody listened, nobody changed and nothing happened. But what do 'assessment', 'alignment' and 'change management' mean?

# ASSESSMENT

Understanding where you are today is critical to success. A shared understanding between the executive decision makers is best achieved through a rapid, yet formal and consistent, assessment that is based on evidence and fact rather than internal corporate myths. For example, the Customer Management Assessment Tool (CMAT) (Starkey, Woodcock and Stone, 2002; see also Woodcock, Stone and Foss, 2003 for more on the general methodology) helps you identify the difference between management intentions (what we want to achieve, or even what we think we have achieved) and execution or deployment progress and the delivery of business improvement results. With a shared understanding of the practical issues, the executive team can more easily agree on the priorities, actions and responsibilities in the change roadmap, based on clear understanding of dependencies and likely ROI results. Sometimes the existing 'strategy' is unexecutable. At other times execution can be improved to ensure an appropriate strategy is successfully deployed.

# ALIGNMENT AND MANAGING THE CHANGE

Perhaps you are crystal clear on what you wish to achieve and why, but who else cares? You need the support of your whole organization – the functions, the management and those involved in implementing KAM in front of the customer. Alignment involves developing a common vision, listening to the views of others, taking on new perspectives and evolving a KAM policy and practice that all agree to. It must be sponsored and championed at the most senior level, with a cross-business steering group to ensure alignment, co-operation and success.

Cross-business alignment is vital to avoid the frustration of KAM being simply a 'sales initiative'. This involves activities that become more complex with the size of the organization and the significance of the change. You may be involved in meetings, persuasion, negotiation, seminars, workshops, newsletters and more. Creating a KAM business environment involves much effort – from you and others. It involves change to ideas, practices and priorities that may be long established and favoured by many in the organization. So, why do people change? Why do they buy new products, sign on to new ideas or change the habits of a lifetime? The notion of a *change equation* helps us understand both the process of change and how you can manage it. The 'equation' starts with something that Thomas Edison realized in his pursuit of innovation: *discontent is the first necessity of progress.*

# THE CHANGE EQUATION

People don't buy products just because they are good. The insurance seller knows that people need to be persuaded of the risks of not being covered. Many financial services are of low interest for most people. Some persuasion is needed to make people dissatisfied with their existing situation. The key to customer purchase is often people's dissatisfaction with what they already have. We have used buying a product to illustrate this idea, but it applies equally to new ideas, attitudes or behaviours. People are most likely to change, as shown in Figure 18.1, if:

1.    They are dissatisfied with how things are now.
2.    They have a vision of some better way of doing things in the future.
3.    There are some simple first steps that will get things under way.
4.    All the above are greater, both in reality *and in their mind*, than the costs of change – and remember, cost is not just money, but time, ego, status and so on.

*Figure 18.1    The change equation*

## Establishing dissatisfaction

For an organization to align with the idea of KAM, there must be some pressing reasons – dissatisfaction with the current situation. Where organizations set out to implement KAM and fail, this is usually due to *lack* of dissatisfaction with how things were before. Once the effort and the pain involved become clear, it is all too easy to fall back on old ways. Sometimes this can cause an organization to leave major change until it is too late, so how can we initiate successful change while we still have time? Table 14.1 listed the 'deadly sins' that stand in the way of successful KAM, which included 'complacency and inertia'. So we need to probe these areas:

- What sort of dissatisfaction are we talking about?
- Are we losing sales?
- Are competitors gaining ground?
- Are profits falling?
- Are we missing new opportunities?

- Is customer dissatisfaction growing?
- Are there any examples of failure?
- Could the customer be made happier?
- Is our organization 'creaking'?
- Are internal squabbles leading to customer failure?
- Even if things are OK now, will this be the same in the future?

Perhaps your desire to implement KAM is particularly visionary – all is well at present, but _you_ see how times will change. This makes managing change more difficult – there is no dissatisfaction with the current situation. Your task is now to project dissatisfaction into the future, perhaps demonstrating how things will be if KAM is _not_ adopted. It is a technique that any insurance salesperson knows well: 'Have you considered what will happen to your family when you die?' they ask cheerily, practising the principle of _anticipation_. This demands ability to discuss possible futures. The worst complacency that can stand in your way is 'If it ain't broke, don't fix it.' For FS companies, envisioning risk for loans, investments or insurance is a core competency, so it should not be culturally difficult to apply the same degree of anticipation to the question of forecasting and responding to change in the market place for their services.

## Sharing the vision

Stirring up doom and gloom is not of course the aim. Scared or depressed people are no easier to change than the smug and complacent ones, and you will soon be an unwelcome Cassandra if all you do is scare or depress people. You must create a vision of how things might be. The key to alignment is securing a _shared_ vision of that future. This is where the purpose and objectives of KAM must be made clear, with some understanding of what is involved:

- What will KAM do for us?
- What benefits will we get?
- What benefits will the customer get?
- What will KAM look and feel like?
- Will it be worth the effort?

## First practical steps

Despite the advice of some business 'gurus' that the role of leaders is to foment upheaval and chaos, it is best to avoid revolutions. Rather, agree some practical steps to get things going. These do not need to be dramatic – better if they are not. A sensible start might be a gathering of interested parties to identify objectives, obstacles and what we might call the *critical success factors*.

# CRITICAL SUCCESS FACTORS (CSFs)

These are the things that you and your business will need to do, or have in place, *in the broadest sense*, in order to make progress on your KAM journey. If an FS business is to be truly aligned behind KAM, then it will need to agree these CSFs at an early stage.

## A possible process

1. Gather a wide cross-section of interested parties – heads of functions, potential practitioners, etc.
2. Ensure that sufficient dissatisfaction with the current situation is apparent to all and that KAM is regarded at least as one of the potential visions for the future.
3. Ensure the principles of KAM, its purpose and practice, are understood.
4. Identify the objectives for KAM and the obstacles to progress – your own list of 'deadly sins'.
5. Identify the 'things that must be' if those obstacles are to be overcome – your critical success factors.

## Some tips and some warnings

- Use an independent assessor, consultant or facilitator – it is important to escape from the confines of current thinking. You *do* need to sort out the wood from the trees.
- Stay objective, but don't ignore people's perceptions and feelings – remember, you are trying to change attitudes and behaviours.
- Listen to all views, including those in opposition (never exclude the possibility that they might have a point!). Alignment will involve compromise, modifying your own vision, perhaps even improving on it.
- Seek alignment across *all* functions and departments.
- Involve senior management at the earliest stages.
- Remember, *you* have probably been thinking about this longer than they have. Don't expect instant alignment – be patient. The alternative to alignment is the probable stillbirth of your KAM plans.

## CSFs – an example list

Below is a list of CSFs, identified by a company at the early stage of embracing the KAM philosophy. The list resulted from analysis of the particular problems and obstacles that stood in the way of its KAM implementation:

- KAM must be a cross-business process, supported at senior levels, with objectives and responsibilities that supersede those of individual functions or departments.
- All team members must understand and share the purpose and objectives of KAM.
- The KA team must understand and sign on to their purpose as increasing customer prosperity, and so our own competitive advantage, in order to secure key supplier status. They must focus on the customer's processes and the customer's markets.
- There must be a system for cross-business communication (including the customer) and the necessary skills and disciplines to make it work.
- Team members must have the right skills and understanding to carry out a customer-intimate role – interpersonal skills and commercial awareness are top priorities.
- We must all understand the dynamics of team working.
- We must have enhanced skills of project management.
- Attention to detail. We require relevant, customer-focused operational excellence from all functions.
- There must be a system for measuring progress on the KAM journey and for assessing the benefits to our customers and ourselves.
- There must be a written and easily updatable KA plan.

## Taking the time to plan and prepare

Books like this always urge you to plan and prepare – hard to do when faced with the urgent need to do. However, the importance of careful planning for KAM implementation cannot be overstated. It pays to know where you are now and what the real focus of your combined efforts should be. Anticipating obstacles and problems before they arise pays dividends. Waiting for a crisis to arrive and then proceeding on the grounds that people will react if they really have to is unwise – people in crisis tend to freeze, like rabbits caught in headlights.

# Part IV

# Identifying Key Accounts

# 19

# The 10-step process

Many FS businesses are put off the notion of KAM simply because they find the task of selecting the key accounts too daunting. The problem is, of course, which accounts don't you select? You would be right to be cautious, but wrong to give up. What is required is a process that helps to navigate the journey, while avoiding the traps that lie in wait. This is the 10-step process shown in Figure 19.1.

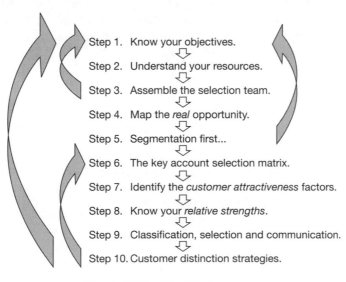

*Figure 19.1*   *The 10-step process*

The 10-step process is shown as a flow chart, indicating that, while the steps do form a broadly linear process, there are several points where you need to go back to some earlier decisions, using your steadily increasing knowledge to challenge the assumptions behind those decisions. This is of course a good thing, and it does allow you to make a start somewhere without prejudicing all future decisions. Some would argue, and with much justification, that you should start with step 5, the marketing plan and segmentation, or perhaps step 3, the assembly of a project team. Either is fine, if you wish it so, provided that you really do start with a clear marketing plan, or that a project team can easily be assembled as the first step in the process. Whatever the case, the flow chart takes you back to step 1 from either of those starting points. Chapter 3 addresses these points, essential foundations to get right. The next chapters, 20 through to 22, cover steps 4 through to 10. The rest of this chapter will deal with step 3.

## STEP 3 – ASSEMBLE THE SELECTION TEAM

Getting the right people to work through this process is perhaps, along with step 5, the most important part of the process. In a sales-oriented FS business it is tempting to rely on the sales team to do this, but that way may lie problems. First, salespeople naturally have positions to defend, and careers to build. They all want their own accounts to be key, because they think this might help their promotion. A broader, more strategic perspective is required. Second, KAM requires the support of the whole business, and if the selection of the key accounts is left to the sales team, how might that be viewed elsewhere? Perhaps you think you know your key accounts, maybe you are certain, but what if the rest of your business doesn't seem to see it your way?

### Getting everyone to agree...

The case of a global supplier to investment banks provides a good example of different perspectives on key accounts from different positions in a large and complex organization. The equity trading division of the supplier had one set of key accounts, while the screen-based products division had another. Normally, this caused no problems, as the two divisions tended to sell to different functions within their customers. However, it was not always possible to keep the deals separate, and conflicts could arise. For example, the New York sales team had a potentially very large deal on screen-based products in negotiation with one of the largest US global banks, but to clinch the deal the bank required the supplier to modify its equity-trading software. The equity-trading division was unwilling to do this, having a policy of only providing standard software because of issues of support. Both parties had a strong argument, from their own points of view. However, the potential customer's perspective was quite simple. It was dealing with one organization – why couldn't it agree the deal? In the end the disagreement had to go up to senior levels in the supplier for resolution. They decided to stick with the standard software policy. This showed that the supplier was not working in a coordinated manner towards a key account, and this reflected a deeper lack of strategic coordination.

## The ideal team?

The ideal team is only ever ideal for the purpose for which it is formed. There are two purposes for this team:

1. To identify and select the key accounts based on a combination of intimate customer knowledge and a clear vision of future strategy and goals.
2. To give that selection sufficient authority for it to mean something across the business. Selection without implementation will be meaningless.

## How senior?

Identifying key accounts is the responsibility of the senior management team. Consider two scenarios. In the first, the team is a group of senior managers who approach the task with their eyes on the recently agreed five-year plan. 'Vision' abounds, but 'What do they know about our customers?' say sales and customer service personnel. In the second, it is a group from sales and customer service who make up the selection team. Their efforts reflect their intimate knowledge of customers. 'Fine,' say the bosses, 'but what about tomorrow's customers? Where's the vision?' The ideal team must combine vision and knowledge. Knowledge exists in many places. Gathering it all together in one team would be unworkable. Perhaps the solution is a core team, probably with a bias towards 'vision', which calls on the knowledge of others as and when it is required.

# 20

# Segmentation

Perhaps alarm bells are already ringing with regard to implementing KAM in your organization. Not only will it call for enormous effort and significant change, but there are also some other potential problems:

- If KAM implies some kind of special treatment for one customer compared to another, does this mean you will be helping to put some of your customers at an actual disadvantage?
- If customer intimacy implies not only understanding your different customers' specific and varying needs, but also acting on them, how will you avoid being pulled apart at the seams by the competing activities?
- How do you hope to focus your organization on anything if the rules of the game seem to be: 'Every customer is unique; there are no *standard* standards'?

The answers to these and many similar issues will be found by taking a few paces back. We need to put KAM back into its wider context: the management of markets through some process of segmentation. By doing this we discover that KAM brings together sales and marketing planning. Forget the idea, popular with some marketers, that sales is just the tactical front of the marketing department, with sales managers subservient to marketing managers. Forget also the equally unhelpful drive to make KAM dominant over every other function in the business (including marketing!). Forget the idea that KAM is a sales initiative that seeks to 'do something' to the customer. KAM and market segmentation come together to ensure a greater focus of effort, on a strategic level. However, first, let's consider one more problem.

## THE PROBLEM FOR SUPPORT FUNCTIONS IN AN UNSEGMENTED BUSINESS

Functions, left to their own devices, are often tempted towards extremes. Either they campaign to drive every cost, frill or excess (their perception!) out of their activities in the pursuit of 'leanness', or they aspire to deliver a Cadillac when a Ford would do. 'Left to their own devices' means, of course, 'managed separately from the rest of the business and from the rest of the supply chain, a long way from the market and the customer'. Requests for variations from the norm lead not only to inefficiency, but also to confusion. See it from their angle. Why does one customer call for fewer frills and a standardized product when another criticizes us for a lack of new product development? Why does one customer accept the standard level of service while another claims it will go under if it doesn't have an immediate response? Why, when the majority of customers have been happy for years, does one customer find our offer unacceptable?

The core of all these problems is the same. FS businesses sell to customers with varying needs: varying because they operate in different ways, with different challenges and aspirations, in different markets. The problem occurs where a business does not distinguish between its customers in any way: not by size, style, the nature of their market or their use of your product. To this type of business, all customers are equal and, of course, as customers are always right, they must all be treated the same. Functions asked to service customers in this situation will always have a hard time. Tell them that you intend setting up a KAM process that will focus even more intimately on specific customer needs and you might expect a rebellion!

In FS, as in most sectors, there are *never* enough resources. Although in theory it would be nice to invest in understanding all customers, this is not possible either. We must focus on those issues or opportunity areas where our customers reward us with value. This means segmenting customers, resulting in stronger focus, improved understanding of needs, improved offers, a more responsive service and better customer retention.

# WHAT IS SEGMENTATION?

## Defining segmentation

Let's start by defining what we mean by a market segment. Here is one definition: 'A market segment is a grouping of customers with similar buying needs, *attitudes* and *behaviours*.' We stress 'attitudes' and 'behaviours', as if we only looked at needs we would limit our understanding and options. FS is used by almost every organization in the world, but there are dozens of segments, at least in part because of the many different ways that FS is used by different organizations in a variety of situations. Organizations displaying particular requirements make up a range of different segments. Just consider a few of these possible groupings in the FS market:

- small businesses – ranging from individuals doing consultancy to building contractors;
- medium businesses – from a building contractor to the computer company that could be the Microsoft of tomorrow;
- large companies – from regional operators to global multinationals;
- different business sectors – retailers, wholesalers, manufacturers;
- public sector – from government institutions, educational institutions through to charitable trusts;
- financial intermediaries – from supermarkets to specialist reinsurance brokers.

This list could go on and on. Companies within each of the categories above could be further segmented according to different criteria. Small businesses could be also segmented by size, type of business, potential for growth, products purchased, etc. However, segmentation involves making choices that will prove to be both actionable and useful, and that is the art and the science of segmentation.

## The 'viable' segment

A segment should be viable, ie stand up to a few simple tests:

- Is it large enough to justify focused attention?
- Are the customers' needs, attitudes and behaviours similar enough to be aggregated together?
- Are the needs, attitudes and behaviours specific enough to be distinguishable from other segments?

- Is it possible to design an appropriate marketing mix for the segment (see below)?
- Is the segment reachable? Can it be identified, measured, analysed, communicated to and sold to, discretely from other segments?

Affirmative answers to these questions mean you are looking at a viable segment.

## Segmentation and the marketing mix

Segmentation is a three-step process:

1. deciding on what basis to 'slice' the market into segments;
2. choosing those segments that you wish to be active in;
3. targeting each of those active segments with a unique _marketing mix_.

Deciding how to segment is a strategic issue, involving definition of key markets, of areas where growth can be achieved, where retention is important, where cost reduction is vital, etc. Theoretical segment definitions are helpful, but too much analysis before action can be very wasteful. Segmentation should be based on success, ie from where your company has been able to select, acquire, retain and manage customers through profitable relationships in the past. It may be useful to use 'discovery'-based segmentation methods (such as data mining) to identify core segments and their needs, aligning market research efforts to key segments discovered, to understand needs, behaviours and value, etc. The supplier aims to influence demand and gain competitive advantage by applying the marketing mix to targeted segments. In service marketing this is known as the seven Ps – product, price, promotion, place, people, processes and physical evidence, illustrated in Figure 20.1.

By preparing a different and specific marketing mix for each segment, the business ensures that it will meet the needs of each grouping of customers in a more focused way. At the same time, it increases its chances for maximizing profits through premium pricing, or differentiation, or the offer of a lowest-cost option – whatever the dynamics of the particular segment demands. The most advanced practice is to integrate knowledge of customers with operational action. This involves learning how to act in different relationship stages, how to personalize and how to develop value from relationships. This operational approach is accompanied by setting appropriate business targets, developing appropriate offers by segment, and setting up measurement systems to track the delivery of value, so that you can decide whether to repeat the process, improve it or invest elsewhere.

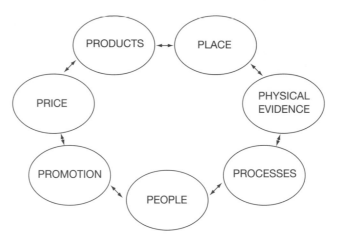

*Figure 20.1* *The marketing mix*

In theory, segments can be as small as an individual customer, with its own unique needs, attitudes and behaviours. In practice it is helpful to aggregate customers together under more general definitions. This enables you to divide your activities up – enough to meet market needs, but not so far that they become fragmented.

## Commercial banking: a classic segmentation

The commercial banking sector provides a classic example of segmentation. Customers are divided into small, medium and large classes by turnover. Small customers are given call centre services more akin to mass-market retail banking. Medium customers receive a similar remote service, but with closer attention for those with more profit potential. Large customers merit far more relationship attention, increasingly from specialist units with expertise in their particular sector. In this way, the banks seek to automate and centralize the servicing of low-turnover business, while focusing resources and expertise on larger businesses providing a greater return.

# The benefits of segmentation

There are many benefits of segmentation:

- an enhanced understanding of the market dynamics, particularly with regard to understanding the needs of different industries or sectors within FS or as clients of FS;
- an enhanced understanding of competitor strengths (the competition will differ by segment) and so the opportunities for competitive advantage;

- greater understanding of the needs, attitudes and behaviours of customers;
- a better chance that you will see how to develop your business's capabilities so as to match those needs;
- a basis for organizing and structuring your business – focusing the whole supply chain on the customer;
- improving your ability to manage the marketing mix in a customer-focused way;
- enhancing your opportunity to add value, gain competitive advantage and build barriers to entry for competitors or substitute products;
- enhancing your opportunity to create, maintain and defend price premiums.

The aim of segmentation is to focus limited resources on opportunities that will take you where you wish your business to be and represent the best chance for you to gain competitive advantage. Failure to segment results in missed opportunities and, worse, inability to gain competitive advantage and long-term security.

## METHODS FOR SEGMENTATION

Segmentation based on historical sales is likely to be short-sighted – a recipe for tripping over. To avoid this, you must understand the *whole* market and not just the bit you happen to occupy, by following these steps:

1. market mapping – identifying opportunities, identifying 'levers';
2. understanding buyer behaviour in context – who buys what, how, when and where;
3. making the cut – selection of segments and positioning through the marketing mix.

## MARKET MAP

This illustrates all the routes to market for your product or service – what we might call the 'market channels'. Figure 20.2 shows the main routes (much simplified) for an insurance company. The map presents some options and choices for segmentation. The next stage is to focus on the best means of segmentation.

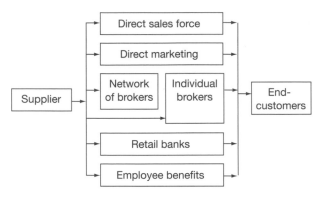

**Figure 20.2** *A market map*

## Opportunity analysis

Note the size of the market and your share at each 'junction' along the different channels. The measurement used depends on the nature of the service. It could be done as percentages of turnover or sales volume, although profit may be more illuminating. Note the size of your own business, and the percentage share, at the same points. Note your competitor's size and shares at the same points. Doing this helps you compare your historical performance to the total opportunity and who you are up against in each area. Segmentation must start with the whole market, not your historical sales – otherwise, you will not only miss opportunities, but also ignore potential threats.

## Where to segment – leverage points

There are many choices. Statistics get us only so far – we must engage our brains. Examine the market map for what we might call 'leverage points'. These are points in the chain where critical purchasing decisions are made. Decisions are made at every point, but where are the big ones, the fors and the againsts, to buy or not to buy?

- Are decisions made globally, regionally or locally?
- Where are corporate decisions made with regard to the use of different types of FS?
- What are the servicing needs of the different sectors?
- Where intermediaries are involved how do they make product choices?

## Push or pull?

If your product or service has a strong reputation, a good brand name and a decent market share, you are in 'pull' marketing. Your marketing efforts create demand that pulls customers into the channels of supply. Without such reputation and market position, you will be more used to 'push' marketing, persuading channels to use your products and services. Most situations will require a combination of these, but it is useful to understand the relative balance at different points of the chain. For companies selling through intermediaries, there may be a case for segmenting by end-consumer and using a pull strategy. Or a push strategy might be called for, with emphasis on segmentation by channel of distribution. The smaller the segment, the more it is possible to meet the segment's needs. But remember the test questions from the start of this chapter: will it be a viable segment?

Getting a full understanding of leverage points goes beyond market size and percentage shares. A new set of questions will help you understand your market dynamics. In our example of a market map for an insurance company the main leverage points might be found at:

- the head offices in the banking channels;
- the corporate customer in the employee benefits channel;
- the individual broker and the end-customer in the independent channel.

Leverage points differ in each of these. Buying decisions are made, and can be influenced, in different ways. However, there are more questions to be asked.

# UNDERSTANDING BUYING BEHAVIOUR IN CONTEXT

In the excitement of all this analysis, remember a simple truth: *markets don't buy – people do!* We must understand the circumstances and the environment in which decision makers operate. There will be much trial and error in finding the right basis for segmentation, and for each possible 'cut' you should aim to understand:

- context and its implications for behaviour;
- attitudes and perceptions;
- motivations;
- needs;
- buying behaviours.

A couple of examples will demonstrate the different contexts for segmentation in FS, the first from the insurance intermediary sector and the second from global investment banking.

## Adding value through segmentation in the insurance industry

A major insurer reorganized its customer management, implementing a new segmentation strategy. This reorganization was stimulated by various factors. On the customer side the adviser market was changing and required a closer working relationship with certain key accounts to manage these changes successfully. Four strategic account groups were set up, representing different types of business areas. There is a banking group dealing purely with the advisory business of a few major banks. Another account group deals with the business of just one advisor network. However, this network is highly complex and made up of many members. These two account groups are poles apart in their buying behaviour and servicing needs. The bank advisors operate within the processes of large corporate organizations, with all that entails in terms of coordination and bureaucracy. The advisor network involves servicing a wide variety of members, but also dealing with a shared infrastructure and policies from the network owner. The new approach is designed to enable the account managers to gain a closer understanding of the businesses they are managing. It is recognized that there are many hurdles to overcome, particularly in balancing demands of the strategic accounts for tailor-made solutions with the need to provide low-cost generic solutions across the organization. Still, the new segmentation provides a strategic framework for allocating resources and making these difficult decisions. For the insurance company, the reorganization is a first step in ensuring that in a changing market it is backing the winners.

## Segmentation in investment banking

Recognizing the value of proactive relationship management, an investment bank reorganized radically to allow it to serve global clients worldwide while developing and strengthening local relationships. Prior to the change the bank had been organized according to broad geographical areas, within these by product and within this by client. The focus of the business was on revenues for each product in each geographical region. The bank recognized that to serve its clients globally the existing organizational hierarchy needed to be turned on its head. The starting point had to be the client rather than the region. Central to this was recognition of the need for a disciplined and segmented approach to relationship development. The bank had to develop an understanding of the relationship between the level of effort and time expended on the client and the return achieved. Its clients were plotted on a relationship development curve and segmented by potential revenue. This model now provides the basis for relationship planning, and activity and resource tracking. KAMs act as the focal point for the account, responsible for orchestrating local account teams, who service the client's local subsidiaries. The business is now truly global in organization and processes, but services are at a local level, where intimate knowledge of local markets is required.

(Adapted from Findlay *et al*, 2002)

# MAKING THE CUT

Once attitudes, behaviours and context are better understood, return to the market map and re-examine leverage points. Do supply channels or buying behaviour of end-users drive buying decisions? Which should be the focus of your marketing mix design? What are the costs involved in servicing the different channels? In our insurance company example, the bank channel ranges from major national banks down to savings and loans institutions. These not only vary in size, but also operate in different ways, requiring different types of support. Depending on the scale of the supplier, we *might* be looking at two or three businesses to be segmented, or we might be looking at two or three segments to be divided into more manageable sub-segments. Detailed work may be needed to research the needs of the different segments and relate this to the type of support required in areas such as systems, administration, training, compliance, etc. Deciding the final basis for segmentation involves a mix of factors. In making decisions on sub-segments, remember to ask, 'Is it viable?' If the groups are large enough, if messages can be targeted and if profits can be made, sub-segments will help you apply focused marketing mixes.

## The 'adopters curve'

This segmentation method is useful in identifying key accounts when launching a new product or service. Some customers may buy, perhaps regardless of the product's merits. However, if a product is to succeed, it must go beyond that narrow following and find a wider audience. It must progress beyond *innovators* to find *early adopters*. Rogers (1962) captured this idea in his 'adopters curve' (Figure 20.3).

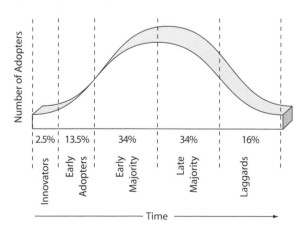

***Figure 20.3*** *The adopters curve*

215

The curve shows how most new products or ideas go through stages of adoption, first by the innovators, then by early adopters. Then the early majority provide the volume sales that cut costs and turn the product into a mass-market one, making it attractive to the late majority. Laggards resist till the very end. This model works very well in financial services. Corporations vary in their attitude towards innovation and new ideas. If your offer is new, leading-edge, challenging or risky, find your key accounts among the innovators and the early adopters of the market. If your offer is well established, secure, safe, perhaps even a little staid, then look at the other end of the curve. However, be wary of innovators who absorb your resources but prove fickle and promiscuous when the next new thing comes along. Early adopters and early majority types may be your most secure targets in the long run.

## SEGMENTATION AND KAM IDENTIFICATION

Your business should have a planning hierarchy, from business plan to marketing plan, segment plans and key account plans, as illustrated in Figure 20.4. The process is not just top down. Valuable input comes from the bottom, or the balance between objectives, resources and opportunity (Chapter 3) will not be found. Still, segment plans must be subsets of marketing plans, and KA plans should be subsets of segment plans.

**Making sure that you avoid 'sizeism'** Without segmentation, selection of key accounts tends to suffer *sizeism*. The next chapter shows how comparing the attractiveness of customers and assessing your strengths in their eyes provide a basis for identifying key accounts. Without segmentation, most markets are too large and diverse for this to be workable; what is attractive in one part of the market is not so important in another, so scale of business becomes the only truly

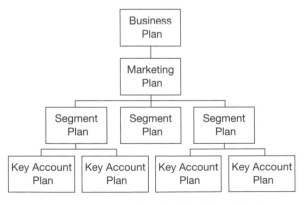

*Figure 20.4* *The planning hierarchy*

comparable factor – hence sizeism. The 20 per cent of customers that supply 80 per cent of the business are the key accounts.

Here, it is helpful to develop a customer value index to segment markets **Defining and** and customers. The largest customers may bring revenue but little profit **analysing your** owing to their negotiating power. Mid-size customers may be more **target market** attractive. So, find indicators of current and potential profitability and act on them during targeting, acquisition, retention and development. Defining target markets and identifying where growth can be achieved, where retention is important and where cost reduction is vital give direction to your planning, integrating the different levels from marketing plan through to the individual key account plans. With segmentation, and the close identification of needs and attitudes within each segment, the selection of key accounts can be made on a broader basis than just size.

Let us reconsider the situation of support functions. If everyone in the **Operational** business understands that the market is divided into segments that have **segmentation** different needs, they will understand why different customers, and salespeople, might have different needs. They will be able to develop their own plans and strategies to maximize value added to each segment. Integrating knowledge of customers with operational action is advanced segmentation practice.

In theory a segment could be as small as an individual customer, with its **All customers their** own unique needs, attitudes and behaviours. In practice this may become **own segment?** possible through KAM, provided that there are not so many customers that the supplier will be pulled apart at the seams.

If a segment is a group of customers with the same needs, attitudes and **The 'lead key** behaviours, and if you segment properly, would you need more than one **account'?** key account in any segment? The idea here is that, by devoting energies to one customer and learning the right solutions for that customer, these solutions should also be appropriate to all other customers in the segment. There is much to recommend such a view, provided you really do segment properly. For instance, an insurance company might choose to work closely with a leading accountant to develop products for clients in this sector. Provided the accountant chosen is representative of other accountancy firms operating in the same market, there may be much to be gained from focusing in this way.

## BENEFITS OF SEGMENTATION FOR KAM

- It allows you to select key accounts because of their importance within particular segments, not just because they are the business's largest customers.

- It enables you to identify the 'winners' within each segment with greater certainty.
- It allows you to focus your efforts as a total business (sales, marketing and support functions) on to clearly identified sets of needs.
- Where customer needs can be expressed as 'segment needs', it gives you a better chance of achieving economies of scale or efficiencies in operation.
- It allows clearer definition of standards, providing focus for support functions.
- It allows you to identify and support more customers as long-term business partners.
- It helps you work with customers that compete with each other, through differentiated support packages.
- It allows KAM to drive business processes without descending into the chaos of 'anything goes'.
- It helps to align the business behind the KAM concept.

The next chapter goes into more detail on how to identify key accounts within specific segments.

# A NEW TYPE OF MARKETING PLAN? KAM AND RELATIONSHIP MARKETING

We have shown key account plans to be subsets of segment plans, which are in turn subsets of the marketing plan, but it should be emphasized that this will be a new kind of marketing plan. Traditional marketing, the management of the Ps, has been criticized as too short term, too tactical and too 'transactional'. In its place, many argue we should put relationship marketing – aligning the whole business towards customers by focusing on the relationship between supplier and customer. This is, of course, very similar to the aims of KAM, as it focuses on:

- moving away from transactional selling to relationship management;
- relationships based on trust and value;
- maximizing future value of customers and market segments;
- developing customer loyalty and retention;
- changing organization and attitudes to fit the customer;
- cross-business processes.

KAM is mainly concerned with managing customer relationships in a business-to-business environment – it is the delivery of the theory that relationship marketing propounds. Gronroos (1996) calls relationship marketing 'the mutual exchange and fulfillment of promises'. Grand words, but a good basis for partnership KAM.

# 21

# Identifying your key accounts

This chapter deals with steps 4 through to 9 of the 10-step process introduced in Chapter 19.

*(The CD ROM attached to this book contains a software package designed to help with the process described in this chapter.)*

There is a dangerous, self-fulfilling prophecy in sales: 'They're our key accounts because they're key…' If today's largest customers are your key accounts, then it is easy for them to stay that way, even as they start to decline, as they inevitably colour your thoughts about the future. If so, you have the 'trapped by your history' syndrome. Examine most 'once great' businesses now in terminal decline and you will find evidence of this syndrome. Sometimes you get lucky and your largest customers take you where you want to be, but don't rely on it. At its worst, the syndrome leads you into decline simply because you follow your customers' decline. You can't escape the vicious circle. Seeking alternative customers would mean abandoning your key accounts. So, we need to select our key accounts on a better basis than today's (or yesterday's) largest. But is 'select' the right word? Do you select your customers or do they select you? As far as today's customers go, selection is often in their hands. What KAM gives you is an opportunity to start doing a bit of the thinking for yourself. Perhaps 'identifying' would be a better word for this process.

In the end, KAM must involve both activities – identifying and selecting. KAM is about analysis and also about choices. One of the toughest choices in KAM is the final one: who's in and who isn't (we don't say 'out'; there is a place for non-key accounts, as we will see later in this chapter) – which is made simpler by the realization that it is a two-way process. You chase the ones that will take you where you want to go and they chase you if you meet their needs. Marry the two thoughts in the same customer and you have a key account and it has a key supplier. The 'diamond' relationship of partnership KAM is the result of mutual strategic intent (see Chapter 5).

So, what about all those very attractive customers that don't chase *you*? Are they key accounts? And what about all those customers that *do* chase you, but you don't really see *them* as your future? Are they key accounts? You probably have customers, or potential customers, that fit both descriptions. What would you call them?

# AN IDENTIFICATION AND SELECTION PROCESS

## KAISM: the key account identification and selection matrix

You can't call everyone 'key'. Customers are not equal – some are definitely more equal than others. Call them all 'key' and the term fast becomes meaningless. If you remember that the purpose of identifying key accounts is to help deploy business resources and commit to action, then you'll see the value in the matrix in Figure 21.1. The matrix considers two sets of factors, the two sides of the identification and selection process: yours (do you like them?) and theirs (do they like you?):

- *Customer attractiveness* – what makes customers, or potential customers, attractive to you?
- *Relative strength* – what makes you attractive to your customers, in comparison to your competitors?

Having answered these questions, you might end up with four 'categories' of customer:

- key account;
- key development account;
- maintenance account;
- opportunistic account.

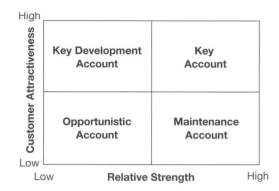

**Figure 21.1**   *The identification and selection matrix*

## Key account

This is it; you want them and they like you, but don't relax. They are central to your future and deserve energetic attention from a KAM team devoted to keeping on top of change. Remember, 'nothing recedes like success'.

## Key development account

This is where it *could* be, if only you could improve your performance in their eyes. The KAM team must focus on finding out what makes the customers tick, what they want, and committing the business to providing it. Such customers could be hard work, with all the 'chicken and egg' problems imaginable, but success will be well rewarded. Only remember; you have limited resources, so don't spread them too thinly. How many key development accounts could your business chase simultaneously? Some businesses appoint their most junior people to manage these customers, or attach them to the responsibilities of account managers already burdened by too many top-right key accounts. Where this is done because the business doesn't see much prospect of progress, they are usually right – they make no progress, but because this prophecy is self-fulfilling! Another common approach is to make such customers the responsibility of the telesales team. It is almost impossible to develop relationships that will enhance the customer's view of you by telephone.

Success with such customers comes from applied effort, not from starving them of resource or expertise. If these are the 'jam tomorrow' customers, then there should not be so many that progress is made with none, or so few that there *is* no tomorrow – a fine judgement indeed, but one that will mark the winners from the losers. There will often be more customers in this category than can actually be developed into key accounts, through either lack of resources or lack of opportunity. This is natural if you are in a market with a wealth of attractive prospects. This gives you choices – increase your resources or 'pick them off' as specific customer opportunities arise. Be prepared to experiment, to trial and to allocate resources as 'test cases', aiming to learn from each experience. Be prepared to put some on hold on the famous 'back burner' and, finally, know when to admit defeat, as an inconvertible customer can hardly be called 'attractive'.

## Maintenance account

This is the hardest category. These are good customers; perhaps they have been loyal for years. Almost certainly they are personal favourites of plenty of your team. The tough decision, but the right one, is to pull resources and energy back from such customers – you need it elsewhere. The clue lies in the category's name, 'maintenance'. This is where you 'win' your time and your resources to invest in key and key development accounts. Some people (and very often the manager responsible for such customers) might say you are abandoning them. Salespeople in particular don't like the idea of 'dropping' customers, not after all the work that has gone into winning them, and who would blame them? But this category is not about abandonment; it is about finding ways of looking after customers that won't trap you and your team into time-consuming commitments. The objective here is to reduce costs and maximize *sustained* earnings. This is often where technology can be used for cost-effective servicing combined with sympathetic, responsive handling of the transition. Often, the success or failure of dealing with newly identified maintenance accounts lies in how the transition is handled. Compare two alternative approaches to such a transition, where local sales support is being centralized:

1.  Apologies are sent to the customer, including a letter from the MD thanking them for their loyal support and hoping that it will continue, despite the need to operate from now on through a call centre and the internet. Once the new process is decided on, and the necessary meetings concluded, the previous sales contact has no further contact with the customer.
2.  The supplier makes a presentation on the advantages of the new way of operating. This includes a discussion with regard to the customer's concerns over the new arrangements and the development of a plan of support in order to overcome any difficulties identified. The sales contact then stays in touch during the handover period, liaising with the call centre and the customer. Investing time in managing the transition is worthwhile in freeing up your time and your team's time in the long run by selling the changes to your maintenance customers, *positively*.

*Opportunistic account*

These are customers you will service willingly as and when it suits your priorities. You should not make wild promises that you cannot keep, nor should you treat them like nuisances. Be pleased with their custom, but recognize it for what it is – income that helps you develop your key and key development accounts.

# IS ALL THIS REALLY NECESSARY?

We have been asked this many times by people reluctant to categorize or label their customers. The reluctance is healthy, but if it helps you do the right things when there are tough decisions the approach is justified.

### Why not just chase hot opportunities?

A large home loans company once risked a number of its key relationships with introducers because it was over-eager to secure a large, but one-off, deal on a tranche of fixed-rate funds with a major broker. It had a system of customer categorization that put the major broker in the opportunistic box. The extra business required a certain amount of changes to standard procedures and needed to be processed over a limited time period, and the operational and administrative people had to put in a superhuman effort to meet the deadlines. They made it and they felt pretty good about it, until the complaints started to flow about the deterioration in the service levels from many of their regular introducers, their *real* key accounts. They had all taken their eye off the ball.

So, identification and selection of customers into these kinds of categories do not necessarily imply abandonment of some for the sake of the rest. They imply planned allocation of resources. For some businesses, the people resources required for KAM teams seem large, so they must identify the candidates for such support with care. Other businesses may have the people, so many customers could enjoy the 'diamond' of partnership KAM, but operational resources would not cope with the resulting commitments. Remember the need to balance objectives with market opportunity and business resources (Chapter 3). The 'bow-tie' relationship is perfect for many customer relationships, representing the right match of supplier and customer strategic intent.

In the end, decide using judgements, not four-box matrixes. The matrix is a tool, a focus for discussion and a guide, no more. Perhaps you can play variations on the theme – a relatively large number of KAM teams with 'diamond' relationships in the making, but a recognition that at any one time only a few of these will be able to commit the business's resources. Or a large pool of development key accounts with 'skeleton' or 'virtual' teams waiting for the opportunity to form and take action with a much smaller number of active KA teams. Or…

One consideration in developing expertise in a particular sector is that **Avoiding shooting** it may lead to clashes of interest. For example, a global food company **yourself in the foot** that likes to work with its suppliers on the basis of long-term relationships has a policy not to use FS suppliers that work with its competitors. This is understandable. Developing a close relationship results in the exchange of much commercially sensitive information. However, with consolidation and mergers on both sides of the fence (with customers merging in many sectors and FS suppliers coming together) it is becoming harder to avoid this situation. For the supplier, there may be pressure from the customer to make choices on which key account to stick with and the KA selection process is one tool for aiding such decisions. The key is in defining the attractiveness factors and comparing potential customers against those factors in the long term. In many cases there is no need to make such stark choices, but there *will* be a need to recognize customers' sensitivities. One solution is to ensure that KAM teams serving such competitors are not composed of the same people. In this instance (and perhaps the only justifiable occasion), the building of some *walls* within the supplier's own organization may be of benefit rather than a barrier.

## Important health warning

Choosing key accounts involves thinking. It should *not* be done as guesswork, or in five minutes on the back of an envelope. It is about how and why you deal with customers and how it might change over time, not about labelling them for ever. And yes, you can break the rules and the definitions – provided you can explain why.

Some opportunities are less obvious and take more time and effort to **The identification** materialize. Take the example of an FS supplier looking to take on back- **and selection** office functions currently run by departments in the potential client's own **matrix is designed** organization. The potential client may need to take a considerable **to help our** 'journey' in its thinking to recognize even the existence of the opportunity. **thinking, not to** It may be taking a big risk in making such a change. First there is the like- **replace our** lihood of discontent and employment disputes if jobs are at stake. Even **brains…** more importantly there are the risks involved in losing control of customer interactions. To take this opportunity, the supplier needs to persuade the client of the quality of the service offered; its employees' ability to represent the client to its end-customers (this may involve reassurance on the quality of recruitment and training and demonstration of customer empathy by staff); the compatibility of the technology employed; the integrity of its customer data management; the legal compliance of its procedures, etc. This involves addressing the concerns of many decision makers and influencers, and demonstrating competency across all these areas. The supplier may need to demonstrate a cultural match between the two organizations, for the client really to trust it. So there may be a long gestation period before the relationship develops to the point where it pays the dividends promised. Sometimes you just have to wait, and prepare – and manufacture your own luck.

# THE PERFECT INVESTMENT PORTFOLIO?

Any successful business needs a balance of customers: key accounts, key development accounts, maintenance accounts and opportunistic accounts. If all customers were key accounts, then, even if the term didn't become meaningless, the effort involved to manage them properly could quite conceivably create greater costs than the income enjoyed. If all were key development accounts, then the chances of this happening would be all the greater. A business with too many maintenance accounts, while enjoying handsome returns today, should worry about its future. Could its customers be holding it back? A business with too many 'opportunistic accounts', while it may be very profitable, could be heading nowhere. It is all a question of investment and return.

Figure 21.2 shows the expectations you might have of where the resources are invested and where the returns come from. The customer portfolio should be seen as a managed flow of time, energy, resources and money around the business. Time and energy saved by more efficient means of handling maintenance and opportunistic accounts could be invested in future development, as could the revenue and profit from those customers. As with any managed investment, KAM must focus not just on the 'star' earners, but on managing a portfolio of customers, balancing short- and long-term income, and balancing the resources and the returns. Seen in this light we can see another capability that the KAM approach demands – an appreciation of the dynamics of investment and return.

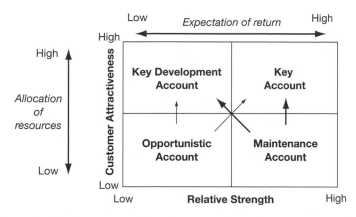

**Figure 21.2**  _Investments in and returns from the customer portfolio_

# THE SELECTION FACTORS AND THE SELECTION PROCESS

To recap, the two axes of the identification and selection matrix are:

- _Customer attractiveness_ – what makes customers, or potential customers, attractive to you?
- _Relative strength_ – what makes you attractive to your customers, in comparison to your competitors?

Each consists of several individual factors, quantitative and qualitative, unique to your business situation. Defining these factors and using them as measures is crucial. If the matrix is to guide you in allocating resources, deciding priorities or determining customer relationships, then much thought should go into this exercise. The most value to be gained from this matrix is not in the final outcome, but in the thinking and the discussions that went into its origination. The matrix provides an opportunity for cross-functional teams to meet and discuss, sharing the viewpoints of their different perspectives. As such, this exercise is a key part of gaining cross-business alignment and is of huge value even if the outcome tells you nothing particularly new or startling.

## Customer attractiveness factors

These are factors that should relate to your longer-term goals as a business. If your competitive advantage is to come from some unique added-value element in your offer, then consider customers that value that element as  **What makes _you_ want _them_?**

227

attractive. If individual solutions to clients' specialist problems are your proposition, then expect your most attractive accounts to be those that value such solutions and are prepared to pay the price. These are also factors that take account of the market opportunity. If your future is providing services that are currently provided in-house by most businesses, your most attractive accounts may be those that have a positive attitude towards outsourcing such services. And there are factors that will recognize the limits to your own business resources. An attractive customer may be one that is easy to gain access to, perhaps because of geography or existing relationships. The factors for customer attractiveness go back to the idea of managing the future (Chapter 3), of seeking a balance of objectives, opportunity and resources. It is the balance of a *range* of factors that determines the ranking of attractiveness. The range of factors might include any of the following:

- Size – volume; value; profit opportunity.
- Growth potential – volume; value; profit opportunity.
- Financial stability – will they be there in the future and will they pay their bills?
- Ease of access – geography; openness.
- Closeness of existing relationships.
- Strategic fit – do they see the world the same way as you? Will they take you where you wish to be?
- Are they 'early adopters' – do they pick up on new ideas and products, or wait until the market tests them?
- Do they value your offer? Is it relevant to their needs?
- Level of competition – low being attractive.
- Their market standing – industry leader, credibility, prestige and so on.

Your own business circumstances must determine your selection and the *weighting* you give to individual factors. Working with a client in Russia, we spent a great deal of time identifying a list of six factors, but there was one that stood head and shoulders above the others: will it pay its bills? It was a crucial aspect of its market circumstance and without it there was little point proceeding – some factors are absolute 'must haves'. If you are offering new ideas, solutions and products, then customers with a tendency to buy into new ideas will clearly be attractive – we might call them 'innovators' or 'early adopters'. Whatever your final choice, you must be able to apply these factors to each of your customers, measuring them against each other. It will become clear at this stage how important it is to segment your market (Chapter 20), as this is the only way to make these comparisons on any kind of equal basis. The choice of attractiveness factors will almost certainly be different for different market segments, and so will your ultimate identification of key accounts.

**Remember the golden rule: segments first, key accounts second**

An insurance company provides private health insurance indirectly through smaller brokers, through employers' schemes and through a tie-up with a big retailer. Consider the scale and profitability of these different channels. The retailer tie-up is a low-cost way to access a significant amount of business, but it is also low-margin. The employers' scheme requires a lot of relationship management, with the returns taking some time to come through. The smaller broker business is high-margin, but can be costly to service. Here the key accounts may be the main broker networks. Different segments call for different objectives and different attractiveness factors.

# Relative strength factors

This is where you must view things through your customers' eyes. What are **What makes *them*** *their* critical success factors in dealing with suppliers? What are they looking **want *you*?** for and what makes them prefer one supplier above another? Judging this is no easy task, as you are dealing not only with measurable 'facts', but also with perceptions – something much harder to judge. Identifying these factors will require great honesty. It is tempting to select all those things that you just happen to be good at, and you will feel very pleased with the outcome, only it will be worthless. The perceptions of different functions in your business will be of great value to the debate – each will know what goes down well and what causes complaints.

The more you know, of course, the better. If you find this part of the exercise hard, then it will at least have highlighted a priority action for your KAM implementation programme – find out! Given the propensity for most of us to either pat ourselves on the back or whip ourselves unreasonably it may be useful to get independent insight as a route to the truth in this matter. Consider formal and independent market research into customers' views, needs and levels of satisfaction. Using research as a way of talking to customers will be a good antidote to a common failing – talking to yourself. Research companies have tools to identify and measure customer needs, customer value, customer experience and satisfaction, from surveys to interviews and beyond. Making use of such expertise may well prove to be one of those early investments that pays handsome dividends in the long run. The range of factors (seen from your customers' perspective) might include:

- price (confidence that they are negotiating the 'best deal');
- service quality (what service agreement you will commit to);
- speed and effectiveness of response (how quickly and well you sort out problems);

- relationships and attitudes (experience of dealing with your staff and managers);
- competence and experience (technical ability of your staff);
- systems compatibility;
- legal and compliance support;
- training support;
- attitude to exclusivity arrangements;
- trust and confidence – ethical standards and behaviour.

These factors are individual to each customer. It is against these factors that you can improve your performance, turning a development account into a key account and achieving key supplier status into the bargain.

# THE SELECTION PROCESS

The CD ROM attached to this book has a software package that takes you through the process described in this chapter. However, it is sensible to start with a paper exercise, however rough. This quickly identifies holes in your knowledge of your customers, facilitates a team-wide analysis and engages the brain rather than your typing fingers. Tables 21.1 and 21.2 help you identify where your customers sit in your portfolio. They give a 'first cut' analysis, but you may wish to go further than this. Weighting of individual factors is the obvious next step and it may be that at this point you should turn to the CD ROM for help – the mathematics start to get quite involved! The portfolio represents the relative positions of customers within a specific market segment and you should have completed a segmentation exercise (Chapter 20) before moving to this stage. In Table 21.1, you rate and compare customers against *your* chosen list of customer attractiveness factors. In Table 21.2, you assess your relative strength, using *their* measures to see how they rate you in comparison to your competitors. The outcomes will be plotted in the identification and selection matrix.

In Table 21.1, enter your chosen customers across the top of the table. It is advisable to select a list of about six factors – of course, more will exist, but this helps focus the analysis. Enter a score from 1 to 10 for each customer, against each attractiveness factor. The higher the score, the better your customer meets that aspiration. Try to set a benchmark of what is 'good' and 'bad' before starting to score and try to stick to it! (It is all too easy to uprate your 'favourite' customers.) Calculate the average score. This will be used once you have completed Table 21.2. If you want to weight your factors according to their relative importance, add a weights column and multiply each score by the weight before totalling.

**Table 21.1** _Customer attractiveness factors – CAFs_

| Attractiveness Factor | Customer A | Customer B | Customer C |
|---|---|---|---|
| Factor 1 | | | |
| Factor 2 | | | |
| Factor 3 | | | |
| Factor 4 | | | |
| Factor 5 | | | |
| Factor 6 | | | |
| Total | | | |

**Table 21.2** _Relative strength versus the competition_

| Customer Critical Success Factor | You | Competitor A | Competitor B | Competitor C |
|---|---|---|---|---|
| Factor 1 | | | | |
| Factor 2 | | | | |
| Factor 3 | | | | |
| Factor 4 | | | | |
| Factor 5 | | | | |
| Factor 6 | | | | |
| Total | | | | |

For each customer under consideration, identify six critical success factors (CSFs) that represent their main needs from their FS suppliers and by which they would judge you in comparison with others. Complete Table 21.2 for each of the customers selected in Table 21.1 – it is quite likely, of course, that each customer will have its own distinct set of CSFs. Place you and your competitors across the top of the table and enter a score from 1 to 10 for each supplier, against each factor. This is how the customer views you and your competitors, fact and perception – so be honest! The higher the score, the better the supplier meets the customer's needs.

**Completing the matrix**

Using the information from these two tables, you can place each customer on the identification and selection matrix, shown again at Figure 21.3. From Table 21.1, if a customer scores higher than the average score then it will be in one of the two upper boxes; if lower than average, it will be in one of the two lower boxes. To identify which of the two, use the results from Table 21.2. Where you score better than your *best* competitor, you will occupy the right-hand box, and the left-hand box if you score worse.

**Figure 21.3**   *The identification and selection matrix*

# HOW MUCH EFFORT AND HOW MUCH DETAIL?

In some cases there may be companies that will clearly be key because they are the top players in their sector – you know before you start the exercise that they will score highly! But remember, it is the thinking behind this exercise, rather than the outcome, that is important. The main effort should be put into identifying the measurement factors and then in seeking to make good assessments. Calculations to two decimal places that shift customers a tiny amount on the matrix are unlikely to add much to your understanding.

*Top tips:*
– **use the exercise as a spur to what you must now find out**
– **involve the team**

Where you do not know the answers, perhaps in looking at your relative strength, make a note to find out. A benefit of this exercise is that it shows what you don't *and must* know. Seek professional advice on researching customers' needs and satisfaction. Do the exercise repeatedly, each time seeking more completeness and greater certainty in your assessment. Over time, you and your team will appreciate much better how you view your customers and how they view you. This exercise is not easy, which is why sometimes it doesn't get done. Involve a cross-section of people – you will discover just how different functions see your customers in different lights:

- Folk in administrative departments like customers who fill in forms correctly and provide a regular and consistent flow of business.
- Folk in financial control like those customers who pay on time, and the few that pay early are *very* special.
- Marketing and product development may like those customers who are keen to test-market new ideas.
- Sales managers like the ones that will help meet their sales targets, especially those that will give large orders just before the end of accounting periods.

Try to relate perceptions to the overall business circumstances. If you are in a low-margin, high-turnover line, where cash flow is crucial, then your friends in financial control have a point. The exercise will help clarify what you really *do* want. If it is possible, involve the customer, but do not build unreasonable expectations.

**Which of these views should predominate in determining customer attractiveness?**

KAM has been described as an outward-facing process, but one aspect should remain internal – these labels of customer categories. Telling key accounts they are such is one thing, but how about being told you are in maintenance, or are viewed opportunistically?

**Should we tell the customer?**

## KEY ACCOUNTS AND MULTIPLE BUSINESS UNIT SUPPLIERS

An interesting challenge for KAM is where the supplier consists of several business units, working independently and selling to common customers. This is becoming more of a problem as FS suppliers merge and operate across a number of divisions. Who are the key accounts here, and who has responsibility for them?

In the UK, government has expanded higher education with an ultimate aim to achieve 50 per cent participation of school leavers. A specialist unit of a national bank is targeting higher education institutions for long-term lending and one of its key development accounts is University X, a modern provincial university seeking to expand its campus. University X also uses the same bank for its transactional business, partly for historical reasons and partly because the bank maintains a branch on the campus and therefore dealing with cash is convenient for the university's finance division. Is University X defined as a key account for its transactional business? Probably not. Is there scope for 'difficulty' here? Absolutely. What if the retail arm of the bank, under pressure to save costs, restricts the opening hours of the on-campus branch? The transactional arm of the bank may well not be concerned because University X is not a particularly profitable

**Should companies with multiple business units act in concert in front of shared customers?**

customer from its point of view. The university's threats to move its banking business fall on deaf ears in the retail arm of the bank. The lending arm of the bank may be so separate that it is blissfully unaware of the problem in the relationship. *Plenty* of scope for difficulties here and little hope for the lending arm in closing a potentially important piece of business.

One solution to this problem is to insist that any one business unit's KA must be regarded as the same by all other units. Seems logical, but just wait for the fights to start. There is a larger question. Does the supplier have anything to gain by acting more in concert? The answer to this will come primarily from the customer's perspective. Does the customer buy separate FS or does it work closely with a key supplier to meet its range of needs? Some businesses try to solve this by using hierarchies of key accounts. They consist of:

- the global key accounts that cross all business and regional boundaries;
- the regional key accounts;
- the business unit key accounts;
- the national key accounts;
- sometimes even the sales representatives' key accounts.

There are two dangers in such hierarchies: confusing yourself and confusing the customer, which is quite enough confusion for anyone! If such designations also come with clear definitions of responsibilities and accountabilities, then they may yet succeed. Who will get first call on the resources available? Where will we aim to forge diamond relationships? How far will we allow the account to drive business decisions? Where does the ultimate responsibility for this customer lie? What is expected from support functions?

# 22

# Customer distinction

Having gone to all the effort of classifying your customers, you must now move to step 10 in the process outlined previously – doing something that makes a difference! If you don't manage each customer type differently – developing *customer distinction* – then three dangers await you:

- *An academic exercise with no buy-in.* It is all too easy for the KAISM exercise to become an academic one, taking lots of management time, building expectations across the organization that something big is about to happen, and then there is nothing. The process easily becomes discredited and it will take some time before people will be convinced to revisit such ideas.
- *Service creep.* Key accounts get top-level attention – the best ideas, best services, best everything. In time, the salespeople servicing the other categories of customer want the best for their own. It is like allowing sales reps to give discounts – sooner or later everyone gets them. The problem here is that these extras cost money. The chances are that the returns you got from key accounts, which initially justified the level of service, will not come from other customers.
- *No energy for the key account challenge.* It is not unusual for most of your customers to be in the bottom right-hand box of the KAISM (see Figure 21.1) – maintenance accounts. It is here that most of the sales team's time is taken. The task of KAM is time consuming. So where is all this new time and energy to come from? From freeing up energy

from the non-key accounts, as shown in Figure 22.1. Without new ways of servicing maintenance accounts, this will not happen. For many, the real challenge of KAM is not managing key accounts, but looking after the others!

# DETERMINING DISTINCT STRATEGIES

For KAM to be effective, energy and resources must be liberated from non-key accounts. Distinct sales and service strategies must be developed for each customer type that allow for that reallocation of resources. Figure 22.1 suggests a possible broad-brush approach by using the terms we discussed in Chapter 5 – the 'milk round', the 'hunters' and the 'farmers'. Key development accounts require an approach that can see the opportunities fast, and can pounce on them and make something happen – some quick wins, a very typical 'hunter' approach. Key accounts will not thrive with such an approach, however, and at some point in the journey it may be necessary to hand over responsibility to a more 'farmer'-oriented KAM. Or, by developing the KA team, the team itself provides that longer-term 'farmer' approach. Maintenance accounts just need to be maintained, and often a 'milk round' approach can do this very well, through a traditional sales force, or perhaps through an outsourced team, or increasingly by other means – customer service staff, call centres, the internet, etc.

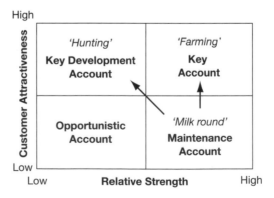

**Figure 22.1** *Freeing up the energy for KAM*

# THE STEPS TOWARDS CUSTOMER DISTINCTION

Identify the possible bases for distinction – the things by which you will distinguish your offer, your services and your proposition to each customer type. Figure 22.2 lists some of the most common bases:

Sales and service strategies must be designed for each customer type, distinguishing across a number of bases, perhaps including the following:

● profitability and the time horizon;
● frequency of contact;
● level and depth of contacts;
● nature of commitment to the customer;
● contracts – _long or short, or none at all_;
● allocation of resources;
● nature and number of projects;
● provision of services;
● charging for services, or part of the package;
● terms and pricing.

**_Figure 22.2_**   _Customer distinction bases_

1. For each possible base, how would this be applied to a key account – can you identify a minimum and a maximum range of application? For example, if the base in question is frequency of contact, for a key account you may decide that this should never be less than once a month, with a maximum of once a week. Similarly, for level and depth of contact, you should always aim to know and meet with, let's say, the CEO, with as a minimum the functional directors or vice-presidents.

2. Repeat this exercise for each of the other customer classifications. If we repeat the example from above but this time with an opportunistic account, we might decide that frequency of face-to-face contact will be nil but the relationship will be maintained through a call centre, providing service support and proactively contacting the customer on a regular basis.

3. Steps 1 and 2 will result in a table, an example of which is shown in Table 22.1. You can now use this table as the basis for preparing specific sales and service plans by customer (in the case of key and key development accounts) or for preparing generic plans for the maintenance and opportunistic categories.

**Table 22.1** Customer distinction options by base

| | Key Account | Key Development Account | Maintenance Account | Opportunistic Account |
|---|---|---|---|---|
| **Profitability and the time horizon** | – Measured over a minimum two- to three-year period.<br>– 'Lifetime value'. | – Be prepared to invest up front.<br>– Have a clear timetable for anticipated returns.<br>– Regular reviews. | – Constant attention to enhancing profitability.<br>– Take an 'accountant's' viewpoint on costs. | – The prime measure of success.<br>– Returns must be instant. |
| **Nature of our commitment to 'understanding the customer'** | – Fully understand the customer's business strategy: its vision, drivers, market position, USPs, attitude to risk, attitude to costs, competition.<br>– Fully understand its view of our competitors.<br>– Know its vendor ratings. | – Make full use of analytical tools to assess and anticipate the customer's business strategy – Ansoff matrix, PLC, Porter, Weirsema's value drivers. | – Continually monitor for changes in its business strategy that might cause us to reclassify the account. | – Understand its market position.<br>– Understand its competitors. |
| **Nature of our contractual commitment** | – Full contract designed to promote trust and confidence, as a platform for developing full partnership. | – 'Letter of intent' approach, outlining aspirations and expectations.<br>– No financial penalties. | – Full contract designed to protect current business and build barriers to exit. | – No contracts. |
| **Relationship and level of contacts** | – Full diamond relationship.<br>– Formal KA team.<br>– Full contact matrix for each DMU.<br>– Formal GROWs for all KA team members. | – Targeting a diamond relationship.<br>– Building the KA team.<br>– Focus on the key sponsors and influencers in the DMU.<br>– Aim to understand their organizational structure at the earliest opportunity.<br>– High level of senior contact up front. | – Seek increasing efficiency of contacts.<br>– Use of virtual and automated communication methods.<br>– Make greater use of support staff.<br>– Reducing the account team while maintaining DMU contacts.<br>– Focus on the key sponsors and influencers in the DMU. | – Bow-tie relationship. |
| **Account plan** | – Full written KA plan.<br>– Focus on long-term growth and long-term profitability. | – Full written plan.<br>– Focus on long-term growth and long-term profitability. | – Full written account plan.<br>– Focus on improving profitability and building barriers to exit. | – No written plan.<br>– Standard budget / forecast. |
| **Customer's perception of us** | – Its no. 1 'helper'.<br>– A strategic supplier.<br>– Supplier of over 60 per cent share. | – A bringer of specific and targeted improvements.<br>– A key supplier. | – Steady and reliable supplier.<br>– Eager to keep our business. | – Commercially astute.<br>– 'We can do a deal with these guys.' |
| **Allocation of resources** | – Resources formally agreed with providers on an annual basis (minimum).<br>– Agreed and provided as part of a clear written KA plan. | – Allocated against clear and realistic targets.<br>– Clear timetable of returns.<br>– Regular review of progress.<br>– Be prepared to withdraw. | – Adopt a 'common-sense liberation' of resources over time.<br>– Aim to regulate the offer on clearly defined levels.<br>– Appoint a techno / commercial account manager? | – Limited commercial effort.<br>– Occasional short-term bursts of commercial activity: sales drives.<br>– No technical resources unless paid for (and even then, take care not to stretch our resources). |

| | | | | |
|---|---|---|---|---|
| **Provision of services** | – Formally agreed levels of service.<br>– Full briefing of the internal providers on 'expectations'.<br>– Formalized access to research and technological support.<br>– Technical openness.<br>– Formal training support.<br>– 24-hour hotline.<br>– Tailored support material.<br>– Tailored products. | – Superior research and technological access.<br>– Full briefing of the internal providers on 'expectations'.<br>– Technical openness.<br>– Selective provision of training support.<br>– Selective provision of tailored support material.<br>– Selective tailoring of products. | – Standard technical support.<br>– Standard customer service.<br>– Standard products. | – Minimum technical support (charged).<br>– Standard customer service.<br>– Standard products. |
| **Nature and number of projects** | – Projects formally agreed by the account team.<br>– Financial investment where required. | – Small list of highly targeted projects (mainly tech).<br>– Clear criteria for success.<br>– Clear timetable for returns.<br>– Ensure we learn from the process. | – Provide 'copy/paste' projects. | – Only short-term projects.<br>– No financial support. |
| **Availability of technology** | – Provide latest technology developments in close partnership.<br>– High speed of delivery.<br>– Long-term development. | – The no. 1 priority.<br>– Tailored 'new' technology.<br>– Top speed of delivery. | – Limited support on 'modifications'.<br>– Medium speed of delivery. | – Existing 'off-the-shelf' technology.<br>– No development work. |
| **Pricing** | – Market based.<br>– Benchmarked to the key accounts competition.<br>– Aiming to help it 'win' in its market. | – Value based. | – Cost plus.<br>– Based on attributes. | – Tactical, penetration. |
| **Knowledge sharing** | – Technical: full sharing.<br>– Commercial: high level.<br>– Provided on the basis of 'partnership'. | – Technical: high level.<br>– Commercial: high level. | – Technical: high level.<br>– Commercial: high level.<br>– Used as a deliberate 'barrier to exit'. | – Technical: none.<br>– Commercial: low level. |
| **Telling the customer its classification?** | – Yes, when benefits are tangible. | – Not until benefits come on stream. | – No. | – Yes, as a piece of negotiation 'positioning'. |
| **Overall sales strategy** | – Farmer.<br>– Long-term focus. | – Penetration (breaking down immediate barriers to entry). | – Seeking 'lock-in'.<br>– Raising barriers to exit. | – Hunter.<br>– Short-term focus. |
| **Outcomes to avoid…** | – Higher-than-justified cost to serve.<br>– KA bureaucracy. | – Getting locked into commitments with little or no return. | – Becoming complacent.<br>– Treating the customer as second-class citizen. | – Destabilizing the market.<br>– Irresponsible reputation. |

# SOME COMMENTS AND ADVICE

## Removing resources

Don't give people unwanted Christmas presents! Chances are that history has brought you to a point where you already do too many things for too many customers. Here, the impact of a customer distinction strategy is more to do with removing than adding – never easy. So, take it slowly, pilot, experiment, discuss with customers before doing anything dramatic – don't abandon your customers overnight. Use the practice of KAM to improve your understanding of what customers really want and value, and how that differs from the things that they take but perhaps couldn't care less about! Figure 22.3 shows what we mean by this.

Many financial suppliers give customers features they don't want or value. This is usually because once they wanted them, but no more – they just never got around to telling you. There are at least three big problems with this:

1. These things cost you money.
2. These things sap your strength.
3. Customers don't value you more for these things; they value you less! What do you think of people who give you unwanted Christmas presents? That's what they think of you.

All members of the KAM team should be charged with keeping their ears and eyes open for any indications that help you determine what is north and what is south of the line in Figure 22.3.

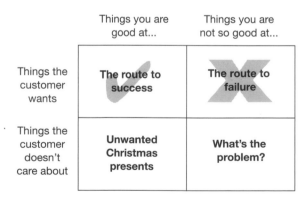

*Figure 22.3*   *Avoiding unwanted Christmas presents*

# Charging for services

You probably give services free that you should charge for. You may not be able to do much about this for things already committed to, but you must get it right for all new services. The customer distinction process forces you to consider this whenever you introduce anything new – who will pay, who will not?

# Using key accounts to develop solutions for the rest

This may sound in direct contradiction of the point about 'service creep' made earlier in this chapter, and perhaps it is, but there are some circumstances where you can see your key accounts as a kind of test bed for the rest. Develop new ideas with those customers, and then let them filter down to the others. This avoids the criticism of service creep if it is done in a planned way – if it was in fact the intention from the start.

# Outcomes to avoid

You will see from Table 22.1 that the last line shows 'outcomes to avoid'. This is particularly valuable in such an exercise as there are some potentially dangerous tendencies. One is the tendency to overdo the reduction of resources or the toughening up of the stance against maintenance and opportunistic accounts. Remember, maintenance means just that – these are not customers anyone wishes to lose. Another danger is the tendency to create too good a package for key and key development accounts. We may well be in unwanted Christmas present territory here. Remember, the whole purpose of this is to improve profitability, not just increase costs.

# Part V

# Entry Strategies

# 23

# The customer's decision-making process

We have done our homework; we know what we are trying to achieve and we know that we are chasing the right customer, but the customer isn't buying. Why? Is our offer going to have a positive impact on its business? This is an important question, which is addressed in Part VI, but let's suppose for the moment that it will and the customer still isn't buying. Why? Do we have the right *entry strategy*?

## ENTRY STRATEGY

Anyone confronted by a new customer has a daunting task. Who should you talk to in its organization with so many departments, functions and sites? This applies whether you are a professional salesperson or, as is often the case in FS, a manager finding that sales is now part of your role. The path to the real decision makers can seem like a maze, only most customers will not allow you the luxury of exploration. There are rarely second chances if you take the wrong turning. While in many business-to-business buying situations the supplier may deal through a buyer, this is often not so in FS. Where a buyer is nominated to deal with sourcing an FS product, the buyer may be operating outside his or her core area of expertise and relies heavily on others in his or her organization to make the decision.

**So who is making the decisions?** Your main contact, whether a professional buyer or not, may claim to be all-powerful and promise a glowing future. In FS, new suppliers may have operational, compliance, training or risk implications. The contact may be just part of a larger, more complex jigsaw. Taking on a new supplier may mean more work in the short term for administrative functions. The IT people may have concerns about systems compatibility. Human resources may be concerned about how it might interfere with their very tight training programme. Here is the seller's quandary – where is the real focus of power and what concerns must be addressed across the organization? How can you talk to the right people without antagonizing the primary contact? You need to find the answers to these questions: 1) how does the company make its buying decisions? and 2) who is the right person to talk to? As the answer to the second depends entirely on the answer to the first, let us start by understanding how a customer makes its decision to buy.

# THE BUYING DECISION PROCESS

Most buying decisions go through three stages:

- realizing that there is a need;
- looking at the options;
- clearing up concerns and making a choice.

Of course, not all customers realize they have a need. Here lies fertile ground for salespeople able to develop such a realization, but without it the prospect of a sale does not even glimmer.

Most sales are made on three levels:

- by meeting business needs;
- by meeting personal needs;
- by understanding how the organization operates and makes its buying decisions.

This is shown in Table 23.1.

## Finding the right level

It is easy for FS specialists promoted into sales-related roles to make a basic mistake – they forget that customers are human. They can easily lose the sale by reciting the features and benefits of their product while irritating the customer with their arrogance. By only considering one of the three selling

**Table 23.1** _Sales/buying process_

|  | Business Needs | Personal Needs | Organizational Decision Making |
| --- | --- | --- | --- |
| Need exists | What are they? | Understanding style and values. | Who has the need? Who makes the decisions? |
| Options are considered Concerns are resolved | Presenting benefits. Negotiation. | Matching style and values. Rapport. | Influencing the decision. Giving the decision-making unit (see Chapter 24) a means to decide. |

levels, they lose the sale. However, professional salespeople have the personal side of the job under control – they know their customers better than their own families (and they probably see them more often!). Yet, they too can lose the sale by thinking that _this_ is all that matters. They have been immersed in the customer for so long that they might even have 'gone native', forgetting to sell on the other levels. Some salespeople can even fall into the syndrome of thinking they are a nuisance to their customers by suggesting change – time for a change themselves. The KAM must work on all three levels. Most importantly, with complex accounts, the KAM must be able to work on the level ignored by so many, inexperienced or experienced: the customer's _organizational decision-making process_. Think back to the KAM model and the idea of moving from the 'bow-tie' relationship to the 'diamond' or beyond. This implies a more complex set of relationships and it recognizes that the buying decision in FS is often made with reference to a range of interests and considerations within the context of a complex organization. This requires an understanding of a strange entity – the DMU.

# 24

# Selling to the organization – the DMU

## DMU – THE DECISION-MAKING UNIT

Most decisions, or at least the important ones, are made by decision-making units. In some companies, these may be quite formal – project teams, sourcing teams or a committee; in others, they may be so informal as to be unidentifiable, eg some members of the finance function in a large corporate or partners in a brokerage firm; but they are there all the same, working with various degrees of formality. There are three broad types of DMU:

- authoritarian DMUs;
- consensus DMUs;
- consultative DMUs.

### The authoritarian DMU

Here, a key individual makes the decision – perhaps the boss, very often the owner of a smaller business or the major partner in an intermediary. The decision is imposed on colleagues and staff, sometimes even against their better judgement. For the seller, this can be the easiest DMU to influence. You simply have to identify that individual and go for him or her, with the right message, ensuring that you meet his or her personal needs. Of course, this may upset other people in the organization, particularly if you ignore their views and just look after the boss. For the unwary, short-term success may be followed by a concerted campaign against the supplier. The wise person will target the key decision maker, but be sure to keep the rest involved.

## The consensus DMU

Here, the decision is made through some kind of process of 'democracy'. Ideally, all members of the DMU agree or, if not, the majority decides. Typically, consensus DMUs are found in cooperative organizations, institutions, government bodies, voluntary groups and so on. For the seller, it is hard work, involving influencing at least a majority of members, if not all. Such decisions are usually taken in private, with no access to the 'committee' for suppliers. The problem here is that you don't always know *why* the decision was taken. Even when you succeed, not knowing why is a handicap. When you don't, knowing why is invaluable. The temptation is to forget it and move on to the next opportunity, but wise suppliers search for the reasons and try to learn from them.

## The consultative DMU

Here, there is an appointed decision maker – a senior manager or partner, or a specialist in a particular area such as the finance department. The decision is based on views of the key DMU influencers, whom the decision maker consults. This can result in a minority view prevailing, but a minority that has the clearest reason to be consulted, perhaps because they are likely to be strongly affected by the product or service being supplied or have particular expertise. For the seller, the key to success is identifying those issues that carry most weight and identifying the interested parties to whom these things matter most – and then influencing them towards your viewpoint.

# INTERESTS AND INFLUENCES – ENTRY STRATEGIES

In each of these DMU types, but most challengingly in the consensus and consultative, it is important to consider:

1. What is your key contact's role?
2. Who else is in the DMU and what are their interests and influences?
3. Levels of seniority.

To sell to a complex organization you must plan and develop your entry strategy:

- whom to see;
- who should see them;
- in what order they will be seen;
- what you will be saying to them.

# THE ROLE OF THE KEY CONTACT

First establish your key contact's role in relation to the rest of the DMU. The supplier may have one key contact in the buying organization. This may be a professional buyer, but often in FS a functional specialist, perhaps from the finance function or product management. Key contacts may suggest they are the kingpins and, of course, they might just be. Even if they are not, but simply 'gatekeepers', then take care not to ignore them or to be seen to ignore them. Of course, you *must* get past them to make contact with the *real* decision makers, but you must not go around them. This is not the time to be insensitive. Key contacts may not decide *for* you, but upset them and don't be surprised when they lobby strongly against you. The KAM must identify what role the key contact actually plays and, based on that, determine what further actions should be taken. Figure 24.1 indicates some of these roles, based on a combination of the level of interest demonstrated by the key contact and his or her level of involvement in the process:

- *Lead.* The key contact plays a pivotal role. The decision may affect his or her performance measures – stay close.
- *Specifier.* This often applies where the contact has professional expertise that leads to his or her involvement and is interested

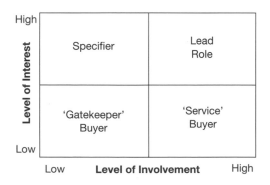

*Figure 24.1*   *Key contact roles*

enough to set guidelines for the decision. This means that he or she is involved early on. Then the involvement wanes. The person has been asked to take part in a decision that is really made elsewhere. If so, then that is where you should seek more information. The interest of the specifier is worth maintaining, as he or she may be a useful ally and could give you valuable advice – keep him or her involved, ask advice and report on progress.

- *Service.* This refers to where the contact is performing the role on behalf of someone else, typically where a buying professional is involved. The issues and the outcomes of the decision may not affect his or her own personal performance measures, so you should not expect strong interest in discussing them. This makes it hard for the seller. The buyer is perhaps only concerned with price, whereas you suspect that the final user, the *real* client, is far more interested in a range of aspects. You must go beyond this type of buyer, but only with his or her permission. This will not be granted if your reasons are self-interested. You must demonstrate that you can be trusted, and that you can help make the buyer's job easier by discussing 'nitty-gritty' issues directly with the user. If you are seen to perform a service for the buyer, then access will be more forthcoming.

- *Gatekeeper.* It is not uncommon to find individuals put up as your main contacts when they have no great interest or involvement themselves, yet they deny you access to those with more. The reason? Perhaps you are a minor supplier, or not yet a supplier to them, so the contact is acting as gatekeeper, protecting the organization from the 'interference' or 'nuisance' of overzealous salespeople. If this is how he or she sees it, you have work to do:

  - Rule one: recognize the person's reservations and don't go behind his or her back.

  - Rule two: keep pressing to find other points of contact, but always with the relevant contact's permission, perhaps using other members of your own team.

  - Rule three: patiently work on winning the contact's trust and confidence, giving reasons to allow you in – reasons that mean something *to the contact*.

# CHANGES IN BUYING

Changes in organizations and the buying revolution have changed the buying process for many financial services. As the buying role becomes more sophisticated and as you deal with more complex organizations, you might expect to encounter more complex purchasing situations, for example where adviser networks have taken over negotiations on product terms on behalf of individual advisers, or where, with corporate consolidation and mergers, buying operations may extend over more than one business or country. Buying processes and roles may have changed and existing arrangements cannot be taken for granted, so you must understand who makes which decisions where. Table 24.1 shows some variations and trends in buying mechanisms and responsibilities. Of course, in many organizations, buying functions aim to increase their buying power and the value they bring to the business by extending their activities beyond individual sites, territories or businesses. If we think back to the supplier power/buyer power positioning model from Chapter 9, then we can see how aggregating several local buying decisions into one regional decision will increase buyer power and the buyer's negotiating position.

Where the attempt is made to purchase on a wider front, the change is often made through a 'lead role' or 'sourcing team' approach. A lead role is where one site, business or territory takes on the main responsibility for buying for a wider group. The lead may be chosen for a number of reasons, eg expertise, largest share of purchase value, particular supplier relationship and so on. The other sites, businesses or territories are expected to fall into line with the lead. A sourcing team is where a group of interested parties gather to pool their expertise, buying power and resources. Decisions will be taken by consensus, perhaps with greater allowance for local variation than the lead approach. The shared service is a buying arrangement where a unit is set up, independent of all businesses, sites or territories, to provide service to all. This might be for all buying or, more usually, for some particular aspect – perhaps one requiring special

**Table 24.1**  *Buying responsibilities*

| Responsibility | Local Responsibility | Regional Responsibility | Global Responsibility |
| --- | --- | --- | --- |
| Individual site or territory | Standard role | | |
| Individual business | Standard role | Increasing role | Possible role |
| Lead business, site or territory | | Target role | Possible role |
| Sourcing team | | Target role | Possible role |
| Shared service | Option | Option | Option |
| Outsource | Option | Option | Option |

expertise or additional after-purchase service, such as IT. This is an attractive option to large, widely spread organizations where several smaller entities are too small to support their own purchasing unit or to have the necessary expertise in all areas. The outsource option is where the organization uses an external body for buying, perhaps for its particular expertise. For example, a company might outsource all its insurance requirements to a broker or its pension arrangements to a specialist pension provider.

# GLOBALIZATION

**As power in organizations shifts from local to global (and possibly back again), so entry strategies must change**

The implications for FS suppliers can be enormous. You must understand what decision-making roles and responsibilities exist and how the customer hopes to develop them. If your relationship is based on an individual site or business and the responsibility for decisions on suppliers or products is given to a wider body, perhaps a global office in another territory, then you will have to start from scratch. You will almost certainly find yourself up against a competitor already 'well in' with that global office, even though on a local basis. The competitor may well gain first option to bid for global business, perhaps only because of a common language with the buyer. If you want to influence specifications, product listings and so on, then you must establish relationships with lead sites or businesses, or with the sourcing teams. This may involve you moving, not only outside your territory, but also outside your particular area of expertise. However, the global trend does not mean the end of national suppliers. In many areas of FS, global suppliers are not strong because there are still big variations in local regulations and conditions. But 'national'-minded FS suppliers should take notice – there is an increasing need to think globally. The worst you can do, worse than ignoring the trend, is to fight against it.

If your customers go global, or centralize their decision making because of organizational rationalization, you must follow. Ignoring central edicts and carrying on as normal on a local basis will be frustrating and, in the longer run, terminal. The more you do to help companies with this rationalization, the greater your reward – though there will be discomforts. Your local contacts, trusty and loyal for so long, may well resent the shift in power and try to persuade you to stick with *them*. They will remind you of favours done and the good old times. You need to steer a middle course through such transitions, meeting the head office requirement while providing local support. Once again, *think global and*, as the cliché continues, *act local*.

---

**Managing a global reinsurance business**

The director responsible for global clients at a reinsurance company made these points concerning global KAM:

- Be prepared to match the style of the client – don't force a global solution on a client that has a decentralized approach, because it won't work.
- Being global doesn't mean being highly centralized – a global business is still the sum of local organizations; the actual business is done in local organizations.
- Centralization only works up to a point.
- Recognize that global account management requires additional skills – a good local KAM will not necessarily make a good global KAM. The global KAM is dealing with many different people with varying goals; from different cultures; operating against varied targets, etc. The global KAM must be able to reconcile these differences, managing complex relationships internally and externally. At the same time the global KAM needs to keep the big picture in mind in moving the business forward.

---

# OTHER INTERESTS AND INFLUENCES

As well as the key contact, there are many other members of the DMU. Formal members may include people from other departments; informal members – important influencers of any decision – may include people outside the customer's own company – *its* customers, government bodies, regulators, local communities, etc. Remember that there are many different types of interested party, each playing its own role in the DMU, each bringing its own particular influence to bear, each requiring its own kind of attention. Below we describe different tools for identifying and defining those influences, to help determine your entry strategy. These are:

- influence through involvement;
- influence through interest;
- influence through acceptance;
- levels of seniority.

We illustrate the tools with the case of a supplier of a new flexible home loan to a big broker.

## Influence through involvement

**Why are they involved?**

We might identify four main types of involvement common to most sales situations – the 'user', the 'specifier', the 'economic' influencer and the 'sponsor', as shown in Figure 24.2. These involvement types might exist as different people, or an individual might have more than one type of involvement. Whichever the case, it is important to identify the different motivations that result.

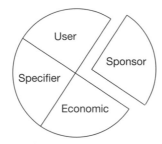

**Figure 24.2**  *Main types of involvement*

## The specifier

This is where standards are specified – a crucial element of any decision process. If you can influence the specification, then you have a good chance of success. However, this activity may be far removed from your normal contact and might happen well before you are involved. In our flexible home loan example, it might be a product expert and someone involved in training, if the requirements for frontline staff expertise is a major issue. The specifier's role is sometimes almost neutral. He or she does not make the final decision, but sets the ground rules for how the decision *will* be made. In this role, the specifier effectively 'selects out' non-conforming suppliers.

## The economic buyer

Economic buyers focus on costs and profits. They may have a short-term view, setting short-term costs against uncertain longer-term returns. They are typically finance or commercial managers, who control budgets. However, their decisions will be based on the options put before the buying company. If one supplier can provide better overall value through support, then it may win the day, despite not offering the best price.

## The user

Users have to do something with your product or service, so they will probably have strong views on what they want from it. They are important influencers, but not always easy to contact. In our example, the users are the salespeople who deal directly with the end-borrowers. They will want features and pricing that appeal to their customers, a product that is easy to understand, sales material to help them with their job, and perhaps easy set-up and administration. The supplier that understands and meets these needs will have a better chance of success than one that only talks to the person with the money.

### The sponsor

Sponsors ease your path through the complex buying organization, perhaps even pointing you in the direction of the specifier, the user and the economic buyer. Why? Perhaps they are above day-to-day operations, with a more strategic vision. Perhaps they like you and your company. Perhaps they want to ensure action. In our example the sponsor could be a senior manager in the broker who sees advantages in the longer-term customer relationships created by flexible products that adapt to changing circumstances. The sponsor has a reason to want something done. He or she points you in the right direction, provides support and endorsement and, above all, is listened to.

## Influence through interest

**Are they receptive? Do they have problems? Do they have power?**

The 'involvement' model looked at influencers by their function in the decision. The 'interest' model enhances that analysis, seeking to identify broader and perhaps more fundamental reasons for the person's likely attitude and subsequent influence. In this model, we look at three broad categories to explain people's interest in the decision:

- those who are receptive to the supplier's ideas or approach;
- those who have problems with their own current situation;
- those who have power regarding the final decision.

Those who are *receptive* listen to you, perhaps already like your offer and agree with your proposal, but may have little to do with the decision to buy. In our example of selling a flexible mortgage, there might be a particularly receptive salesperson in the team, perhaps someone whom you knew previously when he or she worked for a rival broker. This sort of person is valuable in helping you build your case, identifying which messages will work, with whom. He or she may introduce you to those who have *problems*, those whose objections must to be met. So, those responsible for training may be worried about how to resource the training needed before introduction of the new mortgage. Help solve these people's problems and they sell for you, to those with *power*. Those with power have the authority to act, perhaps through seniority, perhaps through holding the purse strings. They are often hard to meet. Your sales proposition may rely on getting those with problems to sell to them for you. The commercial manager may be the final decision maker in our example, but we must be careful about approaching him or her first. It is better to do your homework by understanding the issues and difficulties that the front-line staff will face in selling the new product. That way, you are more likely to put a convincing case when you do find yourself in front of the final decision maker.

## Influence through acceptance

People take up new ideas at different rates. Some like anything new – the 'innovators'. Others are last in line for change – the 'laggards'. There is a spectrum of attitudes between these two extremes, and you need to consider the number of people in a typical audience who represent each attitude. This spectrum is shown in Figure 24.3, a model (from Rogers, 1962) that we saw before in Chapter 20 when examining segmentation, but is also useful here. This model is used in marketing to ensure the right message and approach. It helps determine whom to talk to, and how. *Innovators* and *early adopters* are easier to sell to. They like novelty, risk and experiment. It is harder with the *late majority* and *laggards*. They want evidence and proof. They want to see a track record of success, to know that somebody else has ironed out all the problems. The *early majority* represents the people who come knocking on your door in floods once the idea or product is fairly well established. Use acceptance of your ideas, where you can find it, first as a point of entry and then as a base for approaching the next stage in the curve. Don't start with the laggards – you must build a case first. If you have to start with them, at least be realistic about the obstacles ahead and meet their needs for proof, evidence or whatever.

**Why might they think it a good idea?**

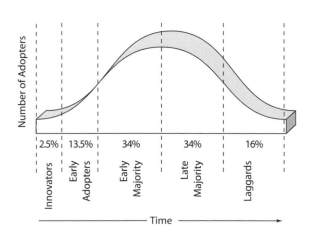

*Figure 24.3   The adopters curve*

Having determined the order of contact, the model indicates the type of approach you might need to take. When you get to the laggards, don't talk about risk and excitement but show them the proof, show them their colleagues' comments and affirmations. With the innovators, don't bore them with case study after case study – they just want to hear what's new. But remember, innovators like new things, your competitor's new things as well as yours. So they may not be loyal or reliable. Worse, they might be regarded as 'suckers for anything new' by their early or late majority colleagues and their views dismissed by the laggards! Selling your ideas to innovators may be easy, but it can sometimes hold you back with the rest of your audience.

## Levels of seniority

Don't get stuck at too junior a level, but don't cause resentment by only attending to the bosses. Understanding the attitudes that come with different levels of seniority can be very valuable in weaving through the DMU. Junior contacts have targets to meet and rules to conform to and a dozen other suppliers to see. Their boss, who set the targets and made the rules, may feel more inclined to ignore or break rules – it demonstrates his or her seniority. Junior contacts may be focused on tomorrow, while the boss may have the luxury of considering next week. A useful exercise is to compare the wants and needs of these different levels ('wants' are desires, 'needs' are necessities). What do the junior contacts need, what might they want and perhaps even what do they dream of? Do the same for their boss and compare notes. Do they correspond? Do they conflict? What does this tell you? Does your offer suit one more than the other? For example, the operations manager in our example of the flexible home loan may not be at all enthusiastic, seeing it as more work for hard-pressed administration staff, while the senior manager takes a more strategic view, seeing the long-term opportunity for building customer relationships.

There are different opinions on the value of making contacts at senior levels. Many salespeople resist involving their own boss and refuse to allow their CEO anywhere near the customer (perhaps experiences like the tale of the CEO in Chapter 5 have had an impact!). Such attitudes can be a major weakness in a KAM strategy, as involving your senior management may be the best, perhaps the only, way to make contacts at the customer's senior levels. The strongest relationships and the longest-running partnerships have in common contacts at senior level in both supplier and customer. Seeking such contacts should be a goal of a managed entry strategy. It is the KAM's job to ensure that he or she works without mishap. Each level of seniority in the customer's organization has its own role to play in the relationship. A good KAM recognizes this and acts accordingly at *all* levels (see

Figure 24.4). Junior levels of contact are what make the machine run, meeting expectations. Middle management contacts manage the relationship, ensuring satisfaction. Senior management contacts can forge loyalty and commitment, the key to long-term security.

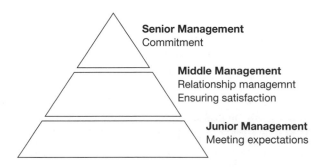

**Figure 24.4**  *Influence by levels of seniority*

# ENTRY STRATEGIES

Breaking down the DMU, by any of the tools described, is of great importance when deciding your entry strategy. The questions to resolve, as raised at the start of this chapter, are:

- whom to see;
- who should see them;
- in what order they will be seen;
- what you will be saying to them.

It is natural in selling to head straight for those with power: the budget holders, the actual decision takers, the boss – but take care. Once thrown out, it is hard to get back through the door. Use the analytical tools to plan your contacts. Start with friends, the receptive ones in the organization, the ones who will tell you things. Try to identify a sponsor. Make sure you are involved with the specifiers. Move on to those with problems, perhaps the users. Try to identify the level of acceptance for your ideas. Use the adopters curve to tailor your approach and build support by stages. Remember, the buyer's boss may be working to a different agenda. If you do all of this well, you will go a long way to getting the customer's DMU to do your job for you – selling to the people with power. Indeed, with a disciplined entry strategy, you will have the DMU *demanding* to be given your solutions!

# THE CONTACT MATRIX AND GROWS

In any key account plan this is perhaps the most important element of all – who sees whom and for what purpose. In Chapter 5 we noted two tools, the contact matrix and GROWs, that provided the simplest way to ensure the success of a diamond team. They are in fact the tools that will help you to manage your entry strategy.

## The contact matrix

Things can get complicated when more than one person from the supplier is involved in front of the customer. It is what we should regard as 'good complication' because of what it brings us, and the job of the KAM is to manage that complication. The KAM must direct and coordinate the team as it is used against the customer's team – he or she is managing a matrix of contacts. The KAM should prepare a contact matrix, as shown at Figure 24.5. This lays out clearly each team member's contacts, and enables us to show the purpose of each contact. If a spreadsheet is used for this tool, use the 'comment' facility, to add information to the matrix – details about the customer, its influencer type, personality, interests and whatever else is useful to you to know. The same can be done for the supplier's team, showing its all-important GROWs (see below). The matrix is not a static

|  | Key Account Manager | Your team member | Your team member | Your team member | Your team member | Your team member |
|---|---|---|---|---|---|---|
| Final decision maker | XXX | | | | | |
| Their team member | XX | Graham Nugent<br>G - Secure order for xxxx<br>R - Present solution yyyy<br>O - Brief team on progress<br>W - 3 July, London | | | | XX |
| Their team member | | XXX | | | X | |
| Their team member | X | | | XXX | | X |
| Their team member | | James Lewis, Operations Manager<br>Specifier<br>Problem holder<br>Laggard | | | | |
| Their team member | | | | | | XXX |
| Their team member | XX | | | | XXX | |

*Figure 24.5   The contact matrix*

tool; people come and go, and it needs to recognize these changes. One way is to indicate who is involved at different stages of the buying decision, by splitting the left-hand column into the four stages we noted in Chapter 23:

- awareness of needs;
- comparing alternatives;
- selection;
- post-purchase concerns.

Customer contacts will change as you move from one stage to the next, and the team members used, listed along the top, will also change to reflect that. Of course, in a complex relationship, with several buying processes going on at once, each at different stages, it may become too complex to capture this all on one matrix. You may then have a matrix for each DMU, or for each sales project. Use this tool to suit your own circumstances.

Every time the team meets the matrix should be reviewed. This simple discipline will probably do more than any other to ensure that your diamond team keeps on track.

**Keeping on track...**

## GROWs

The matrix shows the fact of a contact, but what about the purpose of those contacts? There are many purposes, of course, but they can be summarized under four main headings:

- to get information;
- to promote your solutions;
- to build credibility;
- to build trust and rapport.

Everybody involved with the customer should know their purpose, and their boundaries. Without definition of role and purpose, you will experience all the perils and pitfalls of the diamond relationship (as highlighted in Chapters 5 and 6). We recommend a simple acronym, GROW (borrowed from a project management process), to ensure that the necessary elements are captured:

- *Goal* – the overall purpose of this contact, the ambition.
- *Role* – the nature of the activities undertaken to achieve the goal.
- *Obligation* – the responsibilities, in particular to the rest of the team.
- *Work plan* – the details of dates and actions.

Each contact should have an attached GROW, either written on a separate page in the plan, or perhaps using the 'comment' facility within something like Excel.

## How many contacts?

Preparing the matrix will raise another important question: how many people can you justify putting in contact with the customer? Common sense should prevail, but here are some guidelines:

- Do nothing that causes the customer to consider you a nuisance, a time waster or a burden. Try to avoid the mismatch of strategic intent seen in Chapter 6. By all means create your KA team but, until the customer matches your strategic intent, be wary of putting the team in front of the customer too often.
- Consider the decision style of the DMU – how many people do you need to see?
- Use the tools to identify the influencer types to focus your attentions rather than seeking blanket coverage.
- Go as far as the customer lets you, no further – often it will invite you in, if it sees you as a key supplier.
- If your main need is information, then throw your net wide.
- If your main need is to influence views, then focus your contacts on the key influencers.
- Don't force contacts where there is bad chemistry. It is the KAM's responsibility to coach team members who encounter difficulties, regardless of their seniority.
- Never go behind your main contact's back – always let him or her know who is seeing whom and ask permission before initiating new contacts.
- Make sure information from contacts is communicated within your team and back to the customer.
- Consider your own organization's resources and remember that the members of your team may also be involved with other customers.
- Don't force your team to make promises they cannot keep or commit time that they do not have.

# CONTACTS OVER TIME

Every contact counts – never abandon one. The right contacts change over time. At the early stages of the sale, while the customer is still identifying a need, the contacts might tend to be sponsors and users, those who are receptive, and innovators and early adopters. As the sale progresses and options are considered, expect to meet with the specifier and economic interests, people with problems, and perhaps some of the early majority or beyond. Once the sale is complete, *don't disappear!* This is when continued contact is most important of all, to help things bed in. Demonstrating that you can handle early problems well leads to repeat business and a long-term relationship. As in marriage, it is how bad times are handled that defines a relationship's success or failure.

Many successful sales are tarnished (sometimes even reversed) by a tendency to move on to the next project once the sale is made, as illustrated in Figure 24.6. The gap, post-sale, is a chasm, from the harassed and disappointed customer's perspective. Above all else, remember that the customer's need for contacts is not the same as yours:

1. Respect this at the early stage and try to avoid being a burden.
2. Don't disappear when the customer needs you most – post-purchase concerns.
3. Have a contact plan for *all* stages of the sale, before, during *and after*.

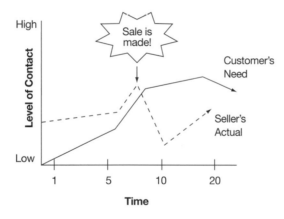

**Figure 24.6** *The need to maintain contact after the sale*

# DEALING WITH THE DMU – HINTS FROM THE FRONT LINE

We are grateful to Peter Le Beau, an experienced FS professional with extensive involvement in KAM, for the following thoughts on dealing with decision makers in FS.

## Honesty in your approach

I think it's very important to try to put yourself in your customer's shoes. I do a thing called profile mapping, which is to try getting an idea of what their competitive landscape looks like. I sometimes deal in markets that I do not know much about but I say to people, give me 10 of your clients and can I talk to them, and then give me 10 non-clients, and then I ask them for their perceptions of the different players in that market place. The variation in opinions can be quite amazing. You do get some fairly clear issues coming through, and they are very often a surprise, and what I tend to find is that there is a huge amount of corporate myopia. Companies really quite fundamentally misunderstand their position in the market place, so you as an account manager can play a very important role in helping people to appreciate their deficiencies. I think that one of the good things about an account manager is they will be able to have an honest relationship both ways and you should alert your client to some competitive problems that might be arising.

I think honesty in approach is absolutely fundamental because, I have to say, almost always I found that companies have quite a warped perception of where they stand in the market place. I think account management does need you to be able to understand where your client is, and if the client has got a real problem in where they're positioned, I think you have to work that out with them. They might not always thank you for telling them, though if you are going to be effective in the way you support them in whatever your thing is, you have to sometimes do some stuff that might be quite difficult. It all comes into the issue about having the right relationship with your client.

## Try to avoid large meetings with unbriefed participants

I went to a meeting a few weeks ago with one of my clients and we were seeing a company, hoping to do some business with them, and this company, my client, had prepared a very good paper, which was quite innovative; they were really looking to develop a new product which was quite ground-breaking. But there were a number of problems in getting the sales pitch across. Firstly the meeting was with no less than 10 people from the other company. Ten people from one company are just too many. Secondly and more importantly it transpired fairly early on that not one of these 10 people had read this paper. Obviously as a supplier you cannot control the size of your customer's meetings, but perhaps there may be opportunities to prepare the ground better by talking to the key participants beforehand to ensure that they understand the proposal.

# Avoiding complacency

If you know someone very well there is a tendency sometimes to work in a sloppy way: not to have any minutes or details of recent meetings and perhaps let deadlines slip on stuff you've agreed to do. I think that good account management just doesn't let that happen. So I think that good account management is about always being aware that they've got a choice to go elsewhere and being acutely aware of that, and bad account management is being complacent and taking your client for granted. It's very important to be able to develop a rolling action programme and make sure as you go through so that you can see that you're making progress in the relationship. Then if you have an issue, you bottom it out and then you move on to the next thing; so there's a clear progression.

# Part VI

# Meeting the Customer's Needs

# 25

# Meeting the business needs – beyond benefits

We are now with the right customer, with the right contacts in front of us and the right team member beside us. Now all that remains is to ask the right questions, talk the right language, make sure they respect you and make a successful proposal. This is more than fancy presentations with slick PC-assisted slide shows. You need to get right to the heart of the customer's needs, going beyond mere benefits, giving it solutions, perhaps even satisfying its *total business experience*. These are fancy words, so what do they mean? Remember that first sales training event you ever went on, the one about *features* and *benefits*? Well, we need to start there, and then make a little progress besides. There are four stages that a company's sales approach might go through. This is not a preordained progression. Development over time will be the result of nurture, not nature. It is a development that takes time, patience and an understanding of where you are and where you are going. Of course, you may already be well beyond stage 1 or 2, but take time here just to be sure by checking against Table 25.1. KAM takes us beyond benefits to solutions, and beyond that to the 'total business experience'.

**Table 25.1**  *Stages of a sales approach*

|  | Stage 1 | Stage 2 | Stage 3 | Stage 4 |
|---|---|---|---|---|
| **The offer** | Features | Benefits | Solutions | Total business experience |
| **Customers** | All | Segmentation | Key account by types | Individual key accounts |
| **Sale approach** | Traditional 1:1 | Enhanced 1:1 | Partnership KAM – the team sell | Synergistic KAM team collaboration |
| **Competitive advantage** | Perhaps none | Specific benefits | Quality of solutions | Quality of relationships and key supplier status |
| **Supplier organization and focus** | Sales focus | Marketing focus | Customer focus | Total business experience focus |
| **Typical skills** | Journey planning | Questioning, selling benefits | KAM project management | Business management, strategic influencing |

# WHERE ARE YOU WITH YOUR CUSTOMERS?

Let's take as an example a bank providing commercial banking services:

- *Stage 1 – Take it, because that's what I'm offering and I know you want it…* You regard your customers as the same. You deliver a standard service. You talk 'features'. Your product is a standard transactional, savings and loans banking service with advice from the local bank manager on occasions.
- *Stage 2 – It's all in the presentation…* You uncover customer needs that allow you to present those features as relevant 'benefits'. The product or service remains much the same, perhaps with some minor cosmetic changes, but you recognize your customers as different from each other, expressed through customer segmentation. You segment your market, perhaps by transactional requirements. You recognize that there is a sector, for example local stores, that has particular cash-flow problems. You make small amendments to short-term credit terms to make it attractive to them.

- *Stage 3 – Tailored just for you…* You uncover a deeper set of needs. This gives you the opportunity to develop services that recognize the customer's individual needs. You present your offer as a tailored solution. You do this only for a small group of customers – your key accounts, perhaps even types of key account. For example, as a result of government policy to expand university education, you discover that universities need to borrow much more for building and other capital projects. You establish a team with specialist expertise in this sector to work with universities to find the best way to fund their expansion.

- *Stage 4 – Managing the customer's total business experience.* Working closely with a large customer you uncover a breadth of needs that allows you to understand the customer's values and aspirations in full. This is not just with regard to your offer – you understand their total business experience (TBE). Your tailored banking solutions are now designed to have a positive impact at all levels. Your customer regards you as more than a simple supplier; you now add value in many ways – you have achieved the status of key supplier. For example, you have worked in a close relationship with a global food manufacturer over many years. There is an intricate web of relationships between your organization and this business, and many of your managers have worked with this client for a long period. Indeed the client admits that in some areas your managers understand more about their business than they do. Your charges are partly linked to their results, and the profit that you make on this customer is closely connected to the customer's success.

The key to success here, in moving from stage to stage, is the ever-improving understanding of what your customer wants. Features tend to be supplier focused; benefits begin to consider the customer; solutions are about meeting requirements. But addressing the total business experience requires you to go beyond this, beyond expectations to anticipating customers' needs. You understand their aspirations, not just with regard to your products as a supplier, but also with regard to their entire business. You can help them achieve these aspirations. Corporate FS is a means to an end. For instance, a line of credit allows a business to expand.

## TBE in intermediated markets

An insurance company found that working closely on understanding the processes operating in a banking intermediary's relationship with its end-clients paid dividends. By going beyond the immediate relationship with the bank into understanding how it interacted with its end-customers across a wider range of relationships it became possible to map out improvements to the sales process. Through this understanding, the insurance company drew up a picture of how the bank could be at the centre of managing a number of different strands in the client relationship. The insurance company then worked with the bank to identify the internal obstacles to achieving this. Out of this it established a plan to overcome the obstacles in the processes. This involved working closely with relevant business teams within the bank to develop the referral generation process and in particular to ensure that the appropriate staff were equipped and motivated to do it. This meant changing the focus of several people's jobs quite significantly. The model for achieving referrals was at first created to solve a local problem within the bank, but proved so successful that it was extended across the organization. In fact the bank then recruited an extra 70 people to build the business using the model that had been created.

## TBE and value

Providing solutions and enhancements to the customer's TBE is an excellent way of moving the relationship away from price and squarely on to value, as described in Chapter 10. The debate over open-book trading (also Chapter 10) becomes less pressing, or at least it is no longer a threat to the good supplier. How many customers you can do this for will depend on your business and market, but it is unlikely to be more than a few. The importance of identifying true key accounts becomes even more apparent. Many of these TBE solutions will be giving customers competitive advantage compared to other of your customers. Can you therefore do it for all? Is there any point? Would the customer let you?

## THE CUSTOMER'S TOTAL BUSINESS EXPERIENCE

Sometimes we tell our customers what they need. Sometimes we are lucky and we get it right. But, *sometimes* isn't enough. We know that we have to learn to ask. But now we find some new problems:

- What if our customers don't know what they need?
- What if things are changing around them so fast that they can't see a clear way forward?
- What if the things they keep telling us they want are just what they think they *should* be saying? After all, everyone wants a lower price, a better product and slicker service.

When Alexander Graham Bell invented the telephone, he toured the USA, showing it off to businessmen. After one such session, an apparent enthusiast approached him: 'Mr Bell, I really like your new toy. It's my daughter's birthday party tomorrow and I would be very grateful if you would come along to show it.' Well, the great man was incensed: 'It is not a toy!' he exploded. 'Don't you realize that this will revolutionize communications and your business? Just think, with one of these you can talk to a customer 300 miles away.' The businessman thought for a moment and then answered: 'But, Mr Bell, I don't have any customers 300 miles away…' Of course this businessman could extend his business reach many times with this new technology.

Telling them isn't enough. But sometimes even asking your customer is not enough. Who knew that they needed Post-it notes before they were invented, or the internet, or a telephone, or even a computer? The job of the KA teams is to try to identify and understand what the customers might want (based on their latent needs) and then aim to provide it and to sell them the vision.

How do you gain this new insight? Benchmarking? Useful, but has **How to gain** everyone else seen the light? Anyway, we want competitive advantage, **insight** not a 'me too' solution. Market research? Of course, but asking traditional questions will get traditional answers. Yes, of course they want a lower price, a better product and slicker service: hardly an *insight*. Anyway, asking rational questions about needs that might be irrational has its limitations. Research sometimes doesn't tell the whole story. Ask any manager who buys FS why he or she chose a particular supplier. The answers will probably be very rational – value for money, product innovation, service support and all the rest, but this is probably not the whole truth. The truth of the matter is that the supplier chosen was the least likely to make him or her look foolish. It is their reputation that is on the line if something goes wrong and the risk of failure is an important dynamic. So it is important to get customer-intimate and to be able to see life from the customer's side of the desk. This is what you must do for your customers if you are to match their total business experience. Ask yourself the following of your customers:

- What are they trying to achieve? Is it a strategic or tactical move?
- Are they seeking to reduce costs by improving their processes? And why?
- Do they want to break into new markets? And why?
- Do they need additional support or services? And what might these be?
- For intermediated FS: Do they need to improve their service to their own customers? And how could you help them to achieve this?

Answer these sorts of questions and you are well on the way to uncovering what they *really* need and, from there, you are staring competitive advantage in the face.

**So, shouldn't we do market research at all?**

None of this argues against market research. Research is vital if we are to understand our customers and their needs. What this argues for is the *kind* of research required. In a KAM situation, when dealing with sophisticated organizations that talk of supply chains and value, and when you seek to go beyond benefits to solutions and enhancements to TBE, you need to research customers' motivations, aspirations and values. And beyond that, you must uncover the things that they didn't even know themselves. In intermediated markets this may require understanding their end-customers better than they do. Remember, customers can be lazy in that they seek the simplest solution to a problem. For customers, the simplest solution to many problems is to ask the supplier. Customers may find it difficult to articulate their desired total business experience; they may even lie to save themselves time, money or effort. It is the supplier's responsibility to avoid laziness itself and to understand its customers well enough to be able to articulate that experience for them and to argue for the appropriate activities to meet it, not just the simplest. The following chapter looks at one way of doing this and one way of structuring your market research – *positive impact analysis*.

# 26

# Positive impact analysis (PIA)

The purpose of this tool is to link deeper understanding of customer needs for value with a move to action. It asks what activities in your organization will result in *positive impact* on the customer's *total business experience*? The impact on the business experience varies according to whether your offer is aimed at the corporate customer or whether the key account is an intermediary. We will deal with each in the next two sections.

## IMPACT ANALYSIS FOR CORPORATE CUSTOMERS

Identifying the customer's total business experience (TBE) involves putting yourself in the customer's shoes and considering what it is like for the customer to do business with you at all stages of the relationship. You list all the activities your customer has to go through to do business with you and to achieve its TBE. This can be called a 'process chain' or a 'value chain'. You then try to understand everything that can go wrong at each stage, and what could make each stage a burden or a frustration. You then identify the activities that could have a positive effect on the customer's TBE. Of course, not all of these will work, nor should we seek to attempt them all, so we describe a screening and selection process, though remember that this stage of the process is a brainstorming one, expanding our horizons before narrowing in on our choice of activities.

**The business process review**

A bank has developed a simple consultancy product to analyse the day-to-day banking needs of its customers. This involves putting a cash manager, who is an expert on cash and processing, into the client for a couple of days. The service is offered to selective clients free of charge. Working with the finance director and finance team, the cash manager looks at money in, money out; information requirements; reconciliation requirements; how things are done within the organization; how they might like to improve things in the future, etc. At no cost to the customer the cash manager produces a report summarizing the situation and making recommendations for improvement. This service is appreciated by clients. It shows ways to work more effectively. The bank often uses it when the account is coming up for tender. It helps both sides understand what is really happening, aiding the bank in putting the tender together and the customer in evaluating it. It is also used in tendering for new business, where the process also has the benefit of establishing a relationship from the outset.

# IMPACT ANALYSIS FOR INTERMEDIARIES

## The value chain

At various points in this book we have referred to the idea of the value chain. This concept applies particularly in intermediated FS, in understanding the steps that your product or service goes through right up to the end-customer. As your sales approach moves towards solutions and beyond, the significance of the chain increases. The interface with end-customers may be a crucial point in the sales process, but historically many FS suppliers have been distanced from this, seeing customer contact as being 'the intermediary's responsibility'. Indeed intermediaries have often encouraged this view. The good news for most providers of FS through intermediaries is that, unlike the market chain for industrial raw materials, their market chain tends to be short – only one or two steps. So, researching the process through to the end-customer is straightforward. Also, suppliers of intermediated FS often have access to information through end-customer records required for administration and control. Obviously this information must be used sensitively and according to data protection legislation and to the constraints on direct customer contact specified by the intermediary.

## Products or solutions?

Where the supplier has a poor understanding of the steps in the customer's value chain, or perhaps only knows about a small portion of the chain, then the chances are that it is selling products, and only that. If, however, the supplier has a wider understanding, and has found how to influence the chain at many points, then the chances are that this supplier is selling solutions. Of course selling solutions requires joined-up thinking by the supplier. Often the left hand of a large FS supplier does not know what its right hand is doing, and there are in fact many positive influences, but nobody is joining them up into one coherent proposition.

### Getting 'inside the head' of an organization

A supplier of health insurance schemes has built its business by getting close to its end-customers in corporate schemes. The company works very hard to build and maintain a network of relationships in each corporate customer. This works at different levels in the chain, from the gatekeepers on whom it depends to get access to sites, through to local advocates with access to smaller groups. Through running advocates' events and meetings it adds value and gets extensive feedback on the products and service experienced by its end-customers.

## The total business experience through the chain

In dealing with intermediated businesses, the analysis of the total business experience takes on two dimensions. It demands understanding both of the intermediary's experience of dealing with you as a supplier and of the end-customer's experience. As we noted, access to end-customers depends on the relationship with the intermediary. In Chapter 3, we looked at the idea of the opportunity snail, a representation of how ideas develop in a business and how the practice of KAM seeks to penetrate into that process. In our example of an FS supplier selling through an intermediary we observed that if the supplier could gain access to the marketing people, it would enhance its opportunity to add value, gain competitive advantage and be seen as a strategic supplier. The problem was gaining access. Why should the marketing people want to see the product supplier? The idea of the value chain answers this question. Perhaps the best way to gain access to the marketing people at an early stage is to demonstrate your value to them. If as a product supplier you understand their end-customers' needs and preferences and if you can demonstrate this expertise, for example through providing research reports, then you might be invited into a dialogue to discuss future trends – the beginning of the opportunity snail.

# SCREENING AND SELECTING POSITIVE IMPACT ACTIVITIES

## Screening to focus your limited resources

You now have several *possible* activities that *might* make a positive impact on the customer's TBE. You cannot work on all at once and, anyway, no customer is likely to want them all at once. You need to screen them, selecting the priority actions. The following checklist of questions may be useful in undertaking this screening:

- Does it remove or reduce the problem?
- What value does the customer put on this?
- Does it impact on the customer's core values?
- What does it cost the customer – time, money, other?
- Would the customer pay for it as part of a service? If so, can you charge enough to cover cost, or make a premium?
- What will it cost you to provide?
- Can you secure your fair share of the value added to the market?
- Do you have the capability? If not, can you work with a partner to bring in the capability?

As a more general test of an idea, we might look for those that provide the best win-win outcome, which means that there is something in it for both sides. This is, after all, one of the tenets of working in partnership.

## Using a selection matrix for screening activities and projects

If the number of potential activities is large or complex, you may want to go further than asking the screening questions so as to identify the runners. You could use a modified version of the key account identification and selection matrix shown in Figure 21.1 (and included as a software package on the CD ROM attached to this book). The vertical axis will now be attractiveness to *us* of the project or activity, the horizontal one measuring the attractiveness of the activity or the project to the *customer*. As with the key account identification and selection matrix, each axis of this matrix is made up of several factors, which could include the checklist questions used in the screening process and any additional factors that apply in your own circumstances.

Attractiveness to _us_ might include:

- Will revenue earned (or protected) outweigh the costs to us?
- Do we have the capability? If not, can we develop it – is there a partner to provide the capability?
- Does it give us competitive advantage?
- Does it enhance our service to other customers or markets?
- Does it give us lock-in?

Attractiveness to the _customer_ might include:

- Does it reduce or remove a known problem?
- Does it impact on our (the customer's) core value drivers?
- Does it reduce risk?
- Is it of high value (using the customer's definition of value received)?
- Is it of low cost to us?

Use a similar weighting and rating system to the one described in Chapter 21 to complete the matrix. You can, of course, use the software package included in the CD ROM attached to this book. Projects in the top right-hand box are most likely to be progressed, those on the bottom left most likely to be dropped. When a project is in the top left-hand box, the next question to ask is: could this be made more attractive to the customer? It is important not to imagine attractions that do not really apply. Similarly, question projects on the bottom right: are they really so unattractive to you? If they benefit the customer so highly, can this also be turned to your advantage? It's not another excuse to lie to yourself; it's simply a double check.

# LOCK-IN

This is very important. Any supplier can do things of value to the customer, but do they bring sustainable competitive advantage? Improved financial terms are certainly of value to a customer, but easy for a competitor to match or surpass. Such added value is short-lived, the competitive advantage is not sustainable and, worse, it can start a price war. Sustainable competitive advantage comes from activities that encourage loyalty and that competitors cannot match without costly effort. _Buying_ loyalty rarely works. The secret of lock-in is to find an activity or service that customers value and would rather not perform themselves, that the competitor doesn't offer and that doesn't involve handing the supplier too much power. It is a delicate balance – lock-in implies supplier power, and suppliers should tread carefully. In certain cases, lock-in may be encouraged by legislation, as for instance in the case of tied agencies in the UK life insurance market, where suppliers had to make the connection (and so lack of choice) very clear to consumers. In other cases, legislation forbids suppliers from tying in their intermediaries, so as to ensure independent advice for the consumer.

In FS it can be hard to lock customers in with product features because of the ease of copying. It is usually impossible to patent a new idea in FS! It is probably most effective where systems and other support are provided that would take a lot of time and effort for the buying organization either to set up themselves or to switch to another supplier.

**Hooking in like Velcro**

The most effective lock-in for many FS suppliers is where the relationship is intimately connected at different levels: the classic diamond-type relationship, where the different connections between the organizations can be seen to hook together like Velcro. To keep the relationship alive and well the supplier should be consistently adding value at all levels of contact, for example adding value by analysing data that come out of the process and making improvement recommendations. This situation can often be planned right from the initial sales pitch by thinking through how you might make it difficult for the customer to disengage. So from the initial pitch, you are stating that as part of the relationship you will do these added-value things – a more holistic approach than the traditional 'Look at us, we're good guys and we're cheap!'

## GAINING A SHARE OF THE VALUE

You do a thorough PIA, select an activity and come up with an innovative approach that adds much value to your customer's business. Will you get your fair share of the added value in the market? Of course, one of the PIA questions was just this, but how to judge? If you supply to the 'owners' of an intermediary market, then your definition of 'fair' may have to be modified. 'Owners' tend to get the lion's share. However, that doesn't make it a bad move because it secures your position with that 'owner'. You might consider that good value. Your best chance of getting a fair share is by doing the analysis ahead of customer demands. If you wait for them to ask, the potential reward from your activity diminishes. By being proactive and by offering solutions to problems your customers are only just becoming aware of, you increase your chances of *fair* reward.

# Gaining advantage or avoiding disadvantage?

The PIA process helps identify those activities that add most value to your customer's business. Some may be unique to you, the _differentiators_, and they provide a real source of competitive advantage. However, do not think that all added-value ideas have to be big and bold, and that small, nitty-gritty activities are too mundane to be worth anything. While big ideas may well gain you advantage, you must not suffer disadvantage by failing to attend to the smaller, everyday things. Here we might identify another class of activities called the _givens_. These are the things that must be in place for business to be carried out. Avoiding disadvantage is as important as gaining advantage, and may well involve focus on more mundane activities. Ensuring, for instance, that invoices are raised in a way that meets the customer's needs will rarely win you the account, but it may well help secure your position, and failing to do it will certainly lead to your disadvantage against those who can. It is surprising, and worrying, just how much of the short discussion time available to seller and buyer can be occupied by such shortcomings. The customer may be reluctant to listen to your ideas for adding value if it feels you are letting it down on everyday matters. Failure to attend to them leads to a perpetual round of catch-up and fire-fighting that saps a supplier's energy and dulls a customer's enthusiasm.

By understanding the customer's _total business experience_, and by looking at ways to make a _positive impact_ on that experience, you identify activities that gain you advantage (the differentiators), and those that help you avoid disadvantage (the givens). List them separately and pay close attention to the givens, if you think they might be ignored in all the excitement! As outlined in Chapter 8 the customer's total business experience in FS will be formed by factors such as the reliability of the service provided; the responsiveness of the supplier in dealing with problems; the degree of accountability on the part of the supplier's employees; the level of empathy and trust built up over time; and the level of proactiveness. This last point may cover a wide range of initiatives from improving processes and procedures to the benefit of the customer at one end of the spectrum through to coming up with new business ideas at the other. A strategy to cover these factors must combine both givens and differentiators – the result will be a very powerful package indeed.

# Adding value by removing features

It is easy think, 'To add value you must always do more', but sometimes less really _is_ more. Understanding the customer's TBE and market value chain allows us to ask what elements of its experience with us are valued most (some perhaps hugely so) and what parts valued least (perhaps not at all)? If elements of the experience are not valued at all, they may represent unnecessary costs in the customer's eyes, so why not remove them? The result is a stripped-down offer that truly meets the customer's value needs, with lower costs as well.

# SOME HINTS ON USING POSITIVE IMPACT ANALYSIS

- Involve a cross-functional team so each member sees a different part of the customer relationship, the value chain and thus the different opportunities.
- Establish PIA as a focal part of team membership, with a responsibility on each member to 'fill in the gaps'.
- Use PIA as a means of uncovering gaps in your knowledge and as a spur to further research.
- If possible, involve the customer (but take care not to build unrealistic expectations).
- Examine the value chain from the customer's perspective, covering all stages of its involvement with you.
- Identify activities that are 'givens' as distinct from 'differentiators'.
- Ensure the 'givens' are in place.
- Seek out options for competitive advantage through the 'differentiators'.
- Be open-minded about the need to work with partners.
- For each screening question, set parameters for good, OK and bad.
- Use it to establish priorities: A, B, C activities.
- Use it to determine project teams.
- Repeat the exercise regularly, backed up by market research, customer surveys and customer involvement.
- Once the PIA is complete, you will be in a much better position to select the package of activities required, thus moving from analysis to action:
  - identify the projects;
  - create the project teams.

# 27

# Key account management and the e-revolution

*Much of this chapter is based on the work of Spottiswoode and El Marouani (2002) and Jerome (2002).*

The US Department of Commerce defines e-commerce to include all forms of business transaction through electronic means (Hamilton and Hewer, 2000). It is a broad definition, covering many possible delivery channels including the telephone, mobile phone and more. E-commerce involves applying a wide range of technologies to streamline business interactions. This includes the use of the internet, e-mail, advanced telephone systems, interactive televisions, mobile phones and hand-held digital appliances. Because technology and delivery mechanisms are developing all the time, it is best to define e-commerce as covering various ways of doing business electronically, rather than define it narrowly in terms of particular delivery methods. Whatever the exact definition, e-commerce is rapidly becoming central to commerce in general. E-business is not just about the World Wide Web, but about exploiting e-business technologies to enhance shareholder return by:

- transforming key processes to compete in new, faster, better ways including via multi-channels;
- breaking traditional business model paradigms;
- creating and leveraging brand experiences;

- optimizing interactions with all stakeholders;
- leveraging knowledge to establish sustainable competitive advantage.

(Spottiswoode and El Marouani, 2002)

# THE IMPACT OF THE E-REVOLUTION ON FS

In Chapter 1 we considered why financial services are special. We stressed the effect of technology. FS companies are in an increasingly turbulent environment. Developments in technology have a major effect on delivery of FS. New electronic delivery systems are cheaper than traditional channels such as branches and sales forces. The internet is usually more cost-effective than the telephone. However, the effect of technological developments on FS is far-reaching and not just cost related. The following summary of the impact of e-commerce on FS is adapted from the work of Spottiswoode and El Marouani (2002).

## New distribution channels

New distribution channels are created through pervasive technologies, which allow customers to be reached anywhere, from anywhere. E-business also facilitates disintermediation, bypassing existing agency and intermediary networks, and can disrupt existing value chains. However, FS intermediaries have also adopted these technologies successfully to take advantage of the same value chain disruption.

## New markets

Once a brand has established a significant online following, new markets can be reached and others can be created. FS sites enjoy the luxury of strong repeat business: if companies use a little imagination, it is not too difficult to divert regular retail site visitors to a financial section.

## New business models

E-business enables direct, simultaneous interaction between all value chain parties – buyers, sellers, information providers, regulators, etc. This can create disruptive business models such as e-market places. We see the most radical impact in the capital markets business, where intense competition has accelerated e-business adoption. Much capital market trading is by nature virtual. Expensive brokers are being disintermediated by real-time e-matching of bids and quotes followed by automated trading. The stock trading value chain has collapsed, accompanied by a loss of millions of revenue from the brokers and market makers who used to hold sway.

## Transparent market places

In its ultimate incarnation, the World Wide Web offers unlimited information about an unlimited number of products and services to the entire population of the world. Where this is applied to virtual products, such as banking services, loans or stock trades, the entire value chain becomes transparent. Buyers access real-time information on current options and prices, interest rates and commission charges, and at any time select the most advantageous deal. In a transparent market, only the fittest will survive: only those suppliers with the most responsive products and service coupled with the lowest cost bases will be able to compete.

## E-CRM

Electronic interactions with customers are by nature 100 per cent computer recorded. Every customer action can be tracked, yielding far more information about customers than was available in the past. Coupled with the 'deep computing' capabilities of modern technology is the capability in theory for companies, consumers and key decision makers within companies to be analysed and targeted on a one-to-one basis in a way never possible hitherto.

## Reduced costs and improved service

E-business can support lower prices by cutting operational costs, while enabling better customer service and product flexibility. E-business's impact is not just at the point of customer sales and service. Virtually every process in a financial institution can be made much more effective and efficient through e-automation, knowledge management and self-service. This implementation of 'straight-through processing' is probably the most powerful but perhaps least understood, most under-exploited area of e-business in the FS arena.

# THE E-REVOLUTION AND KAM

The e-revolution is also at the heart of the KAM revolution. Without e-mail, the communications required to deal with complex global accounts would be hard to manage. Today, many software packages facilitate the management of customer contacts; make customer information available to global teams and analyse that information to identify patterns and opportunities; or help measure customer profitability. In dealing with both corporate and intermediary sectors, the use of call centres or the internet or a combination of the two has often taken over from physical calls. Technology has provided new tools for FS suppliers in managing their key accounts, through automated services and remote servicing and support. This means day-to-day personal contacts have diminished, so technological developments have had a significant impact on the nature of relationships with customers. While customer relationships will inevitably change, it is not inevitable that they will be managed more effectively. This chapter helps you consider how the varied aspects of the e-revolution could be harnessed in support of your KAM strategy.

# STEPS IN THE REVOLUTION

How should you make the most of the new opportunities? As ever, how technology is used very much depends on the customer. Does it want to work collaboratively with you? At the risk of being supplier focused rather than customer focused, we might identify five stages through which a supplier can make use of the e-revolution:

1. promotion;
2. efficient service and transactions;
3. locking the customer into your systems and processes;
4. acquiring customer information and knowledge;
5. customization.

These are not in chronological order, nor independent of each other.

## Promotion

Providing information to your customers has never been easier. Indeed, they no longer need to ask. They simply visit your website to access the sort of things that would once have been the subject of long conversations. This is far more than promotion on your part – it is an opportunity for dialogue. Indeed, customers will not thank you for subjecting them to a promotional barrage when all they want is access to information. Company websites should be designed so that customers can find what they want readily and be encouraged (because it will be to their benefit) to enter into dialogue with you. Denying them the full information so they have to ask is one way to do this, but rather clumsy, transparent in its self-interest and ultimately damaging! Given the potential for a valuable conversation, it is sad to see how poorly so many companies use the medium. Constructing the website is often a job for junior members of the team or of the IT department, whose grasp of HTML and the like might be fine but who have little experience in the business of customer relations. For key accounts you should go beyond a simple website, allowing them direct access to your own systems. You might provide an extranet, where key accounts can access information that is too sensitive (or valuable) for open access. This might include details on contacts within the key account team, product details, specifications, technical information, legal and compliance information, or access to training programmes. Access to an extranet will go further than promotion or the provision of information – it encourages self-service and a dialogue that brings the customer closer to you.

## Opportunities for efficient service and transactions

Technology has revolutionized day-to-day administration and transactions in many financial services. Funds can be moved electronically; products can be applied for with customer details entered electronically; progress on loan applications can be monitored electronically. One of the main aims of FS suppliers taking advantage of technology is to become easy to do business with. This requires an intimate understanding of customer needs, including why they use the technology and any support and training needed. With automation, both the supplier's and corporate or intermediary customers' costs should be less in the longer term, but closely managing the transition is required if 'teething troubles' are not to poison the relationship.

## Opportunities for locking the customer into your systems and processes

Automation of transactions between the suppliers and corporate or intermediary customers does not necessarily imply that they are seamlessly processed by either. Incompatible systems and processes create the need for manual intervention, such as retyping information across internal systems. The ultimate prize of e-business is to create a seamless, transparent process across the value chain, transforming internal organizational processes and radically reducing costs. Most businesses have some way to go in achieving this state.

The more suppliers' systems are integrated into those of individual customers or customer networks, the greater the cost to the customer of switching to alternative suppliers. This is not limited to those involved in developing new systems, but also covers retraining staff and adapting existing processes.

## Opportunities for acquiring customer information and knowledge

Knowledge about customers is traditionally stored in everything from card index files to the salesperson's head. Some ways are more reliable than others, but all suffer from two problems: how to get the information back out, and how to do anything constructive with it. CRM (customer relationship management) systems bring together information from many contacts between supplier and customer. Although many supplier/customer interactions are electronic, this should apply also to face-to-face meetings. Modern multimedia contact centres, by their 'one-stop shop' nature, are good places to gather such information and to access it from one point – despite its many forms, which might include text, voice and document images. Every interaction with customers may yield information about their needs, their buying behaviour, their perceptions, their concerns and their frustrations.

This should be a good basis for improving service. However, many KAM and CRM initiatives have failed to deliver improved customer service and indeed in some cases have been to the detriment of customer service. This is because many organizations do not recognize that customer care is a business-wide issue, not the sole preserve of IT experts or software vendors. As the complexity and sophistication of data capture and analytical techniques increase, customer care may be shifted towards the IT experts. KAM and CRM are facilitators, but their systems and processes should never be allowed to become the controllers. A strategic approach to KAM and CRM should recognize the requirement to operate holistically across the organization. This means changes to processes, structures and management, and staff roles. For the KAM the potential for increased understanding of customers is huge, but realizing the potential is not easy.

## Opportunities for customization

Perhaps the most exciting application of new technology for the KAM is in using it to drive the design of the offer itself. The relative efficiency of e-commerce and the information won through KAM and CRM bring the realistic prospect of segmenting markets based on the needs of major customers. The supplier that best understands its customers and has the most flexible systems and processes is best placed to offer such customization. Of course customization can be at the expense of operational efficiency, so you need to balance the benefit of tying in business with a large corporate client or intermediary with the costs of doing so. However, in an increasingly competitive market, customization may be justified by the gain in competitive advantage.

# THE STRATEGIC APPROACH TO E-BUSINESS

The e-revolution has such an important role to play in FS in general and KAM in particular. A strategic approach is needed. E-commerce cannot be approached piecemeal. Let's work it through. This section is adapted from the work of Jerome (2002).

## Vision and direction

This is all about understanding what the business wants to do, understanding what competitors and potential competitors are doing, understanding what is possible and also what might soon be possible. This establishes the basis for positioning the business. The starting point is the current situation and likely future trends in the FS industry, future trends in technology and new business models. This information is then used to construct the 'business landscape'. This analysis sets the scene in which the FS provider company is operating and relates this to needs of its key accounts. It will enable reasoned thought to take place before setting vision, mission and goal statements, by describing what is happening in the industry and what is possible. It includes analysis to understand where competitors are and what options are possible.

Once the 'business landscape' is established, a more detailed analysis of competitors and the way they go to market will be required. Intelligence on competitors is available from many sources, but can be time consuming to assemble. One option is to use a company that regularly collects and analyses information from annual reports, analyst and shareholder statements, press comments, etc. This is 'secondary' information – it has already been collected and analysed. This establishes what the general competitive environment is like. For more specific information on products and services and segmentation used by competitors, you may need to run focus groups or surveys and ask the participants specific questions about their experience of competitive offerings.

Leading e-business companies invest in research to understand what is happening today, what is influencing the future and what may be possible in the future, and hence make projections on what the future will look like. For e-business strategy in FS, trends in the FS industry and in technology should be combined with understanding the business landscape and segmentation, to create a strategic vision. This is then translated into mission and goals, providing the basis for the next component of the strategy – a positioning for the company that has unique, sustainable competitive advantage.

# Positioning

This relates to selecting a positioning that addresses the business vision. Positioning gives a framework to define the value proposition and capabilities needed to deliver it. A systematic approach is needed that considers the combination of all products and services, segments and channels and then makes trade-offs to sustain profitability and advantage. The decisions on the optimum combinations of channels, segments and products must be based on an understanding of customer wants and needs and the supplier's current position. If we review the supplier positioning matrix introduced in Chapter 9, we can consider these different supplier circumstances. To remind you of the four positions, Figure 27.1 reproduces the matrix.

*Figure 27.1    Supplier positioning*

If you occupy the 'tactical make easy' box the strategy is straightforward. Here, e-commerce is an exercise in making it easy to do business and removing costs. This is where much of the activity was at the end of the 20th century as FS companies sought to get the benefits of automation and centralization to provide service at lower cost. Other opportunities for using e-commerce occur in the 'tactical profit' quadrant. The internet has opened up the FS industry to intense competition. Information can be accessed through search engines and aggregation services. Potential customers can identify low-cost suppliers from across the world in a way that was not possible before. Access to suppliers by the means of e-commerce allows customers to look for the best offers, and access to customers gives suppliers an outlet for those offers. The internet opens up new customers, from the unvisited to the unknown, even to the 'unconsidered'. If you occupy the 'strategic partner' or 'strategic security' box, then more advanced forms of e-commerce (perhaps in the form of access to extranets) provide the means to achieving far more intimate systems of supplier/customer communication. E-commerce in this case is much more about adding value through collaborative relationships. If customer experience is weak, a combined channel strategy allows you to optimize costs and benefits across channels.

# Corporate governance

Another critical area to consider in an e-business strategy is corporate governance. This addresses how the products and services will be administered and controlled through the multiple channels and the interactions ('touch points') with the selected customer segments. This has been one of the biggest failure areas for internet companies. These companies often have an excellent sales proposition, but cannot deliver products effectively or handle queries or complaints. In the FS industry, this is often shown through a lack of knowledge of the customer or status of customer activities when passing between channels, as well as problems when addressing complaints. Few banks or insurance companies today can claim to have a fully coordinated multi-channel strategy across traditional and electronic channels. Your governance model needs to address this. It also needs to address the upstream and downstream interfaces in the value system.

# Value proposition

This is about creating a sustainable value proposition for your customers. To be sustainable, it must be hard to copy and flexible enough to pre-empt or respond to competitive moves. Options include:

- exploiting electronic channels alongside traditional channels;
- designing straight-through processes (STPs) that run through the organization and that require electronic facilities to control workflow;
- providing good-quality KAM and/or CRM in all interactions with the customer;
- exploiting technology to create and sustain the choice of segmentation;
- measuring profitability;
- generating flexible products and features using technology to reduce the time to market.

Pricing strategy is important. Value pricing allows for the value provided to the customer. An important consideration in pricing is the balance between the various channels to be able to achieve the optimum cost structure while still providing excellent customer interaction. Creation of the pricing part of the strategy allows a pricing model to be developed that can be used to test different pricing options. The price points generated need to be verified against the customer wants and needs and competitive analyses.

Another value proposition is the 'channel experience blueprint'. This describes the experience a customer will have in using the various channels. Different blueprints are needed for each segment and service, showing interactions across each possible channel. This shows how the value proposition is provided across channels. It is one of the best methods of avoiding the problems of uncoordinated channels in a multi-channel proposition.

## Capabilities required

This involves identifying the capabilities that support the value proposition and the enablers to implement the capabilities. Trends in the FS industry, trends in technology and trends in business models all help to identify the capabilities that will be required. Enablers include business processes, technology, organization or knowledge and can be a combination of all four. The capabilities and their associated enablers then become the key design points (KDPs) used to specify design of the business processes, organization and change management, IT functionality, IT infrastructure and knowledge management. Once all of the KDPs have been identified they must be prioritized according to the contribution each KDP makes to the e-business value proposition. KDPs with similar priority are grouped, as the first step in breaking the implementation into phases. The business, organization, technology and knowledge enablers must be prioritized next, on cost and complexity to implement. Trade-offs can be made between the different enablers. For example, if some IT functionality is particularly hard or costly to implement, it may be possible to use a process work-around instead. If some business skills are in short supply, it may be necessary to use a modified organizational design to optimize access to available skills. The deliverable from this capabilities component of the strategy is a comprehensive KDP document describing the priorities and enablers needed to implement the e-business value proposition. It is also the base that ensures that each initiative, whether following a process, organization, IT or knowledge work stream, will be consistent with each other work stream.

## Implementation plan

This component of the strategy is about creating a comprehensive plan that is consistent across work streams during implementation. It includes initiatives for each work stream, including a strategic roadmap, technology plans to implement the solutions, marketing plans and regulation and compliance plans. The latter are a critical component for e-business strategies as the mechanisms to achieve compliance or gain regulatory approval can be long, whereas e-business implementations are normally short. The business case is also put together here. If the value proposition is well designed, making trade-offs to achieve a sustainable strategy, then the business case should be straightforward, as all the benefits will be traceable back to the original vision. Further trade-offs on costs may be needed if some enablers are unacceptably costly to develop or operate. This is achieved by further actions on the KDPs, ensuring that changes to enablers are assessed for impact on other work streams.

The implementation plan component also includes the governance model for the strategic programme, identifying roles and responsibilities for implementing the e-business strategy, a communications plan and the change management approach. Creating implementation plans for an e-business strategy is similar to creating such plans for a traditional strategy. The difference is in the information used. Each previous component of the strategy contributes to building comprehensive knowledge of what is needed to implement the vision and value proposition. Implementing an e-business strategy demands more coordination between all the work streams and the plans need to reflect this. An e-business strategy will fail if the business process, technology, organization and knowledge work streams are not all kept aligned throughout the implementation.

# THE E-REVOLUTION AND THE ROLE OF THE KAM

The strategic approach described above is designed to help an FS organization plan its e-strategy. The plans for individual key accounts should be incorporated into this process. The development and subsequent use of technology in dealing with corporate and intermediary accounts may have a big effect on how KAMs work in most FS companies, through both sales and service. In the corporate sector, technology can add value to the offer to customers and the KAM role may require a high degree of involvement in developing and implementing a strategic approach to the way that technology is used, as described in the previous section. While the application of technology and centralized support through call centres can impose greater consistency and control over how an account is managed, it also has implications for the distancing of relationships between customer and supplier. The weakness of less informal contact may be that intuitive understanding between individuals is lost and new business opportunities are missed. The effective KAM will of course work at the strategic level to ensure that this is not the case, through jointly developing strategic plans with the customer and ensuring that knowledge is gathered from all touch points between the two organizations.

In the intermediary sector, if brokers can use FS companies' extranets to access and share information on new product launches, plan promotions and gain approvals on below-the-line activity, this affects the role of the

KAM. Conflict between supplier and intermediary can lead to a co-dependent but uneasy relationship between them, requiring significant collaboration, whilst recognizing mutual competitiveness (Moffett *et al*, 2002). However, in the e-world closer cooperation is often required between suppliers and intermediaries, necessitating sharing of large amounts of information on both sides. This may require a big change of mindset in some FS companies, where their relationship with third parties is more adversarial, based on controlling or drip-feeding of information, rather than partnership and open data sharing. This may be culturally difficult for both organizations and requires a planned and long-term approach by the KAM.

# 28

# Making the proposal

## PROPOSALS ARE OPPORTUNITIES TO SHOW YOU HAVE LISTENED

At all stages of the key account relationship, you need to present proposals. At the early stages these demonstrate your understanding of the customer's needs and your suitability as providers of assistance. Resist boasting about your scale, abilities or ambitions. As the relationship develops towards the partnership and synergistic stages, those presentations become less formal – the customer's need to 'test' you against competition declines and the focus is on specific projects. However, this should not lead to complacency on your part. Nowhere is the cliché 'familiarity breeds contempt' better demonstrated than here. However close the relationship, remember that the customer can break it at a moment's notice – although of course its ability to do this depends on the difficulty of setting up alternative systems and administrative arrangements.

Each time you need to make a proposal – a new product launch, a pitch for a greater share of the business or whatever – ask these questions:

1.  Is the customer open to change?
2.  How does your proposal stack up against the alternatives?
3.  How should you put the case?

# OPEN TO CHANGE?

In Chapter 18 we examined the change equation (see Figure 28.1) as a tool for assessing how to influence and manage change in our own organization. This tool is also applicable to dealings with the customer. Let's say we wish our customers to replace an existing service, provided by us, with a new, higher-grade, higher-price version.

*Figure 28.1* *The change equation*

## Does the customer have any dissatisfaction with the status quo?

If so, who and where? Perhaps the customer's function that you deal with is happy with existing arrangements and certainly does not want to entertain price increases. You must look elsewhere, perhaps to the users, who have been finding some problems with the existing service. Prepare a summary of recent complaints or an estimate of the costs of recent problems in the customer's process. (This is, of course, a delicate affair; you are detailing a catalogue of problems with your own service – only a good idea if you have a solution!) Perhaps everyone is happy? Then the future is your only hope – might the existing service have limitations and limit the options for your customer in the future? Perhaps the market may be changing and what might be acceptable today may become undesirable tomorrow.

## Does the customer share your vision for the potential future?

Don't be too sure about this. Remember the problems Alexander Graham Bell (Chapter 25) had with his telephone. Find out how your customers think before making big assertions about how things will be in the future. Perhaps you believe that the market is about to change. Perhaps the customer has plans to make fundamental changes to its own systems and processes that you are not aware of. This kind of information is priceless and can be embarrassing if you are not aware of the full circumstances!

## Does the customer see some first practical steps?

Can you make the transition to the new service painless? Can you provide assistance with systems development and training?

## Is all of this greater than the cost of change?

This depends on where you stand in the customer's organization. For some members of the DMU, it may be more compelling than others. This, of course, calls on the art of selling to the organization (Chapters 23 and 24).

# PROPOSAL ANALYSIS

The change equation helps you assess how your proposal may be received, compared to the buyer's simplest choice – doing nothing. We must now look at how it might stack up against a competitive offer.

## Do you have a competitive advantage in the customer's eyes?

The proposal analysis provides a simple means of making this comparison and then judging where your relative strengths and weaknesses lie. This will be vital when you come to presenting your case or defending yourself against competitors' claims. The example in Table 28.1 assumes that you are trying to sell a credit card service that an organization will offer to its own customer base. Your company offers to own-brand all communications with the organization's end-customers and you are also able to offer sophisticated analysis of these end-customers' characteristics and transactional behaviour. Your competitor is not prepared to offer such extensive own-branding or customer analysis. However, it does offer a differentiated gold card option and a slightly better percentage margin. To ensure that you consider all of your customer's needs (and not just the ones that we think our proposal stacks up well against), we have categorized needs into performance, financial, other and the total business experience. Once the needs are determined, score your proposal in comparison to the competitor's, with a score of two meaning the proposal meets the need well, a score of one meaning it is OK and zero meaning it is poor or doesn't meet the need at all.

Consider the members of the DMU. Might there be differences of need or opinion? Can you find a proposal that suits all requirements? Note a particular interest with X, or XX for *very* significant. In the example in

**Table 28.1**  *Proposal rating*

| Customer's Needs | Your Proposal | Competitor's Proposal | DMU Member, Finance | DMU Member, Marketing |
|---|---|---|---|---|
| **Performance** | | | | |
| Degree of own-branding available | 2 | 1 | | XX |
| Gold card available | 0 | 2 | | X |
| Analysis of end-customer data | 2 | 1 | | XX |
| Low interest rate | 1 | 1 | X | X |
| **Financial** | | | | |
| Margin offered | 1 | 2 | XX | X |
| Set-up costs | 1 | 2 | XX | X |
| **Other** | | | | |
| N/A | N/A | | | |
| **Total business experience** | | | | |
| Good overall deal | 2 | 2 | XX | XX |
| **Total score** | **9** | **11** | | |

Table 28.1, for simplicity we have included just two DMU members: finance and marketing. In real life there will be many more interested parties! So far, it doesn't look too good for your proposal. If the buyer were a computer, you would have lost on points. Fortunately, the buyer is human. You have some choices:

1. Argue with the customer's assessment – 'But you're wrong; ours is a far better offer!' Rarely a good idea.
2. Downgrade the competitor's offer – 'But do you really believe their service promises...?' An even worse idea – this can result in the customer defending the competitor.
3. Raise the importance of those needs where your offer shows a clear strength. The best plan by far.

There are many ways to do this, but let's consider two.

# Consider the DMU

Are there any issues or needs where your offer can satisfy all, or most, of the important members of the DMU? Are there points in your offer that provide a compromise for different members of that DMU? In our example, the willingness to analyse end-customer data on the cardholders is valued by marketing but not by finance. Perhaps there is an opportunity to demonstrate to the finance decision maker the potential longer-term benefits and financial return from understanding the end-customers better, for example through better understanding of risk; ability to be more selective based on potential consumer value; or pricing differentially for profit. A plan could be drawn up showing how the resulting better customer segmentation would decrease direct marketing costs and improve the ability to find and retain more profitable consumers, also achieving cross-sell of other products. In this way you might overcome the objections of finance and tip the balance of the decision.

# Questioning strategy

The best propositions are rarely lectures. Questions lie at the heart of persuasion and are key to building partnerships. Prepare questions and statements that will help you raise the importance, in the customer's view, of those needs where your proposal makes the strongest case. This is a four-part questioning strategy:

1. Understand the customer's strategy fully. What is it trying to achieve in the long term by offering the credit card to its end-customers?
2. Uncover potential or existing problems and issues. How successful has the customer been in cross-selling FS products to its end-customers in the past? Does it have sufficient expertise in this area?
3. Expand the concerns about those problems or issues. What concerns does it have about negative reactions from its customers to this initiative?
4. Suggest possible solutions. Highlight actions that might be taken to prevent end-customer dissatisfaction, for instance offering to clean up the customer's database records effectively.

This is, of course, a great simplification of a questioning process that might take some time. Increase the complexity of the sale and this is a process that might extend over several meetings.

Proposal analysis and the subsequent questioning strategies are best regarded as tools for planning. In front of the customer, take great care not to be seen as laying traps. Moreover, in the heat of debate, questions are never answered as you hoped. The conversation never runs to script. Planning and preparation help point you in the right direction, to see the customer's perspective, consider alternatives and be fast on your feet – great advantages for anyone selling FS.

# 29

# Selling to the individual

In the previous chapter, we considered selling a credit card deal to an organization for its end-customers. On an initial assessment, giving points for performance against identified needs, we lost – and yet we might have made the sale based on a more thorough assessment of what individuals in the buying organization were trying to achieve. Making the sale is partly down to sales technique, but more importantly to recognition that we sell to human beings, not computers. Our drive towards KAM; the technical features of the product or service; the complexity of the customer's DMU; the importance of the sale – these are just a few things that can make us forget one truth about selling, one that has not changed since selling began: customers are human. What do we conclude from this? Not that we can confuse, pressure or propagandize them. Remember, with KAM, you develop more intimate relationships, and increase mutual trust, confidence and security (Chapter 9). Put simply, a key factor for a successful relationship is rapport between selling and buying companies.

The next few pages raise the importance of the issue of rapport and introduce some basic concepts. Fuller coverage is available in various excellent books or, best of all, through training focused on the interpersonal skills of selling (see Chapter 32 for suggestions). When you consider the training needs of KA team members, expect to find 'improve interpersonal skills' a high priority. If the team has members with little previous direct customer contact, but with a strong background in a function based on 'logical process flows' (systems, operations, administration, etc), then expect this priority to be number one. The hardest lesson for non-salespeople to learn (and, for that matter, a few salespeople as well) is that the customer does not always make decisions for logical, let alone rational, reasons.

# LOGIC OR EMOTION?

Most decisions taken in business are taken for 'emotional' reasons. The purchase of a financial service is often a very complex process. The decision may take months, maybe years, involving many people from the buying organization and from various potential suppliers. Even once a decision is made, there may be a long process of determining specific needs and tailoring the supplier's offer. The key decision maker might deal with the chosen supplier over several years. In such circumstances, how far will the key decision maker proceed with a potential supplier that he or she cannot trust, feels uncomfortable with or just doesn't like? Research has shown that, when customers change suppliers, while one might expect the key reasons to be better products or prices elsewhere, the real reasons are human. The biggest killer of relationships is a supplier that shows indifference to customer's needs, problems or complaints. Buying decisions, or making the sale, result from activity on several levels, as discussed in Part V:

- meeting the business needs;
- meeting the personal needs;
- understanding how the organization operates and makes its buying decisions.

Many experienced salespeople would argue that it is the second of these, the personal needs, that makes all the difference. Non-salespeople may find this hard to accept. Consider this situation. Two companies offer the same product, a commodity. The specification is identical, the price the same and the service offered matches. How does the customer decide? Various factors come into play:

- Previous experience of either supplier – good or bad.
- Treatment received from the suppliers during the sale.
- Who does the customer trust?
- Who does the customer like?

In each of these factors, the personal rapport between supplier and key decision maker makes the difference. Consider two banks offering complex solutions to business problems. To develop an appropriate package, the suppliers need to understand the customer in depth, to identify with a series of needs, across different departments and functions. Which supplier is more likely to identify these needs, the arrogant supplier or the supplier that strikes up a personal rapport during a series of contacts? In Chapter 26 we included an example of the use of a business process review by a bank as a way of establishing relationships.

# ENSURING RAPPORT

So, how do you ensure that contacts with your customer are enhanced by personal rapport? The training of all team members in interpersonal skills will be a top priority. Make sure that all members of your KA team recognize the importance of rapport and actually _believe_ in its value. No book will do this for you – hence the limited aims of this chapter. This is a job for training. The themes below are all important in developing attitudes and behaviours that ensure rapport – and don't expect to convince your team just by asserting these points – you need to train them:

- Persuasion skills are much less about objectives and logic and much more about personal feelings.
- The best persuaders recognize three key needs: to focus on the personal needs of others; to persuade through involvement; to earn the right to proceed.
- Earning the right to proceed comes as much from being liked and trusted as it does from being regarded as an expert.
- Sellers with great skills of 'projection' achieve nothing without corresponding skills of 'empathy' with their customers.
- The best sellers speak as little as possible and, when they do, it is to ask a question.
- The best sellers listen to the answers.
- The customers' perceptions matter as much if not more than the facts of the matter.
- Understanding what makes your customers tick, that is, what motivates them personally, is the key to rapport, giving you the opportunity to mould your style to meet their perceptions.

There are many tools for analysing buyer behaviour, personal motivation and the like. The best are the practical ones – they may not be perfect from the point of view of a psychoanalyst, but they provide a KA team with a shorthand for discussing the customer, the members of the DMU and the best way to approach individuals.

# CHEMISTRY

Getting chemistry right is very important. At the 'bow-tie' phase of KAM, the relationship is largely between two individuals, and the supplier often puts forward its trained chameleon, the salesperson. Once we arrive at the partnership 'diamond' relationship, the contacts are numerous and you might not expect every individual to have the same interpersonal skills as that trained salesperson. Training these team members is important, but so is planning for good personal chemistry. Choosing who should see whom might be as much about who will get on with whom as it might be about professional or functional expertise. What makes personal chemistry? Accepting all those marriages made up of complete opposites, the usual route to chemistry and rapport is a matching of outlooks and attitudes. People driven by ambition usually get along best with like-minded souls – those who just want to get through life might frustrate them or leave them cold. Those who thrive in the company of others will seek out similarly sociable animals.

# GETTING MOTIVATION RIGHT

Key accounts are important, relationships are vital and chemistry matters. So do you select your KAMs and teams simply (or primarily) based on geographical location? One of the best tools is that developed by David McClelland, used to examine how people are motivated to interact with colleagues, particularly when making decisions. The model highlights six particular motivational drivers, present in all of us, of which three stand out: motivations for power, achievement and affiliation. With training, you can learn how to observe these motivations in others, and so modify your behaviour so as to match their expectations from you, and so gain rapport. We go no further in the explanation here. This cannot be learnt from a book – it requires training, an understanding of your own motivations and a proper understanding of the limits of such tools. (Chapter 32 provides some advice on how to follow up this issue.)

# Part VII

# Keeping on Track

# 30

# Getting there – timetables and performance

So far, we have seen the effort needed to make KAM work. As with any investment, we need to know how it is doing. In the early days at least, you will face a stream of questions from all parts of the business, all on the same theme – was it all worthwhile?

## HOW WILL YOU MEASURE SUCCESS?

'If you can't measure it, you can't manage it', they say. Measuring helps, but it is not true that if things cannot be measured they are not important. It may be a relief to some not to have to think about relationships, trust, communications and many other vital but hard-to-measure ingredients of good KAM practice. A relief perhaps, but possibly the cause of a disaster. So, how much effort should be put into trying to measure some of the less tangible elements? Trying to measure them helps focus minds on their importance, but perhaps the effort would be better spent elsewhere? The secret of measuring progress is to set out clear targets in the first place. These can be identified from rapid assessments (eg CMAT – see Woodcock, Stone and Foss, 2003) and developing roadmaps for KAM change. You must identify the main objectives of the change. They must be relevant to *your* plan rather than to a generic KAM strategy. Make sure you consider dependencies between different departments when allocating objectives, ensuring the teamwork needed for KAM success. Targets might include:

- customer performance;
- business performance;
- KA team performance;
- project and change performance;
- relationship performance;
- customer satisfaction (including end-customers in intermediated markets);
- KAM implementation.

There will be others that apply to your business. For each, you need to identify where you currently stand and where you wish to be. Only then can you hope to measure progress.

**Good investments result from clear objectives and regular tracking**

Some measures lend themselves to quantifiable analysis. There are sophisticated tools, for instance, for measuring customer satisfaction and its movement over time, although professional expertise should be sought here. It is tempting to send salespeople out with home-grown customer questionnaires, but many factors can make such exercises worse than useless (not least the salesperson's determination to get a good report!). In intermediated FS a further question relates to which level of the channel customer satisfaction should be measured. Is it your immediate customer or the end-customer? Both may be equally important, but the end-customer may be difficult to research if the intermediary is protective of the customer relationship and customer data, even though such measurement is vital. Once you have set performance targets, they should be supported by incentives and tracked over time with mechanisms for review and corrective action.

## TIMETABLES FOR IMPLEMENTATION

You need to measure progress in implementing KAM and to identify hold-ups and bottlenecks. This can only be done if you start out with a clear timetable for implementation. Let's suppose that you are right at the start of your KAM journey, a traditional sales force with traditional selling strategies and a business run in functional 'silos'. You want to establish KAM as a cross-business process with the whole business focused on identifying and satisfying the needs of a carefully identified group of customers. How long do you give yourself? Different sectors of the FS industry change at differing speeds. Some markets have customers more ready for KAM than others, but in any case it will take years, not months or quarters. Such long-term timetables will necessarily be general and simplified, with implementation phases. Each phase requires its own detailed timetable. Of course, when it comes to implementation, you will find that phases are consecutive, but overlap. Some will run together for months, even years, and some that you thought were over will need revisiting. This does not invalidate the original timetable. You can't predict the many turns of fate – a plan that tries to will be unrealistic.

The following _sample_ implementation timetable may seem rather simplistic, but it is a start:

- Phase 1 – Determine your expectations from KAM.
- Phase 2 – Identify the obstacles.
- Phase 3 – Ensure top management support and cross-business alignment.
- Phase 4 – Market segmentation.
- Phase 5 – Customer classification.
- Phase 6 – Identify the KA managers and potential teams.
- Phase 7 – Customer distinction strategies.
- Phase 8 – Ensure the appropriate support systems are in place.
- Phase 9 – Develop the relevant skills and capabilities for each KA team.
- Phase 10 – Prepare KA plans.
- Phase 11 – Continuous review and improvement.

KAM is not simply about getting the sales force to behave differently. But you must have the 'infrastructure' in place. Following the timetable suggested in this chapter helps ensure that you don't rush too quickly into building capabilities and expectations in the sales team that can only be frustrated as they hit a brick wall of obstacles. The setback will not be temporary – people revert to previous behaviours and attitudes that will be all the harder to change at your next attempt.

The example timetable in Table 30.1 is adapted from an insurance **In implementing** company moving into KAM from a regional sales structure. In this **KAM, patience** example, the planning and initial development up to launch took up 12 **really is a virtue** months. It included:

- Development of a business case to determine expectations from KAM, to establish the costs and benefits and to identify the obstacles (Phases 1 and 2).
- Approval of the business case by senior management (Phase 3).
- Consideration of customer segmentation and classification using current and potential profitability and a consideration of the future structure of the industry in defining key accounts and their servicing needs (Phases 4 and 5).

**Table 30.1**   *Example KAM timetable*

| | |
|---|---|
| Prepare initial sales and cost projections for KAM. | Apr |
| Business case for programme prepared. | May–Aug |
| Business case signed off locally. | Sept |
| Business case signed off at board level. | Oct |
| Work commences on streamlining business processes. | Nov |
| Appoint head of new KAM structure. | Nov |
| Define new management structure. | Nov |
| Define what is a key account. | Dec |
| Briefings: national cascade. | Dec |
| Appoint KAMs. | Jan |
| Identify skills and capabilities of KAMs (research into client views and select a training partner). | Jan |
| Define the role of field sales in relation to the role of call centres and e-commerce support. | Feb |
| Develop remuneration model. | Feb |
| Appoint KAM teams. | Mar |
| Initial phase of launch of new structure. | Apr |

- Appointment of KAMs (Phase 6).
- Identifying the skills and capabilities required in KA teams and subsequent appointment of teams (Phase 6).
- Defining the role of support systems, such as call centres and e-commerce in the new structure (Phase 8).

The implementation of training comes in near the end of this process, when those to be trained know where they are pointed and what is expected of them, and that they have the systems in place to support them.

# TRAINING DEVELOPMENT TRACKS

Good training is a vital part of KAM implementation, but must come at the right point in the process. It must be planned, like any other activity, against identified needs and with clear performance outcomes. The first thing is to identify the skills and capabilities required for KAM (see Chapter 15). Then you are ready to audit current performance and competency. This uncovers any 'skills gap' and indicates the training required. This should be done for prospective KAMs and KA team members. A useful tool to consider is the training development track, an idealized training programme designed for KAM implementation. It lists the full range of training available, though in practice it is rarely necessary to take any one individual through the whole programme. It provides a means of relating current skills and abilities against an ideal, back to the 'skills gap' noted above. Table 30.2 is an example of a possible training development track for a KAM at the start of a KAM implementation programme. Spread over 12–18 months, it allows KAMs to apply the learning to their developing jobs. A similar track should be developed for team members, taking particular note of the needs of those from non-commercial backgrounds or with little experience of face-to-face customer contact.

**Table 30.2**  *Example training development track for a KAM*

| Main Track | Key Skills Track | Related Skills Track |
| --- | --- | --- |
| **KAM I** | | |
| Strategy and planning | Marketing awareness | Influencing skills |
| **KAM II** | | |
| Team dynamics | Financial understanding | Face-to-face skills – review |
| **KAM III** | | |
| Project management | Business management | Creative thinking |

## How will you know when you get there?

Most journeys have an end, but not this one. There is no ultimate point of arrival, no perfect state of KAM. Why do salespeople always have annual conferences, but engineers or accountants rarely? The annual conference may be the only time a salesperson gets to feel that things have come to a conclusion, something has been completed and everyone can now gear up for a new start. It is an artificial full stop placed in a sentence that otherwise would have little punctuation at all. Managing customers just isn't like that. If there is no endpoint, the best that can be done is to note where you are headed, keep a log of the journey and hold frequent reviews to see if course changes are required. From time to time the purpose of the journey may change and new destinations appear. One of the arts of KAM is the ability to keep up with such changes, not to regard them as failure of the original plan.

# REGULAR HEALTH CHECKS

Start a 'well key account' clinic. Lately, 'well man' and 'well woman' clinics have boomed. Their main purpose is prevention rather than cure, based on regular check-ups. Perhaps you should start a 'well KA' clinic in your organization. A simple health check along the lines of Tables 30.3 and 30.4 might keep you on track.

Choose your own questions, but perhaps the following categories, or characteristics, are universal:

- internal support and capability;
- KA team dynamics;
- customer relationship;
- key supplier status;

**Table 30.3** *Health check I*

| Characteristic | OK | Could Improve | None | Action Plan |
|---|---|---|---|---|
| **Internal support and capability** Do you have senior management support? Is your KA team empowered to act? Do functional 'barons' present obstacles? Is KAM a recognized cross-business process? Are the right organization and resources in place? Are the right systems in place? Do people have the right skills? | | | | |
| **KA team dynamics** Do team members have clear GROWs? Is communication clear and constructive? | | | | |
| **Customer relationship** Do you understand the customer's DMUs? Do you have broad access to the customer? Do you have integrated processes? Are you part of the customer's communications network? Does the customer want you to succeed? Do you have shared goals, planning and info? | | | | |

**Table 30.4** *Health check II*

| Characteristic | OK | Could Improve | None | Action Plan |
|---|---|---|---|---|
| **Key supplier status** <br> Are you regarded as a key supplier? <br> Is your status improving? <br> Do you know how the customer 'positions' you? <br> Are you acting appropriately? | | | | |
| **Customer intimacy** <br> Is your business customer focused? <br> Do you share the customer's values and culture? <br> Do you understand the customer's value chain? <br> Do you have a positive impact analysis? | | | | |
| **Project management** <br> Have projects been identified? <br> Do they proceed to schedule? <br> Have they been implemented? | | | | |
| **Account profitability** <br> Can you measure account profitability? <br> Is it improving? <br> Do you share the value in the chain? | | | | |

- customer intimacy;
- project management;
- account profitability.

Many companies have used the QCi Customer Management Assessment (CMAT) (Starkey, Woodcock and Stone, 2002) to understand and benchmark their current KAM capabilities against other companies within FS and other best-practice industries. A more industry-specific assessment has been deployed by IBM for financial markets companies. An evidence-based assessment is the most thorough, yet rapid, way to develop a prioritized roadmap for KAM improvements, which focuses on both quick wins and longer-term change.

# 31

# Writing the key account plan

## NO PLAN – NO KEY ACCOUNT

Written KA plans are rare. It is as if there is a fear that in writing down forecasts, predictions or promises they may come back to haunt the KAM, customers being what they are. Salespeople used to living by their wits seem to find it hard to adhere to formal planning. Or is it just that they don't know how or see no purpose in it?

## THE PLAN'S PURPOSE

How big should the ideal KA plan be, that is to say, how many pages long? The answer must have something to do with the purpose of the plan, so let's consider some possible uses:

- a repository for all the data and information on the account;
- getting your thoughts together and validating them with others;
- a means of communicating the importance of this customer to the business as a whole;
- a means of communicating objectives and actions to key account team members;
- the best way of tracking progress against targets and so determining the success of your efforts.

The first use is not the aim of a KA plan. You do need such a record, but do not confuse it with an action-focused document. The same applies to the second use. It is a valuable exercise, but the plan itself is the refined outcome of that process, not the history of your thoughts. A good plan should achieve the third objective, but there will also be other means of raising your customer's profile. The plan is part of a wider influencing strategy and should be written to support rather than hinder the strategy, but this is still not the core purpose of a KA plan.

It is the fourth and fifth uses that are the core purposes. These are communicating objectives and actions, and a way to track progress. If this is the purpose, then the answer to the question 'how long?' is 'as short as is possible'. Plans with dozens of pages and overflowing with analysis and background data are not helpful. They are probably written to communicate the importance and expertise of the KAM (not on our list of uses). The plan should be focused on objectives and actions to achieve those objectives. If this can be said in three or four pages, then even better. However, the plan is more than a list of sales objectives and more than volumes and revenues. It must cover objectives for the relationship, objectives for the team and objectives for the business as a whole, and this may run to a few more pages than the proverbial one side of paper (though there should be a one-page summary).

## A KEY ACCOUNT TEMPLATE?

The CD ROM attached to this book contains a KA planning document. Is this a recommended template? No – there is no blueprint for a key account plan, nor should there be. Blueprints and pro formas tend to result in box-ticking, rather than thinking. They are unlikely to meet your own unique needs. The planning document (and the rest of this chapter) is simply an attempt to provide a framework for your planning activity. In fact, designing your own format is part of the thinking and planning process, determining what is important to you and what is less so. There is nothing worse than agonizing over an analysis, perhaps even commissioning research, simply to fill in the spaces of a model that will never be used. There is nothing better than getting everyone in the account team to agree on the things that matter in your business and what should be included in the plan. Writing the plan should be a team effort and, as such, a source of team cohesion.

# SOME 'MUST HAVES'

So, no blueprint, but there are perhaps a few things that just must be in the plan:

- goals and targets;
- people;
- projects and activities;
- resources, risks and contingencies.

## Goals and targets

Without these, there is no direction, no hope of a common approach and no way of judging success. There should be targets for a number of things and not just the obvious ones of revenue and profit – for how the relationship should progress, for communications, for progress on key projects and for customer satisfaction ratings to name but a few. Just because some are hard to quantify, that does not make them unimportant.

## People

People are what will make KAM work; so don't forget them in the plan. Perhaps the most important part of the plan is identification of who is in the customer's DMU, what makes them tick and who in the KA team will be responsible for them (the contact matrix – see Chapter 24). As well as having a customer-contact role, team members will have other roles and obligations. Identifying these clearly in a written plan – who is on your team and what goals, roles, obligations and work plans (GROWs) they have – will be of enormous help. GROWs are important, particularly when a team sets out on unclear waters. They should be set for each individual but understood by the team.

*Goals* speak for themselves – what is to be achieved for the customer and the team.

*Roles* are important, particularly in a cross-functional KA team. Individuals already have functional roles (the product specialist, the market researcher, the administration or service manager), but they must also take on team roles. What do they bring to the team? Why are they there? How will they do what they have to do? The roles might indicate two separate things. What functional activities will they carry out in the team? What team role will they perform? Dr Meredith Belbin has done a lot of work on this second kind of role, how people behave as team members, and the value those different styles of behaviour can bring. Go through the Belbin team-analysis process to discover your own team make-up and use it to advantage.

*Obligations* are a means of agreeing 'who owes what to whom'. For a KA team to succeed, people must perform tasks for each other, communicate with each other and receive instructions from each other. If responsibilities between the KA team and a function are unclear, start to identify just what these obligations are and what they imply.

*Work plans* are the nitty-gritty of the tasks and projects that team members will be working on. They come in many forms – project plans, critical path analyses and more – but one ingredient is vital to them all: timing. Work plans without time deadlines are work plans that don't get completed.

## Projects and activities

What is going to be done by the team, with clear plans for each project. Vital ingredients include objectives, who is responsible, timetable, and milestones of progress – critical path analysis and ways to measure success. Critical path analysis is just setting out timetables of activities and noting the inter-relationships between them – some activities depend on others being completed. You can then decide what to do first, and so on – the critical path, with clearly identified dependencies. Projects result from value chain and positive impact analysis (Part VI). They include activities for creating the right environment for KAM, overcoming obstacles identified in Chapter 14: modifying structures; developing new systems; adding skills; and finding the right resources.

## Resources, risks and contingencies

A central reason for the KA plan is to identify resources needed and put up a case for them. Resource needs may appear in many guises: new people; additional skills; more access to IT support; greater training support; expansion of operational capacity; investment in new technology; and so on. Only when we know the scope of resources needed to achieve the account objectives can we judge the value and priority of a particular KA. Putting the case is only the start. Of course, aggregate resources required by all the key account plans must be assessed before projects and activities can commence. We must go back to Chapter 3 and remember the balance between objectives, opportunity and resources: the KA plan is an action plan and must be rooted in the reality of the finite. Beyond that, resources may be allocated, but will they bring success? Will the new call centre improve the service support sufficiently to overcome the service problems currently being encountered by the key account? Will additional training provided to your customer's sales staff increase their own sales of your product to their end-customers? Every resource expansion carries risks – of failure, higher expense (permanent or temporary) and so on. The KA plan must assess that risk and propose an appropriate contingency in the event of any such shortfall.

# A FEW TIPS

- Keep it short. Six pages is good; four would be better.
- Keep it updatable (short and in a medium that makes revisions and redistribution easy to achieve).
- Don't write it in one sitting – the best plans form over time, perhaps a long time. Consider the plan from many perspectives over time and ask others to do the same.
- Start off with some strong comments on direction, goals and targets (but note the final tip in this list). People reading this want to know where you are headed.
- Stress the actions resulting from the plan and who is responsible for them.
- Prepare it as a team effort to gain additional inputs and shared commitment – the plan is a practical tool.
- Make it available to the whole business. You are writing it for the people who have to put it into action. The written plan is a key ingredient in ensuring that KAM becomes a cross-business process.
- Consider sharing some or all of it with clients.
- Include an 'executive summary' of the key points – direction, benefits, actions and requirements.
- Make background information on the account available, perhaps as an appendix to the plan, as otherwise pages of data start to obscure the direction and the actions.
- Include your analysis, for instance the customer's value chain, your positive impact analysis, as an appendix.
- Avoid unsupported hype. A good plan will go a long way to winning senior management support for change, new resources, investment and so on, but only if it is balanced and objective.

# A SAMPLE RUNNING ORDER

Here are some suggested headings of a 'typical' key account plan. The exact order and weight of one section or another depends on the level the relationship is working at. If you are at the pre-KAM stage, then the plan will lean heavily towards exploration and information required. If you are already at the partnership stage, then the focus will be more on projects and activities. The running order given below might suit an FS supplier just entering the partnership stage with its customer. Let's suppose it has a history of writing plans heavy on long and worthy analysis with little practical application, so the focus here is on action:

- the key account team – core and full;
- executive summary;
- the profit plan – current profitability and future target;
- opportunities and objectives;
- the contact matrix and GROWs;
- the value proposition – positive impact on total business experience;
- projects – project teams and milestones;
- resources required – actions required by management to commit resources;
- implementation timetable;
- appendices – analysis, information and links.

## Appendices – analysis

At the early stages with a KA it may be important to show more analysis in the body of the plan – the actions part. As a relationship develops and matures, analysis might withdraw by stages to an appendix. How long you have been managing the account determines what is analysis and what is action. Analysis might include:

- market segmentation;
- the KAISM analysis (see Chapter 21);
- historical account profitability analysis – lifetime value analysis;
- the market chain;
- the competitive position – Porter's analysis, SWOT;
- our source of competitive advantage in the market chain;
- customer's purchasing strategy – organization, supplier positioning;
- customer's decision-making process – DMU analysis;
- value chain analysis;
- positive impact analysis and screening;
- proposal analysis;
- Belbin team roles;
- KAM health check (or customer management assessment, eg CMAT).

## Appendices – information

Keeping these kinds of things in an appendix keeps the plan short:

- address book;
- customer's organization charts and contact profiles;
- customer's strategy and market activities;
- customer's performance – sales, growth, shares, profitability, financial status;
- our sales performance – history, current, forecast – and share of business;
- vendor ratings;
- competitor profiles.

# SOME TIPS ON WRITING KEY ACCOUNT PLANS

1. Keep the plan focused on people and actions, not data and history.
2. Keep detailed information in appendices.
3. Use presentation rather than word-processing software. Using word processing leads to paragraphs of unreadable waffle. Using spreadsheets leads to a mass of numbers and budgets. Using presentation software keeps it short and to the point, and makes it easy to present to others.
4. Have as few pages/slides as possible – and then edit further!
5. Don't write this alone – get the team to contribute (especially their GROWs).
6. Could you present it to the customer? With a few subtle edits, this should be an objective (at least in theory), and being able to answer yes is a test of a good plan.

Plans are for making things happen, not for recording history, and certainly not for showing off that you have just read a KAM book and can list all the models! Now you have a plan, add loads of energy, a great deal of resolve, not a little patience and finally a little piece of luck. But don't wait for fate. Figure 31.1 shows why time spent early on analysis and planning pays in the long run. Good planning also allows your team to recognize good fortune when it smiles on you, know it for what it is and turn it to your best advantage. So we don't just wish you good luck on your KAM journey; we wish you the best luck you can make for yourself.

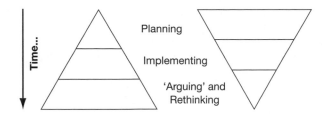

**_Figure 31.1_**   _Why time spent on analysis and planning pays in the long run_

# 32

# Getting further help

Throughout this book, references have been made to professional help and advice, on subjects ranging from analysis of your business environment and customer attitudes to designing implementation programmes for KAM, including training. For help or advice on any of the issues raised, in the first instance contact Peter Cheverton. Peter is a director of INSIGHT Marketing and People, an international training and consultancy firm that specializes in all aspects of KAM implementation, and can be contacted as detailed below:

INSIGHT Marketing and People Ltd
1 Lidstone Court
Uxbridge Road
George Green
Slough SL3 6AG
Tel: +44 (0)1753 822990
Fax: +44 (0)1753 877342
e-mail: Customer.Service@insight-MP.com
www.insight-MP.com

Details of the other authors are as follows:

Dr Tim Hughes is Senior Lecturer at Bristol Business School. He is an expert in the deployment of e-business in FS. He can be contacted at Bristol Business School, University of the West of England, Frenchay Campus, Coldharbour Lane, Bristol BS16 1QY (e-mail: tim.hughes@uwe.ac.uk).

Bryan Foss is Worldwide Banking Solutions Executive (Customer Insight), FS Sector, IBM UK Ltd. He is an expert in all aspects of the deployment of systems and data to meet marketing, sales and customer service objectives in FS. He can be contacted at IBM UK Ltd, Knollys House, 17 Addiscombe Road, Croydon CR9 6HS (e-mail: bryan_foss@uk.ibm.com).

Professor Merlin Stone is Business Research Leader, Business Consulting Services, IBM UK Ltd; IBM Professor of Relationship Marketing, Bristol Business School, University of the West of England; Director, The Database Group Ltd, Digital Data Analysis Ltd, QCi Ltd, The Halo Works Ltd and NowellStone Ltd. He is an expert in all aspects of CRM, particularly in FS. He can be contacted at IBM UK Ltd, Mailpoint SOUTHBANK 2PB2, 76 Upper Ground, South Bank, London SE1 9PZ (e-mail: merlin_stone@uk.ibm.com).

# References

American Bankers Association (ABA) [accessed 9 December 2003] *The Banking Industry: A vital component of the US economy*, www.aba.com

Ansoff, HL (1957) Strategies for diversification, *Harvard Business Review*, Sept–Oct

Cerasale, M and Stone, M (2004) *Business Solutions on Demand*, Kogan Page, London

Datamonitor (2003a) *Banks in Europe*, July, www.datamonitor.com

Datamonitor (2003b) *Banks in the United States*, July, www.datamonitor.com

Datamonitor (2003c) *Commercial Banking in Asia Pacific*, October, www.datamonitor.com

Datamonitor (2003d) *Commercial Banking in Europe*, October, www.datamonitor.com

Datamonitor (2003e) *Commercial Banking in Japan*, October, www.datamonitor.com

Datamonitor (2003f) *Commercial Banking in the United States*, October, www.datamonitor.com

*Direct Marketing* (1994) Profile of Sid Friedman, President and Chairman of Corporate FS, *Direct Marketing*, 11 March, pp 31–32

Findlay, G *et al* (2002) CRM in investment banking and financial markets, in *CRM in Financial Services: A practical guide to making customer relationship management work*, ed B Foss and M Stone, Kogan Page, London

Foss, B and Stone, M (2002) *CRM in Financial Services: A practical guide to making customer relationship management work*, Kogan Page, London

Gronroos, C (1996) Relationship marketing logic, *Asia–Australia Marketing Journal*, **4** (1), pp 7–18

Hamilton, R and Hewer, P (2000) Electronic commerce and the marketing of internet banking in the UK, *Journal of FS Marketing*, **5** (2), pp 135–49

Holland, JB (1992) Relationship banking: choice and control by the multinational firm, *International Journal of Bank Marketing*, **10** (2), pp 29–40

IBM (2003) *Supermarket Banking: Fulfilling the potential*, November, IBM Business Consulting Services

International FS London (IFSL) (2003) *International Financial Markets in the UK*, November, www.ifsl.org.uk/

Jerome, B (2002) E-business strategy or just business strategy, in *CRM in Financial Services: A practical guide to making customer relationship management work*, ed B Foss and M Stone, Kogan Page, London

McDonald, M, Millman, AF and Rogers, B (1996) *KAM: Learning from supplier and customer perspectives*, Cranfield University School of Management

Millman, AF and Wilson, KJ (1994) From key account selling to key account management, Paper presented to the 10th annual conference of Industrial Marketing and Purchasing, September, University of Groningen, Netherlands

Mintel (1999) *Financial Supermarkets Report*, June, Mintel, London

Moffett, T, Crick, P, Stone, M and Jerome, B (2002) Managing marketing in the e-world, in *CRM in Financial Services: A practical guide to making customer relationship management work*, ed B Foss and M Stone, Kogan Page, London

Morgan, RM and Hunt, SD (1994) The commitment–trust theory of relationship marketing, *Journal of Marketing*, **58**, pp 20–38

Porter, M (1980) *Competitive Strategy*, Free Press, New York

Reichheld, FE and Detrick, C (2003) Want to know how to keep expenses low? Think loyalty, *American Banker*, **168** (181)

Rogers, E (1962) *Diffusion of Innovations*, Free Press, New York

Spottiswoode, A and El Marouani, A (2002) E-business impact on customer management in FS: an overview, in *CRM in Financial Services: A practical guide to making customer relationship management work*, ed B Foss and M Stone, Kogan Page, London

Starkey, M, Woodcock, N and Stone, M (2002) Assessing the quality of customer management in FS, in *CRM in Financial Services: A practical guide to making customer relationship management work*, ed B Foss and M Stone, Kogan Page, London

Treacy, M and Weirsema, F (1995) *The Discipline of Market Leaders*, Harper Collins, London

Turnbull, PW and Moustakatos, T (1996) Marketing and investment banking II: relationships and competitive advantage, *International Journal of Bank Marketing*, **14** (2), pp 38–49

Tyler, K and Stanley, E (1999) UK bank–corporate relationships: large corporates' expectations of service, *International Journal of Bank Marketing*, **17** (4), pp 158–70

Woodcock, N, Stone, M and Foss, B (2003) *The Customer Management Scorecard*, Kogan Page, London

# Index

**Also available from Kogan Page
by Peter Cheverton:**

*Key Account Management*
*A complete action kit of tools and techniques for achieving
profitable success*

"A combination of clarity, enthusiasm, and common sense…
reading this is a rewarding experience."

*Professor Malcolm McDonald, Emeritus Professor,
Cranfield School of Management*

"Will help any business focus their sales activities where they matter…
on those (customers) that will take your business where you want it to go.
All in all, this is the essential guide to global best practice."

*Winning Business*

Any organization's key accounts are its lifeblood. This highly practical book puts forward a unique yet simple planning methodology for identifying, obtaining, retaining and developing key customers.

Completely updated and revised with lots of new material to reflect the latest best practice, this edition will reinforce its standing as the premier book on the subject. This is one of very few books to take the long-term, team-selling strategic view of Key Account Management (KAM).

Apart from finding great resonance with business practitioners all over the world, Key Account Management has established itself on many academic reading lists. Translated into five languages, it was also short-listed for Business Book of the Year in Sweden (2002).

---

The above title is available from all good bookshops. To obtain further information, please contact the publisher at the address below:

Kogan Page Limited
120 Pentonville Road
London N1 9JN
United Kingdom
Tel: +44 (0) 20 7278 0433
Fax: +44 (0) 20 7837 6348

order online at:
**www.kogan-page.co.uk**